Reporting Crime

The Media Politics of Criminal Justice

Philip Schlesinger and Howard Tumber

CLARENDON PRESS · OXFORD

Oxford University Press, Walton Street, OX2 6DP
Oxford New York
Athens Auckland Bangkok Bombay
Calcutta Cape Town Dar es Salaam Delhi
Florence Hong Kong Istanbul Karachi
Kuala Lumpur Madras Madrid Melbourne
Mexico City Nairobi Paris Singapore
Tapei Tokyo Toronto
and associated companies in
Berlin Ibadan

Oxford is a trade mark of Oxford University Press

Published in the United States
by Oxford University Press Inc., New York

First published 1994
Paperback reprinted 1995

British Library Cataloguing in Publication Data
Data available

Library of Congress Cataloging in Publication Data
Schlesinger, Philip, 1948–
Reporting Crime : the media politics of criminal justice / Philip
Schlesinger and Howard Tumber.
p.   cm. — (Clarendon studies in criminology)
Includes index.
1. Crime and the press—Great Britain—History—20th century.
2. Crime and criminals in mass media.   3. Mass media—Social
aspects.   I. Tumber, Howard.   II. Title.   III. Series.
PN5124.C74S35   1994   070.4'49364'0941—dc20   93–49445
ISBN 0–19–825838–0
ISBN 0–19–825839–9 (pbk.)

Printed in Great Britain
on acid-free paper by
Biddles Ltd, Guildford and King's Lynn

1299

Reporting Crime

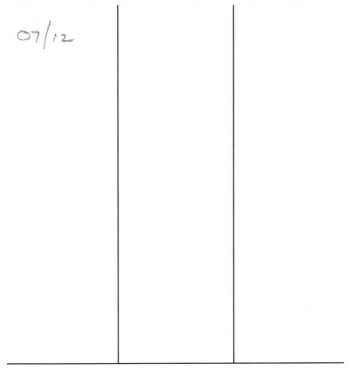

07/12

Please renew/return items by last date
shown. Please call the number below:

Renewals and enquiries: 0300 123 4049

Textphone for hearing or
speech impaired users: 0300 123 4041

FA

CLARENDON STUDIES IN CRIMINOLOGY

Published under the auspices of the Institute of Criminology, University of Cambridge, the Mannheim Centre, London School of Economics, and the Centre for Criminological Research, University of Oxford.

GENERAL EDITOR: ROGER HOOD

EDITORS: TREVOR BENNETT, ANTHONY BOTTOMS,
DAVID DOWNES, NICOLA LACEY, PAUL ROCK,
ANDREW SANDERS

Other titles in this series:

To
Sharon, Hannah, and Tamara (PS)
Hila, Michal, and Judy (HT)
—for putting up with it all.

General Editor's Introduction

IT is not often that a new criminological series emerges. It is now over fifty years since Leon Radzinowicz and J. C. W. Turner began *English Studies in Criminal Science* under the Macmillan imprint, which, after ten volumes, became the internationally renowned *Cambridge Studies in Criminology*. Forty-one further volumes were published under the editorship of Sir Leon by Heinemann Educational Books, led by the distinguished publisher, the late Alan Hill. Ten more volumes, published by Gower and Avebury books, appeared under the general editorship of Anthony Bottoms before the prestigious Cambridge Series was unexpectedly and sadly wound-up.

The Cambridge Institute of Criminology then approached Oxford University Press in the hope that the series could be continued in another form at a time when, co-incidentally, the Press had begun to discuss the prospects for a criminological series with the Mannheim Centre for Criminology and Criminal Justice at the London School of Economics. With the energetic support of Richard Hart, these two institutions decided on a joint venture with the Oxford Centre for Criminological Research in which each would provide the members of the Editorial Board for a new series to be called *Clarendon Studies in Criminology*. I was honoured to have been asked by my colleagues (whose names are listed next to the title page) to be the General Editor for the first three years.

Clarendon Studies in Criminology aims to provide a forum for outstanding work in all aspects of criminology, criminal justice, penology, and the wider field of deviant behaviour. It will welcome works of theory and synthesis as well as reports of empirical enquiries and will be international in its scope. The first titles, Philip Schlesinger and Howard Tumber's *Reporting Crime: The Media Politics of Criminal Justice* and Jon Vagg's *Prison Systems: A Comparative Study Of Accountability in England, France, Germany, and The Netherlands* already indicate the potential range of the Series.

In this book, Philip Schlesinger and Howard Tumber make a distinctive contribution to the politics and sociology of crime reporting. They explore not only the practices of journalists, editors and television producers but also the strategies of those who provide information about crime and criminal justice to the media and thus seek to shape the news for their own purposes: the Home Office, agencies such as the police and probation services, and a plethora of pressure groups. Through interviews with a wide range of journalists, editors and members of pressure groups and through striking case studies, they provide for the first time in this country a multi-faceted analysis of how crime news is interpreted and presented. Their work raises important questions about the production of such news, its effect on public perceptions of crime and fear of it. The Editors are delighted to welcome this valuable contribution to an important topic.

Roger Hood

Acknowledgements

THIS book could not have been written without the help and co-operation of many people. First, we are extremely grateful to all who so generously gave up their time to be interviewed by us. We should also like to express our appreciation to all who gave access to their organizations both for observation and for the collection of documentation. Second, we offer our thanks to those who, in various ways, collaborated in this project: Alison Anderson for her dedicated and efficient research assistance; Graham Murdock for his involvement in planning the research, helpful advice, and contribution to a co-authored journal article; Paul Hartmann for his help with computing; Sally Clark and Clare Taubin for their transcription work, John Wallis for his video-recording assistance, and Cathryn O'Neill and Rachel O'Sullivan for additional research assistance. We are pleased to have had fruitful exchanges of view with Richard Ericson, and have received valued comments on various sections of the study that first appeared as papers from Russell Dobash, David Downes, Herbert Gans, Marjorie Ferguson, Pam Mills, Paul Rock, and Lee Sigal. We also thank the BBC and IBA Research Departments, and the Police Foundation, for providing relevant documentation.

Funding for the project came from the Economic and Social Research Council in its 'Crime and Criminal Justice System' Research Initiative. We gratefully acknowledge the ESRC's support.

The vagaries of life often intervene between intention and realization, and on this occasion we were not exempt. Just as we were completing the empirical research for this study in Summer 1988, each of us found himself moving to another job, and a new set of obligations. Consequently, in the words of steam age television, there has been a brief intermission. It would have been longer had our respective universities not provided us with indispensable sabbatical time to complete this book—a term for Howard Tumber at City in Spring 1992, and a semester for Philip Schlesinger at Stirling in Spring 1993.

During the enforced intermission, some parts of the present work were first published in different form elsewhere. We have drawn freely on the following:

'Rethinking the Sociology of Journalism: Source Strategies and the Limits of Media-Centrism', in M. Ferguson (ed.), *Public Communication: The New Imperatives* (London: Sage, 1990), 61–81;

'The Media Politics of Crime and Criminal Justice', *British Journal of Sociology*, 42 (1991), 397–420 (written with Graham Murdock);

'Crime and Criminal Justice in the Media', in D. Downes (ed.), *Unravelling Criminal Justice: Eleven British Studies* (Basingstoke and London: Macmillan, 1992), 184–203;

'Fighting the War against Crime: Television, Police, and Audience', *British Journal of Criminology*, 33 (1993), 19–32.

We thank the editors and publishers concerned for their permission to use this material.

No list of acknowledgements would be complete, however, without mentioning those who, as usual, have borne the brunt of what we might like to think of as authorial distractedness. For their heroic fortitude, tolerance, and enduringly remarkable patience, we thank our families—once again.

P.S. and H.T.

Stirling and London
July 1993

Contents

Introduction

THIS is a sociological study of crime journalism that is also conceived of as a contribution to political sociology. The political dimension of crime is inescapable because the maintenance of public order through law enforcement is a fundamental function of the state. Since reporting infractions of order is so central to everyday news coverage, and arguably to the public's perceptions of threat and sense of security, the questions addressed here are inherently political in character. We are also concerned with how the distribution of resources affects the access of political actors to public debate via the news media, a recurrent theme in discussions of democracy. By presenting our analysis in this way, we underline our view that crime journalism cannot be seen in isolation from its broader social contexts nor, in particular, from how contemporary political communication is conducted.

This study discusses how crime is reported by the London-based national news media in Britain (on which see Appendix 1). A central contention is that reporting crime is much more than simply crime-reporting: in order to understand the daily diet of news about crime and criminal justice we need to examine not only the practice of specialized journalism but also the media strategies of the news sources that try to influence its production by managing—or attempting to manage—the news. Consequently, this takes us into the analysis of two related, but distinct, worlds. First, there is the rather complex and ramified arena of government, police, criminal justice professionals, and pressure groups whose political activities are focused on crime and its control and management in society. Secondly, there are the journalistic specialists whose task it is to report on the doings of the criminal justice system. Given the often intimate relations that exist between these two worlds, the bulk of our analysis is concerned with an exploration of first, how each operates in attempting to shape the creation of crime news, and second, how they interact with one another.

We emphasize this last point conscious that there has been a long-standing failure in the sociological study of journalism to recognize how central are the relations between news media and their sources of information (a term which one would be well advised to define broadly, to include disinformation and misinformation). Although numerous studies have shown that news media routinely make use of sources, relatively little work to date has begun by *also* looking at the news from the perspective of the sources themselves. Only very recently have questions begun to be asked in a consistent and focused fashion about the tactics and strategies pursued by sources seeking media attention, about their perceptions of other, competing, actors in the fields over which they are trying to exert influence, the resources at their disposal, the organizational contexts in which they operate, their publicity goals, and how they assess their own effectiveness in using the media.

The Aims and Methods of Our Research

We originally conceived this piece of research in terms of the established models and empirical studies in the sociology of the media, to which we have ourselves contributed in the past.[1] One of the most striking things about the tradition of research into news production is its focus upon the practices of newsrooms and of newsgathering. This has resulted in a great deal of new knowledge about how the media work, but at the same time it does have the major shortcoming of neglecting the interrelations between media and the social institutions that they report. This study has forced us to think again about these relationships by what we have discovered in the process of research itself.

Work began in Autumn 1986, and whilst the in-depth datagathering had been completed by Summer 1988, we have included further material collected up to 1993.

There were several aims to our research. Our concern with how news is produced has led us to examine the practices of relevant forms of specialist reporting and programme-making. However, we have given this interest a particular inflection by studying how

[1] See Schlesinger, P., *Putting 'Reality' Together: BBC News*, 2nd edn. (London: Methuen, 1987); Schlesinger, P., Murdock, G., and Elliott, P., *Televising 'Terrorism': Political Violence in Popular Culture* (London: Comedia, 1983); Morrison, D., and Tumber, H., *Journalists at War: The Dynamics of News Reporting during the Falkland War* (London: Sage, 1988).

news sources interact with the news media, an area of study receiving little systematic attention in previous British research. In pursuing this line of inquiry, we have been especially interested to examine how sources in the crime and criminal justice arena have developed and used strategies and tactics of information management when dealing with journalists. For the purposes of the present study, these sources have been divided into three groups:

Official sources. Interviews were conducted with élite personnel in the politically sensitive fields of the Home Office, the Police, and HM Customs and Excise. In addition, access was granted to the Police College at Bramshill where interviews were conducted with those in charge of media training courses. (See Appendix 2 for a full list of interviewees.)

Professional Associations and Trades Unions. Interviews were conducted with senior officials from seven organizations concerned with criminal justice and law enforcement. These were the Bar Council, the Law Society, the Magistrates' Association, the National Association of Probation Officers, the Prison Governors' Association, the Prison Officers' Association, and the Police Federation.

Pressure Groups. Interviews were conducted with personnel from twenty-five groups. Others were contacted by telephone or engaged in short conversations. (See Appendix 2 for a full list of interviewees and Appendix 3 for background information on some key groups.)

Semi-structured interviews were conducted with all of the above in an attempt to learn about their information strategies and their reflections on these. Unlike a survey, where it is essential to undertake a pilot questionnaire, the semi-structured interview schedule could be refined and adapted after the initial interviews to take into account emergent research questions. Our aim in drawing up the interview schedule for the sources was to gather information that could be broadly summarized as: the systems and models used in producing information; how images were monitored; and how images were managed.

For the professionals and the pressure groups information was sought on their memberships, objectives, and sources of funding, as well as their relationships with one another, with government institutions, and with journalists. Where available, other material such as annual reports and accounts, publications, press releases, and cuttings were obtained.

Following the interviews with news sources, interviews were conducted with crime, legal affairs, and home affairs journalists. This phase of the study followed the more conventional route of the sociology of journalism, but was armed with the findings of our interviews with sources. We thus approached the journalists highly aware that they were the targets of others' considered strategies, and pursued lines of questioning germane to this. Our main aim in these interviews was to elicit information in the broad areas of their journalistic careers; their current briefs; and their relationships with sources.

Most interviews took place 'on the record' and verbatim quotations are included in this book. However, some interviewees preferred their remarks to remain unattributable and some wished to go completely 'off the record', allowing us to use information as 'background'.

Our investigation of the content of crime-reporting in both the press and television eventually centred upon a number of case studies selected during sample weeks of news coverage during our research. We have sought to explore how a given story is presented across the whole range of news outlets, and have linked the arguments developed through our examination of the sources and producers of crime news with aspects of news coverage.

Finally, in addition to the interviews with journalists, our research into the production of crime news involved observation of the production teams of crime and legal affairs television programmes. We also attended public meetings and press conferences organized by some of the pressure groups.

The Organization of this Book

Chapter 1 is concerned with theoretical questions in the political sociology of the news media, touching on recent debates on democracy, political communication, and the relations between sources and journalists. It sets out our own position without in any way aiming to offer a comprehensive review of the academic literature.

The book is then divided into two parts which elaborate our empirical findings in the light of our theoretical thinking. Part I,

'Sources in Action', examines the activities and strategies of news sources in the crime and criminal justice field in Britain. To the best of our knowledge, no such investigation has been attempted previously. Chapter 2 offers a glimpse of how the Home Office and criminal justice and law-enforcement professionals relate to one another and to the media in a context of competition and co-operation. The subject-matter of Chapter 3 is closely linked to this and, in a complementary fashion, studies the complex world of the criminal justice pressure groups. To complete this part, Chapter 4 analyses recent changes in the police's management of media relations and considers how this relates to their need to 'sell' themselves.

Part II, 'Making Crime News', concerns the production and content of crime-reporting. Chapter 5 presents a comprehensive analysis of London-based specialist crime journalism, the first new research on this topic for some twenty years. It is followed by three qualitative case studies of news story-telling, each of which ranges across the national press and television news. Chapter 6 takes up the current debate about the impact of publishing crime statistics on fear of crime and poses questions about what the regular disputes about this really signify. Next come two contrasting cases of reporting that concern acts of violence. Chapter 7 discusses the acquittal of a police officer charged with a shooting offence, whereas Chapter 8 deals with the conviction of a sex murderer. Each raises some distinctive issues, not least about both fear of authority and fear of crime. In Chapter 9, we examine the question of the increasingly popular coverage of 'real crime' by way of a case study of the origins, developments, values, and impact of the BBC television programme, *Crimewatch UK*. Finally, we offer a brief conclusion.

1

News Sources and News Media

Crime occupies a great deal of space in public discussion and in the public's imagination. The fascination with criminal activity and law enforcement is at the very heart of popular culture. News-reporting, of course, has a central role to play in retailing everyday stories of murder, fraud, robbery, extortion, and violent—often sexual—assaults. But alongside this journalistic catalogue is the vast array of fictional representations of crime and its detection, which ranges through film, radio and television to the novel.[1] In short, stories about crime and crime-fighting—whether factual or fictional—are an integral part of daily media consumption for virtually all of us. Popular anxieties about disorder are intermeshed with immersion in popular entertainment, of which much news is arguably a part.

How press-reporting of criminality, violence, or disorderly behaviour might affect the wider population has been a long-standing matter of debate and research, and official concern about these matters has also existed for a long time. There are well-established discourses upon social deviance, law and order, and threats to conventional morality which repeatedly come onto the political agenda at times of social crisis.[2]

Our study will obviously be read with these kinds of concern in mind. In Britain, it will also be read in the light of perceptions of growing problems in the criminal justice system: there has been an eight-fold rise in the crime rate since 1950, with a corresponding decline in the overall quality of life, particularly in the worst-hit areas. New forms of crime and deviance have emerged—such as

[1] See Reiner, R., *The Politics of the Police*, 2nd edn. (Hemel Hempstead: Harvester Wheatsheaf, 1992), 183–203, and Sparks, R., *Television and the Drama of Crime: Moral Tales and the Place of Crime in Public Life* (Buckingham, Philadelphia: Open University Press, 1992).

[2] See Kuhn, A., *Cinema, Censorship and Sexuality, 1909–1925* (London: Routledge, 1988) for an account of the early moral and sexual regulation of the cinema. On the tendency to repeated moral panics, see Pearson, G., *Hooligan: A History of Respectable Fears* (Basingstoke: Macmillan, 1983).

hard-drug trafficking, terrorism, and sophisticated corporate fraud. There has been a decline in public trust in police effectiveness since the 1980s. There have also been some quite spectacular miscarriages of justice, most notably in relation to alleged terrorist offences and homicides. The ensuing crisis of confidence led to the setting-up of the Royal Commission on Criminal Justice, which reported in July 1993.[3] Coupled with major prison riots and public concern about prison conditions, there have been good grounds for arguing that the criminal justice system is in crisis.[4]

The news media have had to adapt to the broad changes that have occurred both in patterns of criminality and in the responses of the criminal justice system. There has been a consequent growth in specialist reporting, documented later, that deals with changes in the law, policing, and government policy. In turn, this has occurred in the context of a more intensely competitive media environment in which aggressive marketing strategies have increasingly shaped the performance both of the press and of broadcasting. Moreover, at the same time, political actors have become increasingly skilled at the techniques of selling themselves and their policies in the political market-place of contending parties and interest groups.

Media, Democracy, and the 'Public Sphere'

Much current debate has centred upon how political and economic factors have shaped media systems so that that they tend to privilege the ideological perspectives of the powerful—in particular, those of the holders of state power, exponents of establishment politics, and representatives of major capitalist economic interests. Alongside this has been concern about those whose voices in the political system tend to be excluded.

These issues are coloured by the transformation of the media landscape, most notably by the widespread decline of public service broadcasting since the 1980s and the growing concentration of ownership in the press and broadcasting. Alongside such changes at the national level has been the increasing global dominance in

[3] Runciman of Doxford, Viscount (chairman), *Royal Commission on Criminal Justice*, Cmnd 2263 (London: HMSO, 6 July 1993).
[4] For a discussion of relevant sociological research, see Downes, D., 'Introduction', *Unravelling Criminal Justice* (Basingstoke: Macmillan, 1992), pp. xi–xxviii.

the past decade of transnational multi-media enterprises. These are certainly not new developments, but they have attained a novel importance in the context of the collapse of the communist system, the crisis of socialist theory and practice, and the hailing of liberal democracy as the only viable kind of political regime.

However, liberal democracy at the national level is far from free of crisis in how it represents the diversity of social, political, and economic interests. And this crisis is not unconnected with pressures on national political systems deriving from the globalization of the economy and the loss of traditional forms of political sovereignty. Pressures such as these have led to a re-evaluation of some of the main questions of political theory and attempts to formulate new forms of democracy, in particular to consider the prospects for international democracy.[5]

Arguments about media and democracy are at root about the relative openness and closure of communicative processes, both nationally and internationally, and the broader implications that these have for the conduct of political life. To the extent that given media systems in a variety of ways limit access to the production, distribution, and consumption of information they affect the capacity of the wider public to deliberate and determine decision-making processes in the state and in the wider society. The workings of the media and the capacities of citizens as participants in public life are therefore connected: openness and publicity are means of making political life transparent and accountable.[6] Censorship and secrecy act in a contrary direction. Much debate about this question has centred upon what many academic writers have taken to calling the 'public sphere'.

In the ideal conditions envisaged by the German sociologist Jürgen Habermas, the 'public sphere' is a realm in which 'a time-consuming process of public enlightenment' may take place 'for the "general interest" on the basis of which alone a rational agreement between publicly competing opinions could freely be reached'.[7] A

[5] For discussions of these issues, see Held, D. (ed.), *Prospects for Democracy* (Cambridge: Polity, 1993); McGrew, T., and Lewis, P. (eds.), *Global Politics* (Cambridge: Polity, 1992).

[6] See Bobbio, N., *The Future of Democracy* (Cambridge: Polity, 1987); Golding, P., 'Political Communication and Citizenship: The Media and Democracy in an Inegalitarian Social Order', in M. Ferguson (ed.), *Public Communication: The New Imperatives* (London: Sage, 1990), 84–100.

[7] Habermas, J., *The Structural Transformation of the Public Sphere: An Inquiry into a Category of Bourgeois Society* (Cambridge: Polity, 1992), 195.

key underlying condition for consensual opinion formation, according to this view, is guaranteed universal access to the public sphere for all citizens. Habermas has offered an influential analysis of the historical emergence of a space in which private individuals could debate the regulation of civil society and the conduct of the state, underpinned by the rise of the political press and of new social milieux wherein discussion could occur. The liberal, constitutional public sphere is presented as permitting a rational, well-informed conversation between equals capable of resolving their differences by non-coercive means.

But the normative ideal thus sketched out hardly matches contemporary conditions, as Habermas himself recognizes, and critical research both in the political economy and political sociology of the media has also made abundantly clear. Numerous studies have drawn attention to a variety of obstacles plausibly held to impede the realization of an open communication system to which all have access. For instance, and the list is not exhaustive, trends to oligopoly in media ownership and control, the restriction of entry to the market by virtue of high capital start-up costs, the impact of advertising in shaping media output, centralized distribution systems, the manipulation of the political agenda by political parties and powerful lobbies, the role of the state in regulating media and in enforcing censorship. All have been cited as negative influences and as impediments to democratic communication.[8]

Habermas observed that the contemporary political public sphere had developed beyond the originating bourgeois conditions that constituted the basis for his ideal, and that organized groups rather than individual citizens had become the key actors in political communication in what he called the 'social-welfare state' (itself a political formation now evidently in crisis and apparent disintegration).

---

[8] For pertinent work on this see Curran, J., 'Mass Media and Democracy: A Reappraisal', in J. Curran and M. Gurevitch (eds.), *Mass Media and Society* (London: Edward Arnold, 1991), 82–117; Downing, J., 'The Alternative Public Realm: The Organization of the 1980s Anti-Nuclear Press in West Germany and Britain', in P. Scannell, P. Schlesinger, and C. Sparks (eds.), *Culture and Power: A 'Media, Culture and Society' Reader* (London: Sage, 1992), 259–77; Garnham, N., *Capitalism and Communication* (London: Sage, 1990), ch. 7; Golding, P., and Murdock, G., 'Culture, Communications, and Political Economy', in Curran and Gurevitch, *Mass Media and Society*, 15–32; Keane, J., *The Media and Democracy* (Cambridge: Polity, 1991); Scannell, P., 'Public Service Broadcasting and Modern Public Life' and Sparks, C., 'The Popular Press and Political Democracy', in Scannell *et al.*, *Culture and Power*, 278–92 and 317–48.

In this connection, he pertinently underlined the importance of public relations and political marketing in shaping processes of mass communication. Habermas talked of the public sphere becoming 'refeudalized', being turned into a public display or spectacle, with major interests, political parties, and the state all pursuing their communicative goals through techniques of information management. 'From a critical principle wielded by the public, publicity has been transformed into a principle of managed integration,' he writes, lamenting the loss of critical debate.[9] Whereas some have justly disputed the appropriateness of the feudal analogy in describing how modern media relate to their audiences, Habermas, writing presciently on this theme more than thirty years ago, must be credited with some important insights into the evolution of contemporary political communication, as our findings show.[10]

In response to what they see as the failings of contemporary media systems in the major capitalist democracies, and influenced by Habermas's work, several critics on the left have attempted to envisage a public sphere that contains a diversity of media, representing a range of views and interests, based on different forms of ownership and variously controlled. In some recent thinking, tremendous weight has been put upon the desirability of public service broadcasting as a space wherein a wide range of views and perspectives might be articulated. Here, too, the real falls far short of the ideal. But it has been argued that in a fragmenting culture, those ideals need even more to be taken seriously.[11]

What several recent blueprints for democratic communication have in common is the attempt to institutionalize pluralistic means of expression by advocating a diverse political economy for mass communication, with, for instance, a mixture of free market, subsidized, and state-owned media. Alongside different forms of ownership, a variety of forms of management and editorial control are also proposed. This view is premised upon the argument that the

[9] Habermas, *The Structural Transformation*, 207.

[10] For a relevant critique of Habermas, see Thompson, J. B., *Ideology and Modern Culture: Critical Social Theory in the Era of Mass Communication* (Cambridge: Polity, 1990).

[11] For attempts to tackle the issue of democratic communication see Curran, Garnham, and Keane cited in n. 8 above. It could be argued that the national state now no longer has the capacity to define the scope of a national public sphere, or indeed to defend national cultural and identity. For a contrary view see Schlesinger, P., 'Wishful Thinking: Cultural Politics, Media, and Collective Identities', *Journal of Communication*, 43 (1993), 6–17.

market tends to marginalize oppositional and alternative media and that the state cannot always be trusted to secure adequate diversity by the pursuit of public policy—not least when it may itself be subject to adverse criticism.[12]

Thus, whilst it makes sense to argue that there is a public sphere or arena in capitalist democracies in which space exists for the elaboration of different political perspectives and projects, and for the articulation of a range of interests, it is important to underline its imperfections and limitations if we are to grasp contemporary realities. The scope for diversity and dissent in capitalist democracies is inherently a matter of struggle, its precise composition and extent being determined by the balance of political forces at any given time.

The functioning of the public sphere is an empirically research-able question, as well as one of democratic and media theory. In the present study our aim is to chart in a highly specific way how diverse political actors may articulate with a range of media in the pursuit of their communicative interests. In this respect, our case study of the field of crime and criminal justice may be read as one way of quite concretely examining the workings of the flawed, con-temporary public sphere.

For present purposes, the political space of capitalist democracies may usefully be seen as divided into numerous fields that are sub-ject to ideological struggle. Such conflict involves the incessant mobilization of resources by actors in pursuit of strategies and tac-tics aimed at affecting public attitudes and judgements about mat-ters in dispute. In the case at hand, discourse about crime and criminal justice is produced by contending actors that range from government departments through to pressure groups. Such action is increasingly subject to the constraints imposed by a 'promotional culture' that is heavily mediatized.[13]

---

[12] Consequently, a 'decommodified' space between market and state is envisaged as the site for the public sphere. Whether this is now an intellectually coherent or politically plausible vision is a matter for debate. See Curran, J., 'Rethinking the Media as a Public Sphere', in P. Dahlgren and C. Sparks (eds.), *Communication and Citizenship: Journalism and the Public Sphere in the New Media Age* (London and New York: Routledge, 1991), 27–57; Keane, J., 'Democracy and the Media—Without Foundations', *Political Studies*, 60 (1992), 116–29.

[13] Wernick, A., *Promotional Culture* (London: Sage, 1991).

Communicating Politics

Such promotionalism is particularly evident in the information management strategies that modern liberal democracies employ. Apart from the ever-evolving techniques of political marketing which have characterized election campaigns, governments, and politicians more generally, have increasingly turned to public relations consultants and communications advisers to promote both themselves and their policies. The breaking-down of voters' party identification and partisanship has forced politicians intent upon election more and more to use the wiles of media managers to appeal to the uncommitted voter. Moreover, in order to maintain the coalitions that brought them to victory, to maintain public approval for their policies, and to avoid the risk of a loss of legitimacy whilst in office, governments also have resort to the techniques that first brought electoral victory.[14] The idea of the 'permanent campaign' has meant that a bevy of 'spin doctors' is constantly at hand to assist governments and political parties with their communicative acts.[15] When presidential poll ratings dip, though, the official messenger, namely the press secretary, often gets fired.

Political image-building is not a new phenomenon. Rhetoric and propaganda have long been a means of achieving and maintaining political power. But in the last thirty to forty years there has been a qualitative change in political promotion.[16] The use of negative advertising and news management techniques by the political world in what is euphemistically termed the 'sound bite' culture has become so contentious that 'the manner in which strategy is conducted can itself become an issue, so that promotion itself becomes a topic for promotional politics'—an observation borne out in our empirical study of the media politics of crime and criminal justice.[17]

Whilst the development of mass communication has led political figures to employ the strategies of symbolic construction in order to promote and present themselves as likeable, accessible, and com-

[14] Wernick, A., *Promotional Culture* (London: Sage, 1991) 135; Berkman, R. and Kitch, L. W., *Politics in the Media Age* (New York: McGraw Hill, 1986), 147.

[15] Wernick, *Promotional Culture*, 136.

[16] Harvey, D., *The Condition of Postmodernity* (Oxford: Basil Blackwell, 1989), 329; Wernick, *Promotional Culture*, 134.

[17] Wernick, *Promotional Culture*, 141.

petent, it has also made leading personalities newly visible and vulnerable to mass audiences' judgements.[18] Governments constantly faced with the risk of losing legitimacy can have both their institutional and personal authority deconstructed by the mass media.[19] Whilst stories of scandal involving personalities in politics, business, the monarchy, sport, and entertainment remain a key element in the audience-building strategies of the press, the potential for undermining the institutions such figures represent is now always present.[20]

In Britain, the 1980s and 1990s have seen the rise of publicity in many aspects of the governmental process. Before the election of the Conservatives in 1979, most government publicity had centred on the provision of information about departmental services and benefits, influencing social behaviour, and recruitment campaigns. During the 1980s, selling shares to the public in the newly privatized industries gave a major new impetus to government-sponsored publicity campaigns. The conduct of these led to accusations that the distinction between government information campaigns and party political advertising was being deliberately blurred.[21]

That a culture of promotionalism has invaded many areas of public life is fully apparent from our study of crime and criminal justice. One example is the use of publicity by lawyers. In the USA, many attorneys are using the techniques of media management to aid their clients in litigation. For clients with high public profiles, public relations is seen as an important adjunct to legal argument, and publicists are increasingly representing the rich and famous in legal trouble. The Wall Street dealers Ivan Boesky and Michael Milken (both charged with insider trading), and the Kennedy family member William Kennedy-Smith (charged with rape), all had PR agents to represent them to the media. In the 1991 Senate hearings to confirm the nomination of Judge Clarence Thomas to the

[18] See Meyrowitz, J., *No Sense of Place: The Impact of Electronic Media on Social Behavior* (New York: Oxford University Press, 1985), 273–5; Thompson, J. B., *Ideology and Modern Culture*, 115.

[19] See Ericson, R. V., 'Mass Media, Crime, Law, and Justice: An Institutional Approach', *British Journal of Criminology*, 31 (1991), 233.

[20] Tumber, H., '"Selling Scandal": Business and the Media', *Media, Culture and Society*, 15 (1993), 345–61.

[21] Tumber, H., 'Taming the Truth', *British Journalism Review*, 4 (1993), 37–41, and 'Marketing Politics: The Americanization of Government Information Policy in Britain', in P. H. Melling and J. R. Roper (eds.), *Encountering America: The Impact of American Culture on Europe, 1945 Onwards* (Lampeter: Edward Mellen, in press).

US Supreme Court, both Thomas and the woman who accused him of sexual harassment, Anita Hill, were represented by professional publicists.[22]

In Britain, one of the best-known solicitors to adopt a media strategy as part of his clients' defence was the late Brian Raymond. Raymond's most publicized client was Clive Ponting, the senior civil servant who leaked information concerning the sinking of the Argentine battleship, the General Belgrano, during the Falklands War, and who was subsequently prosecuted for breaches of the Official Secrets Act. A particularly astute and successful media campaign was organized by Raymond as part of the defence's public strategy.

As these last instances show, the field of crime and criminal justice has certainly not remained untouched by wider trends in political communication. In fact, they are now quite integral to its functioning, as we demonstrate below.

Rethinking the Sociology of Journalism

Much sociological debate about communication has developed against the backdrop of wider theoretical disputes between Marxists and pluralists. Throughout the 1970s, and for much of the 1980s, a great deal of academic debate took place in the shadow of two broad socio-political paradigms that offered competing images and interpretations of the performance of the news media and of the democratic credentials of liberal democracy. 'Pluralism' and 'neo-Marxism' provided distinctive and opposed ways of thinking about media power and its connections with the political and economic structure of contemporary capitalism.[23]

In the pluralistic image of a society of competing groups and interests, none predominant, all struggling for influence over the centres of political decision-making and allocation of benefits, the media are seen as so many contending voices in a market-place of ideas and as articulating a range of distinctive views. By contrast, in the neo-Marxist vision, heavily centred upon the role of class domination in capitalist society, the media are viewed as subordi-

---

[22] See Roschwalb, S. A., and Stack, R. A., 'Litigation Public Relations', *Communications and the Law*, 14 (1992), 3–24.

[23] For a useful summary see Curran, J., 'The New Revisionism in Mass Communication Research', *European Journal of Communication*, 5 (1990), 15–64.

nate to the political and economic interests of the dominant class or classes, and, in general, as reproducing their dominant ideological perspectives. This summary somewhat overstates the actual divergence of views, but it does, nevertheless, give a sense of the parameters of recent debate.[24] Amongst Marxists some influential studies have been based upon a 'dominant ideology thesis'.[25] Using, for instance, either a theory of the ideological hegemony of the dominant class or a 'propaganda model', it has been argued that the power of politically and economically dominant groups in the society defines the scope of debate, ensures the privileged reproduction of their discourse, and by extension, significantly determines the contours of what the public may think.[26]

At the heart of the matter is whether the workings and output of the media are seen (more or less sophisticatedly) as subject to the control of the ruling class in capitalist societies or, alternatively, whether they are seen as enjoying substantial autonomy *vis-à-vis* contending forces and interests. Broadly speaking, the choice for researchers in recent years has been between seeing the media as contributing to the maintenance of a dominant ideology or as sustaining a range of contending perspectives. Alignment in relation to this rather simplistic alternative for some considerable time largely determined the questions posed for research and the interpretation of findings.

Latterly, the underlying theoretical paradigms that gave rise to this opposition have shifted substantially. There is increasing awareness amongst radical critics of the media that the holders of power do not constitute a dominant ideologically cohesive bloc,

[24] See Gurevitch, M., Bennett, T., Curran, J., and Woollacott, J. (eds.), *Culture, Society and the Media* (London: Methuen, 1982), 1 and McQuail, D., *Mass Communication Theory: An Introduction*, 2nd edn. (London: Sage, 1987), 58–9, 85–7.

[25] For a critique see Abercrombie, N., Hill, S., and Turner, B. S., *The Dominant Ideology Thesis* (London: George Allen & Unwin, 1980) and *Sovereign Individuals of Capitalism* (London: Allen & Unwin, 1986).

[26] See Hall, S., Critcher, C., Jefferson, T., Clarke, J., and Roberts, B., *Policing the Crisis: Mugging, the State, and Law and Order* (London: Macmillan, 1978); Herman, E. H., and Chomsky, N., *Manufacturing Consent: The Political Economy of the Mass Media* (New York: Pantheon Books, 1988). This is much more the case with Herman and Chomsky. For a critical review see Schlesinger, P., 'From Production to Propaganda?', *Media, Culture and Society*, 11 (1989), 283–306. Hall's work, in contrast, has recognized the potential for interpretations of the dominant ideology that work in opposition to its 'preferred reading'. This has fed into significant work in the field of media reception.

and that there is a need to pay more attention to resistances to domination and ideological competition from outside the centres of political and economic power. At the same time, those committed to variants of liberal pluralism have increasingly acknowledged the impact of political and economic inequality in shaping the contexts in which the media operate.[27]

Holding on to the basic Marxist insight, it is essential to bear in mind the political and economic constraints that undoubtedly limit access to the news media. However, given the contemporary transformation of political communication, it is no less essential to pay attention to the competitive strategies for media attention employed by news sources. This position does not at all preclude our recognizing that political actors are subject to inequality of access and possessed of unequal resources.[28] In precisely such terms, the present book may be read as a case study in the dynamics of unequal access to the construction of the news.

Source–Media Relations

We have set out to analyse the behaviour of political actors as news sources. Crucial to the study of news sources are the relations between the media and the exercise of political and ideological power, especially, but not exclusively, by central social institutions that seek to define and manage the flow of information in contested fields of discourse.[29] Inevitably, in the present study we focus on the institutions of the state's criminal justice apparatus and how these compete for media attention, both amongst themselves and with other, more or less institutionalized, sources of information. Although, as we shall show, official bodies do occupy a dominant position in shaping crime-reporting (as is the case in other journal-

---

[27] Curran, 'The New Revisionism', provides a review of current tendencies. An impression of the shift that has occurred may be gained by noting the present proximity on questions of news management of a pluralist such as Jay Blumler and a radical critic such as John Eldridge. See Gurevitch, M. and Blumler, J., 'Political Communication Systems and Democratic Values', in J. Lichtenberg, (ed.), *Democracy and the Mass Media* (Cambridge: Cambridge University Press, 1990), 269–89 and Eldridge, J., 'News, Truth and Power', in J. Eldridge (ed.), *Getting the Message: News, Truth and Power* (London: Routledge, 1993), 3–33.

[28] See McLennan, G., *Marxism, Pluralism and Beyond* (Cambridge: Polity, 1989).

[29] In personal correspondence reacting to an earlier version of this chapter, Herbert Gans notes: 'Emphasizing the role of sources is the best way, or perhaps the only one, to connect the study of journalism to the larger society . . .' (22 July 1988).

istic fields), we shall also demonstrate that a fuller understanding of competition amongst sources requires us also to pose questions about non-official sources—a theme hitherto neglected.

News Sources as 'Primary Definers'?

Much cited in debate about the power of sources has been the concept of 'primary definition' proposed by Stuart Hall and his colleagues in an analysis of 'the social production of news' that centres upon crime coverage.[30] The media are analysed by Hall *et al.* in terms of a theory of ideological power underpinned by a Gramscian conception of the struggle for hegemony between dominant and subordinate classes in capitalist societies. According to them, 'It is this structured relationship—between the media and its [*sic*] "powerful" sources—which begins to open up the neglected question of the ideological role of the media. It is this which begins to give substance and specificity to Marx's basic proposition that "the ruling ideas of any age are the ideas of its ruling class." '[31]

Hall *et al.* argue that the media give access to those who enjoy 'accreditation'. This is a resource limited to certain social groups which enjoy a special status as sources in virtue of their institutional power, representative standing, or claims to expert knowledge. Specific examples given are government Ministers and Members of Parliament (MPs), and organized interest groups such as the Confederation of British Industry (CBI) or the Trades Union Congress (TUC). As a consequence of professional practices of ascertaining source credibility, the media are held to be structurally biased towards very powerful and privileged sources who become 'over-accessed':

The result of the structured preference given by the media to the opinions of the powerful is that these 'spokesmen' become what we call the *primary definers* of topics . . . [which] . . . permits the institutional definers to establish the initial definition or *primary interpretation* of the topic in question. This interpretation then 'commands the field' in all subsequent treatment and sets the terms of reference within which all further coverage of debate takes place.[32]

Primary definition, then, involves a primacy both temporal and ideological. This is a very strong argument indeed. Taken at face value, its import is that the structure of access *necessarily* secures

---

[30] Hall *et al.*, *Policing the Crisis.*   [31] Ibid. 58.
[32] Ibid., authors' emphases.

strategic advantages for 'primary definers', not just initially but also subsequently, for as long as a debate or controversy lasts. It also asserts that counter-definitions can never dislodge the primary definition, which consistently dominates.

The assumptions just discussed are open to various criticisms. Here we set them out as analytical points, but as the empirical findings of this and other studies show, our critique is grounded in the actual relations between news sources and news media.

First, the notion of 'primary definition' is more problematic than it seems. The broad characterization offered above does not take account of contention between official sources in trying to influence the construction of a story. In cases of dispute, say, amongst members of the same government over a key question of policy, who is the *primary* definer? Or—and it goes against the very logic of the concept—can there be more than one?[33]

Second, the formulation of Hall *et al.* fails to register the well-established fact that official sources often attempt to influence the construction of a story by using 'off-the-record' briefings—in which case the primary definers do not appear directly as such, in unveiled and attributable form.[34]

A third point concerns the drawing of the boundaries of primary definition. Do these shift, and if so, why? Hall *et al.* make reference to MPs and Ministers. Presumably, primary definition is intended to include all consensually recognized 'representative' voices. But access to the media is plainly not equally open to all members of the political class: Prime Ministers and Presidents routinely command disproportionate attention and politicians may also use media strategies to gain attention for themselves in competition with others.[35] There is nothing in the formulation of primary defining that permits us to deal with such inequalities of access amongst the privileged themselves.

[33] A classic instance of policy divisions within the state machine is illustrated in Daniel Hallin's study of the Vietnam war and the news media. See Hallin, D., *The 'Uncensored War': The Media and Vietnam* (Oxford: Oxford University Press, 1986). More recently David Miller has shown the problems of applying the concept of 'primary definition' to a divided officialdom in Northern Ireland. See Miller, D., 'Official Sources and "Primary Definition": The Case of Northern Ireland', *Media, Culture and Society*, 15 (1993), 385–406.

[34] The story of the prime-ministerial voice of the Thatcher years, Bernard Ingham, offers some instructive insights in this regard. See Harris, R., *Good and Faithful Servant: The Unauthorized Biography of Bernard Ingham* (London: Faber & Faber, 1990).

[35] See Seymour-Ure, C., 'Prime Ministers' Reactions to Television: Britain,

Fourth, there is the unconsidered question of longer-term shifts in the structure of access. Writing in the late 1970s, it may have been obvious to talk of the CBI and TUC as major institutional voices. But with the disappearance of corporatism in Britain under successive Conservative governments, such interests have lost their one-time prominence. What this point reveals is the tacit assumption that certain forces are permanently present in the power structure. It is thus an atemporal model, underpinned by the notion that primary definers are simply 'accredited' to their dominant ideological place in virtue of an institutional location. But when these are displaced by new forces and their representatives, it becomes essential to explain their emergence.

Hall *et al.* go on to locate the media in the power structure thus:

The media, then, do not simply create the news; nor do they simply transmit the ideology of the 'ruling class' in a conspiratorial fashion. Indeed, we have suggested that, in a critical sense, the media are frequently not the 'primary definers' of news events at all but their structured relationship to power has the effect of making them play a crucial secondary role in *reproducing* the definitions of those who have privileged access, as of right, to the media as 'accredited sources'. From this point of view, in the moment of news production, the media stand in a position of structured subordination to the primary definers.[36]

Thus, the media are characterized as a subordinate site for the reproduction of the ideological field; in effect, they are conceived as 'secondary definers'.

This now brings us to a fifth objection, which is that Hall *et al.* tend to overstate the passivity of the media as recipients of information from news sources: the flow of definitions is seen as moving uniformly from the centres of power to the media. Within this conceptual logic, there is no space to account for occasions on which media may themselves take the initiative in the definitional process by challenging the so-called primary definers and forcing them to respond. Relevant examples would be cases of investigative journalism dealing with scandals inside the state apparatus or in the world of big business, or when leaks by dissident figures force out undesired and unintended official responses, or when

Australia and Canada', *Media, Culture and Society*, 11 (1989), 307–25; Hinkley, B., *The Symbolic Presidency: How Presidents Portray Themselves* (New York: Routledge, 1990).

[36] Hall *et al.*, *Policing the Crisis*, 59, authors' emphasis.

accidents occur and official figures are caught on the hop.[37] At times, too, it is the media that crystallize slogans or pursue campaigns that are subsequently taken up by the would-be primary definers because it is in their interests to do so.[38] Aside from seeing the media as excessively passive, this way of conceiving of their relations to news sources tends to elide the variations that exist within and between different news media. Access for 'alternative' viewpoints differs as between the press and television, and indeed, as between different newspapers.[39]

A sixth criticism concerns how the conception of 'primary definition' renders largely invisible the activities of sources that attempt to generate 'counter-definitions'. This rules out any analysis of the process of *negotiation* about policy questions between power-holders and their opponents that may occur prior to the issuing of what are assumed to be primary definitions. As we shall see, thinking about such brokerage as taking place within a policy arena does complicate the picture, even though access to that political space is undoubtedly limited. The essentially structuralist approach of Hall *et al.*, however, is profoundly incurious about the processes whereby sources may engage in ideological conflict prior to, or contemporaneous with, the appearance of 'definitions' in the media. It therefore tends to ignore questions about how contestation over the presentation of information takes place within institutions and organizations reported by the media, as well as overlooking the concrete strategies pursued as they contend for space and time.

Although Hall *et al.*'s approach fails to deal with a number of conceptual difficulties, there is still undoubtedly a strong case for arguing that the organization of journalistic practice *generally* promotes the views and interests of authoritative sources. This is a paramount finding of much of the sociology of journalism, which

---

[37] For relevant studies see Murphy, D., *The Stalker Affair and the Press* (London: Unwin Hyman, 1991); Molotch, H. and Lester, M., 'News as Purposive Behavior: On the Strategic Use of Routine Events, Accidents and Scandals', *American Sociological Review*, 39 (1974), 101–12; Tumber, H., '"Selling Scandal"'.

[38] e.g. the press campaign over the 'seal plague' and its political impact. See Anderson, A., 'Source Strategies and the Communication of Environmental Affairs', *Media, Culture and Society*, 13 (1991), 459–76.

[39] For relevant studies see Curran, J., 'Culturalist Perspectives of News Organizations: A Reappraisal and a Case Study', in Ferguson, *Public Communication*, 114–34; McNair, B., *Images of the Enemy* (London: Routledge, 1988); Schlesinger, P., Murdock, G., and Elliott, P., *Televising 'Terrorism': Political Violence in Popular Culture* (London: Comedia, 1983).

will be discussed in the next section. The key point is that because the conception of 'primary definition' resolves the question of source power on the basis of structuralist assumptions, it closes off any engagement with the dynamic processes of contestation in a given field of discourse.[40] It has the signal advantage of directing our attention to the exercise of definitional power in society, but it offers no account of how this is achieved as the outcome of strategies pursued by political actors. That is because 'primary definers' are seen as simply guaranteed access to the news media in virtue of their structural position. To sum up: 'primary definition', which ought to be an empirically ascertainable outcome, is held instead to be an a priori effect of privileged access.

However, the massive investments that have taken place in political public relations and marketing both by state agencies, and by a variety of other interests that aim to establish themselves as authoritative news sources, do require some explanation. Thinking of 'primary definition' as a resolved matter makes us incurious about source competition and what its implications for the workings of the public sphere might be.

The Production of News

The production of news is one of the most well-researched fields in media studies, with work ranging across the political economy of the media, through organizational studies, and into broader cultural concerns with the form and content of news.[41] Most sociological research into news sources has failed to focus upon the

[40] Hall has maintained his views on 'primary definition'. In the opening essay in a critical collection aimed at giving an 'adequate understanding' of media power to those at the receiving end, he put the argument in a less qualified, and therefore more revealing way: 'Some things, people, events, relationships always get represented: always centre-stage, always in the position to define, to set the agenda, to establish the terms of the conversation. Some others sometimes get represented—but always at the margin, always responding to a question whose terms and conditions have been defined elsewhere: never "centred". Still others are always "represented" only by their eloquent absence, their silences: or refracted through the glance or the gaze of others,' See Hall, S., 'Media Power and Class Power', in J. Curran, J. Ecclestone, G. Oakley, and A. Richardson (eds.), *Bending Reality: The State of the Media* (London: Pluto, 1986), 9. Although he concedes that some 'marginal categories get "accessed" all the time' (ibid.), this is basically seen as window-dressing and not as the outcome of source strategies.

[41] For a useful recent survey of the field see Schudson, M., 'The Sociology of News Production Revisited', in Curran and Gurevitch, *Mass Media and Society*, 141–59.

source–media relation from the standpoint of sources themselves *as well as* from that of journalists. In other words, it has been predominantly media-centric.

Empirical studies generally stress the importance to journalistic work of official sources in government and administration, and there is widespread agreement that these play a crucial role in defining and shaping the news agenda through their interaction with the news production process. Consequently, it has been suggested that 'the story of journalism, on a day to day basis, is the story of the interaction of reporters and officials.'[42] Studies examining news-reporting have tended to concentrate on how reporters cover specific institutional areas, although very occasionally a range of different specialisms has been analysed and compared in the same study.[43] Not surprisingly, given its crucial importance, news coverage of the political system has been repeatedly examined. For instance, in the American context, the relations between reporters and officials in Washington has been a major focus of research, whereas in Britain studies have focused on the Westminster–Whitehall lobby system, and in Australia there has been work on media and politicians in the Federal and state capitals.[44]

This predominantly institutional focus has been followed in studies of areas other than political reporting. US studies have long shown how much reporting is routinely centred upon specific 'beats'.[45] Likewise, in British work, the political lobby has pro-

---

[42] Schudson, 'The Sociology of News Production Revisited', 148.

[43] The classical study of this kind is Tunstall, J., *Journalists at Work: Specialist Correspondents, their News Organizations, News Sources, and Competitor-Colleagues* (London: Constable, 1971). Ericson, R. V., Baranek, P. M., and Chan, J. B. L., *Negotiating Control: A Study of News Sources* (Toronto: University of Toronto Press, 1989) also compares different, but more closely related, specialist fields.

[44] On the USA see Sigal, L. V., *Reporters and Officials: The Organization and Politics of Newsmaking* (Lexington, Mass.: D. C. Heath & Co., 1973); Hess, S., *The Washington Reporters* (Washington, DC: The Brookings Institution, 1981); Cook, T., *Making Laws and Making News: Media Strategies in the U.S. House of Representatives* (Washington, DC: The Brookings Institution, 1989); On Britain see Seymour-Ure, C., *The Press, Politics and the Public* (London: Methuen, 1968); Tunstall, J., *The Westminster Lobby Correspondents* (London: Routledge & Kegan Paul, 1970); Cockerell, M., Hennessy, P., and Walker, D., *Sources Close to the Prime Minister: Inside the Hidden World of the News Manipulators* (London: Macmillan, 1984); on Australia see Tiffen, R., *News and Power* (Sydney: Allen & Unwin, 1989).

[45] An early example was Gieber, W. and Johnson, W., 'The City Hall "Beat": A Study of Reporter and Source Roles', *Journalism Quarterly*, 38 (1961), 289–97. For more contemporary approaches see Fishman, M., *Manufacturing the News* (Austin:

vided a general model for the official flow of information to the media in other areas of institutional activity. Hence, for instance, a number of studies have dealt with the relations between various types of reporters and official sources within the state machinery, but usually in terms of how journalists perceive these.[46]

The well-founded recognition of the crucial role of the state (in the form of government departments and the wider political class) as the major producer of information which defines 'the amount, timing and overall direction' of much news does not preclude acknowledgement of some of the further complexities of struggles to influence coverage.[47] The empirical sociology of journalism for the most part has shied away from endorsing a concept of primary definition, although analogous terms can be found in the literature. The pressure of detailed analysis of source activity has tended to result in an appreciation of divergencies within the official camp. The question of alternative views (even if they fall into quite a restricted ideological range) necessarily surfaces as a matter of importance, as does recognition of the fact that official status does not automatically ensure credibility. As Leon Sigal observes, 'The convention of authoritativeness may assure a hearing in the news for those in authority, but it is no guarantee of a "good press" so long as other sources are willing and able to talk to reporters.'[48] It is precisely this latter point that the concept of primary definition ignores: the credibility of given political actors may vary over time, as indeed may the scope for oppositional and alternative views to force their way onto the political agenda.[49] The scope of the public sphere is not fixed for all time, and its relative openness or closure is an outcome of political struggle. Consensual times may give way to those of extreme crisis, and vice versa.

Apart from producing a recognition of possible divergencies

University of Texas Press, 1980) and Hess, S., *The Washington Reporters* (Washington, DC: The Brookings Institution, 1981).

[46] See e.g. Chibnall, S., *Law-and-Order News: An Analysis of Crime Reporting in the British Press* (London: Tavistock Publishing, 1977); Golding, P. and Middleton, S., *Images of Welfare: Press and Public Attitudes to Poverty* (Oxford: Martin Robertson, 1982); Morrison, D. and Tumber, H., *Journalists At War: The Dynamics of News Reporting during the Falklands Conflict* (London: Sage, 1988).

[47] The phrase is Golding and Middleton's in *Images of Welfare*, 121.

[48] Sigal, L. V., 'Who? Sources Make the News', in R. K. Manoff and M. Schudson (eds.), *Reading the News* (New York: Pantheon, 1986), 37.

[49] See Schudson, 'The Sociology of News Production Revisited', who notes in this connection the importance both of historical and comparative approaches.

within the political establishment, engagement with the empirical realities of source–media relations may also enhance awareness of the significance of non-official sources, such as, for instance, of pressure groups which 'serve a twin function. On the one hand they act as research agencies, able to point out the inconsistencies or evasions in official versions of policy. On the other hand they provide hand-wringing reactions to the iniquities of government policy that can be used to "balance" a story.'[50] Although it has certainly not loomed large, built into the empirical sociology of journalism—irrespective of whether it has tended towards pluralism or Marxism—is the potential for investigating the social organization of non-official news sources and of assessing their relationships to the state. This analytical opening has implications for how we think about the wider functioning of the public sphere.

Various writers have tried to generalize about the relations between news media and their sources. Such theorizing or model-building has generally been closely allied to the empirical research at hand. A common formulation is that news sources and journalists are engaged in an 'exchange of information for publicity'[51] or in a relationship characterized as a 'tug of war' in which 'sources attempt to "manage" the news, putting the best light on themselves [and] journalists concurrently "manage" the source in order to extract the information they want'.[52]

At one level, this view presupposes that such interaction is akin to those based on an instrumental economic calculation, where each side weighs up the costs and benefits involved in an activity, and seeks to maximize its satisfactions or utilities.[53] Although an explanation in terms of the coincidence of self-interest on both sides of an exchange relationship is of importance, it does not tell the whole story. Sources and journalists often need to appeal to norms other than those that are purely economic, for they are engaged in a social process that goes beyond simple buying and selling. For instance, such non-economic considerations as trust

---

[50] Golding and Middleton, *Images of Welfare*, 119.

[51] See the discussion in Tunstall, *The Westminster Lobby Correspondents*, 43–4.

[52] Gans, H., *Deciding What's News: A Study of CBS Evening News, NBC Nightly News, Newsweek, and Time* (New York: Pantheon, 1979), 117.

[53] The most fully worked-out version of this position is in Gandy, jun., O. H., *Beyond Agenda Setting: Information Subsidies and Public Policy* (Norwood, NJ: Ablex Publishing Co., 1982).

and confidentiality come into the equation on many occasions. And yet, although personal liking and compatibility may certainly be important at times, such relations are not in any case purely and simply conducted between individuals. They operate at the inter-face between news organizations and news sources, who, almost invariably, are themselves members of organizations with collective goals to pursue.[54]

In this context, relevant questions concern the kinds of control that sources have over journalists and those that journalists, in turn, have over their sources.[55] A number of studies suggest that, on the whole, the advantage lies with sources, given the substantial passivity of the media in information-gathering.[56] Moreover, empirical research does give considerable support to the notion that there is a structured bias towards access for the politically powerful, a view somewhat epigrammatically summed up thus, by the US sociologist, Herbert Gans:

While in theory sources can come from anywhere, in practice, their recruitment and their access to journalists reflect the hierarchies of nation and society. The President of the United States has instantaneous access to all news media; the powerless must resort to civil disturbances to obtain it.[57]

In addition, economic resources play an important role in offering a privileged basis for the routine provision of information. The fact that sources are not generally paid entails an implicit class bias both in terms of self-selection as an information-provider and in the media's selection of given individuals or groups. The social and geographical concentration of news-gathering also brings about routinization of media search procedures.

It is not surprising, then, that in empirical studies there is strong support for that part of the 'primary definition' argument which stresses how the media's use of 'authoritative and efficient sources' leads to a 'cumulative pattern that determines availability and suit-ability' and 'makes the public official the most frequent and regular source'.[58] Nor is it especially startling to conclude that 'habitual access is generally found among those with extreme wealth or other institutionally-based sources of power', with the consequence

[54] See Tunstall, *Journalists at Work*, 185–6.   [55] Ibid. 203.
[56] A view taken by Gans, *Deciding What's News*, Golding and Middleton, *Images of Welfare*, and Sigal, *Reporters and Officials*.
[57] Gans, *Deciding What's News*, 119.   [58] Ibid. 145.

that 'Routine access is one of the important sources and sustainers of existing power relationships.'[59]

To recognize that such advantages accrue to those possessed of advantaged positions, however, does not preclude the need to look *beyond* the powerful in order to see whether, and how, that might affect our understanding of source–media relations. The empirical sociology of journalism plainly shares insights with the structuralist view about the strategic advantages that political and economic power may secure for sources. But on the whole it holds back from characterizing this as primary definition, because it tends to be recognized that those seeking access to the media must engage in the active pursuit of definitional advantage. Powerful sources still have to pursue goal-oriented action to achieve access, even though their recognition as 'legitimate authorities' is already usually inscribed in the rules of the game. This contrasts with the structuralist notion of 'automatic', accredited access resulting in primary definition.

These considerations point to rethinking the methodology of empirical studies of how sources act, an issue that has attracted almost no critical attention at all so far. The available approaches fall into two: the internalist and the externalist. These are not mutually exclusive by any means, but treating them as distinct alternatives helps bring out their separate logics.

Internalists typically produce their analyses of source behaviour either by interpreting what sources do by a reading of media content, or by deriving conclusions from accounts given by journalists of their interactions with their sources, or by combining both. There is nothing wrong with this, but it has shortcomings. If we restrict ourselves to what appears in the media this plainly does not tell us much about the process whereby it comes to be there. Furthermore, if we restrict ourselves to journalists' accounts of how they have dealt with sources the optic is largely limited to how the media organize *their* information strategies.

These limitations can be circumvented by taking an externalist approach. This implies an analysis of the strategies and tactics of sources in relation to the media. Such work exists already, for instance, in the form of *post hoc* reconstructions of particular exercises in news management or censorship. Such evidence is usually based upon a mix of journalistic reflections on experience, pub-

---

[59] Molotch and Lester, 'News as Purposive Behavior', 107.

lished revelations based on leaks or the subsequent coming clean of participants, and the release of official documents long after the event. In short, for externalist accounts involving substantial reconstruction from diverse sources the passage of time is a great help, especially so where the weeders of public records or the feeders of shredders have lacked foresight.

Our argument here is that in addition to using internalist evidence we need to extend the scope of externalist evidence. Our step in this direction has been a simple one, namely systematically to interview news sources. Observational studies are an obvious complement to this approach.[60] All such research, of course, is open to the usual problems such as incompleteness, verification, evaluation, and interpretation. Moreover, since the analysis of sources (like that of media production) is highly dependent upon the co-operation of those studied, serious problems of access or secrecy could arise.[61] Nevertheless, the attempt has seemed worthwhile to us, for not only has it gathered in a different kind of evidence from that normally found in media studies, it has also provoked some reconceptualization and refocusing of the sociological study of journalism.[62]

Source–Media Analysis

A number of significant studies have gone beyond the dominant media-centrism of the sociology of journalism to investigate the media strategies and tactics of news sources. However, such research has tended to be subsumed under the production study tradition without its originality of focus being clearly seen. By drawing attention to this persisting line of investigation, it is not our intention, as might erroneously be supposed, to replace media-

[60] See Ericson et al., Negotiating Control.

[61] As pointed out in Gandy, jun., O. H., 'Information in Health: Subsidized News', Media, Culture and Society, 2 (1980), 114.

[62] This point has been particularly clearly recognized in two studies working within what is still a media-centric framework that both have pushed to its limits. See Murphy, D., The Stalker Affair and the Press (London: Unwin Hyman, 1991), which trenchantly challenges the dominant ideology thesis by using an example of official loss of control over news management. Also see Tiffen, R., News and Power, which lucidly demonstrates the role of political news sources in contending over control of the political arena. This second study is based on an internalist approach coupled with externalist reconstructions.

centred studies with a 'source perspective', as that too would suffer from tunnel vision.[63]

The overall approach that we single out here may be termed 'source–media analysis'. This extends the now well-established focus on how news organizations work. The sociological study of news production developed, at least in part, because of the inadequacies of analysing news simply by looking at its content. Of course, the external analysis of news has much to tell us, for instance, about the textual construction of given stories, or the patterns of attention accorded to given types of reporting. However, as an approach used on its own, external analysis (whatever form it takes) does face the crucial limitation of only being able to make inferences about the production process. By offering an internal vantage-point, therefore, production studies have substantially enlarged the possibilities of studying the anatomy of journalism.

There is a comparable gain to be made by the further shift of focus that we advocate here. Whilst studying the practices of newsrooms and news-gathering has much to tell us about how media work, it still has the crucial shortcoming of offering only a partial view of the interrelations between the news media and the social institutions, organizations, and groups on which they report. Just as research into news organizations has offered an important refocusing of attention from product to process, so has the study of news sources considerably extended the scope of production studies by adding the complicating factor of sources' perspectives.

Over the past two decades, with varying emphases, but essentially subsumed under the mainstream of production studies, a number of researchers have taken a source–media analytic approach.[64] Given its intermittent appearance it is only latterly,

---

[63] The phrase cited is Dennis McQuail's. See McQuail, D., *Media Performance: Mass Communication and the Public Interest* (London: Sage, 1992), 133. Restricted as it is to questions of news production and content, the present study does not constitute a comprehensive account of the process of public communication, nor, indeed, is it intended to. For one, it leaves out any analysis of media reception, although our approach may articulate with analyses of the reception process in which judgements about the sources of public communication by audience members are quite central. For a relevant account see Corner, J., Richardson, K., and Fenton, N., *Nuclear Reactions: Form and Response in Public Issue Television* (London: John Libbey, 1990).

[64] Others might classify the research literature differently. See Tuchman, G., 'Qualitative Methods in the Study of News', in K. Bruhn Jensen and N. W. Jankowski (eds.), *A Handbook of Qualitative Methodologies for Mass Communication Research* (London: Routledge, 1991), 79–92. Tuchman has also

perhaps, that this corpus of work could be identified as constituting a quite distinctive strand in media research. All such work to date has been North American. To the best of our knowledge, this is the first full-scale British study of this kind to be published, and several others are in progress.[65]

Probably the first study to signal the new orientation was the US political scientist Leon Sigal's research on the politics of news-making in Washington. Published in the early 1970s, his work took as its centrepiece the interactions between two bureaucratic worlds: that of Washington politics and that of two élite newspapers, the *New York Times* and the *Washington Post*. Sigal's central thesis was that 'news is an outcome of the bargaining interplay of newsmen and their sources.'[66] To substantiate this, he investigated the routines of news production and showed their conformity to those of routine governmental information flows, with heavy journalistic reliance on authoritative sources in the US government. Sigal also demonstrated the use of what he called 'informational press manœuvres' that involved the tactical and strategic release of information by news sources. Since non-official political actors had serious problems in gaining access to media coverage, he concluded, 'the press will primarily offer news from official sources passed through official channels'.[67]

It was precisely non-official sources—basically ignored by Sigal—that were the focus of the US political scientist Edie Goldenberg's subsequent analysis, conducted in the early 1970s, of 'resource-poor', largely politically radical, interest groups and their relations to the metropolitan press in Boston.[68] This research showed how urban interest groups sought recourse to newspapers in order to influence policy-makers. The resources available to political actors were of major importance in affecting their ability to organize

noticed how source–media analysis extends the scope of more conventional production studies. She differs from us, however, in seeing this shift as only very recent. Moreover, since for her its main importance is to confirm the media-centric view that 'news organizations are heavily dependent on legitimated sources' (p. 86), she overlooks the need to analyse sources' strategies.

[65] Some have appeared in articles or unpublished form. See esp. the research of Anderson and Miller, cited in nn. 33 and 38.

[66] Sigal, *Reporters and Officials*, 5.

[67] Ibid. 190. Sigal's work has been followed by others such as Cook, *Making Laws and Making News*.

[68] Goldenberg, E., *Making the Papers: The Access of Resource-Poor Groups to the Metropolitan Press* (Lexington, Mass.: D. C. Heath & Co., 1975).

media strategies in competition with official sources. Factors such as group size, geographical location, news-management skills, expert knowledge, and finance were all shown to play a role in determining the credibility of a would-be source with journalists. Given newspapers were targeted by sources on the basis of the audiences they were thought to reach, their politics towards given issues, and the kind of coverage that they offered. In comparison with official sources, non-official groups had greater endemic problems in achieving coverage. The routine practices of reporting, which, as Sigal argues, tend to be focused on institutional news sources, tend also to favour official news. Thus, Goldenberg maintained, only under favourable conditions could 'resource-poor' groups gain access to the news media. Such sources needed to establish themselves as credible and to maintain their reliability over time. The type of newspaper targeted, therefore, and its relative openness to non-official sources of news was an important factor. In general, it was concluded that whereas occasional entry into the public arena was possible for those with few resources, it was not secure in the long term.

Two other relevant American studies were published at the beginning of the 1980s. In the first of these, the US sociologist, Todd Gitlin, put the relations between Students for a Democratic Society (a key factor in the anti-Vietnam War movement in the 1960s) and the national news media under the microscope. He showed how a loosely organized movement was obliged to throw up professionalized sources from amongst its leadership in what he terms 'the manufacture of celebrity'. Given the news media's tendency to personalize social groups, individuals in the wider movement were singled out and became, for a time at least, authoritative sources, speaking on its behalf. Gitlin observed how in seeking sources the media made celebrities out of unknowns which in turn fed back into leadership struggles with destabilizing effects, as did polarizing reportage of 'moderates' v. 'militants'.[69]

Both Goldenberg's and Gitlin's studies were concerned with inequality of access to the news media rooted in political and economic relations, and they focused on news sources that were disadvantaged. The question of sources was also taken up in another analysis by the US communications researcher, Oscar Gandy, who

[69] Gitlin, T., *The Whole World is Watching: Mass Media in the Making and Unmaking of the New Left* (Berkeley, Calif.: University of California Press, 1980).

shifted the focus towards what he termed the 'primary sources of media content' by investigating what lay behind the creation of media agendas, particularly by exploring the routine activities of powerful institutions and organizations in political and economic life.[70] Rather than the resource-poor, the interest on this occasion lay in the resource-rich.

Gandy's perspective stresses the crucial importance of inequalities in the economic resources disposed of by news sources, which are rooted in the class structure and hold general implications for power relations. His main concern is with the provision of information by major corporations and government, rather than with the uses of secrecy. Those sources best endowed can, in effect, reduce the price of information to the media and provide them with a subsidy. 'It is through the provision of information subsidies to and through the mass media', he argues, 'that those with economic power are able to maintain their control over a capitalist society.' The issue for him, therefore, becomes one of exploring the 'relatively unknown dimensions of source behaviour and the structural conditions that facilitate the use of information as an instrument of social control'.[71] Although Gandy's work is primarily concerned with resource-rich corporate, political, and bureaucratic sources, as a consequence he notes the economic problems of entry into the policy arena for resource-poor citizen consumers.[72]

Most closely related to the substance of the present research is the work of the Canadian criminologist Richard Ericson and his colleagues who, in a book published at the end of the 1980s, examined how sources and news media in Toronto interacted in shaping the reporting of crime and deviance.[73] Ericson *et al.* investigated

---

[70] Gandy, *Beyond Agenda-Setting*, p. x. This was part of a direct critique of the influential 'agenda-setting' approach in US communications research. Gandy explicitly argued for new priorities in media research. The proposed shift away from the analysis of news content and effects, and towards recognizing the limits of studying news organizations, has offered a productive way into understanding the shaping of the policy process.

[71] Ibid. 7, 9.

[72] Ibid. 33–4: 'persons and groups who take positions at variance with the dominant ideology would require a much larger budget to overcome the pool of existing information, and achieve any degree of conversion.' Also see p. 199. Gandy sees relations between media and sources purely as one-dimensional exchanges based upon economic calculation, and, as suggested earlier, social relations cannot be reduced to economic relations without a loss of broader understanding.

[73] Ericson *et al.*, *Negotiating Control*. This was part of a wider study of news production and content. The companion volumes, by the same authors, are

several institutional arenas in Toronto—the courts, the police, the provincial legislature and private-sector organizations—to see how these differed in terms of their openness or closure with respect to the flow of information, and how these variations affected the kind of media coverage to which they were susceptible. In parallel with the approach developed below, they were concerned with processes of negotiation at the interface between news media and major social institutions.

What Ericson *et al.*'s work has shown is that although—in keeping with previous work—authoritative sources attempt largely successfully to control the flow of information to the news media, their room for manœuvre varies according to the institutional setting in which any given set of source–media relations takes place. Thus the picture becomes more complex than one of across-the-board, largely uncontested, dominance of the news agenda by well-resourced sources. In particular, this research raised questions about seeing news media as simply passive, or as 'secondary definers' responding to others' initiatives. Rather, it was argued that for sources 'the news media are very powerful, in possession of key resources that frequently give them the upper hand'.[74] In this connection, Ericson *et al.* instance the denial of access, negative coverage, and journalistic discretion over how an issue or event is to be represented.

Ericson *et al.*'s approach has also introduced a novel comparative perspective into the analysis of the different sites in which sources and media interact, broadening out from the customary single institutional arena noted above.[75] In addition, the authors also

---

Visualizing Deviance: A Study of News Organization and *Representing Order: Crime, Law, and Justice in the News Media* (Milton Keynes: Open University Press, 1987 and 1991). Fieldwork for the present study was well under way by the time Ericson *et al.*'s first book—on news production—appeared. An exchange of views ensued once we became aware of the striking parallels between one another's work.

[74] Ericson *et al.*, *Negotiating Control*, 378.

[75] The present study does not take the comparative road, and this still remains to be taken in the UK. However, as we do here, others too are contributing to the new wave of research represented by this book. See Anderson, A., 'The Production of Environmental News: A Study of Source–Media Relations', Ph.D. thesis (University of Greenwich in collaboration with the University of Stirling, 1993); Eide, M., 'Strategic Action and the Sociology of News', in H. Rønning and K. Lundby (eds.), *Media and Communication: Readings in Methodology, History and Culture* (Oslo: Norwegian University Press, 1991), 151–8; Miller, D., 'The Northern Ireland Information Service and the Media: Aims, Strategy, Tactics', and Miller, D. and Williams, K., 'Negotiating HIV/AIDS Information: Agendas, Media Strategies and the News', in Eldridge, *Getting the Message*, 73–103 and 126–42.

brought the private sector into their analysis. In this regard, their research principally covered business corporations but also included citizens' interest groups, which, as Goldenberg pointed out, have also become more knowledgeable in handling public relations techniques, but which commonly lack the resource base for equal competition with powerful institutional sources. This latter theme is a line of investigation that we take considerably further below. As will be seen, it is at this point that the largely separate fields of pressure group analysis and media research begin to connect.

Because of their striking preponderance, and consequent attractiveness for analysis, sociological studies, with few exceptions, have looked almost exclusively at powerful sources. Ericson et al. have recognized the consequences of this neglect, commenting that the present preoccupation 'with news sources in government legislatures, bureaucracies and criminal law-enforcement agencies . . . has the effect of limiting our understanding of how private-sector institutions and organizations participate in the news system'.[76] In the present book, as well as considering the perspectives of official sources, we also seek to remedy the dearth of sustained investigation into *non-official* source competition. Whilst this is of interest in its own right, it also opens up a further dimension: namely, that of the interaction between different types of source, official and non-official, and what this tells us about the workings of the wider policy arena. This has been ignored by conventional media research, and has therefore remained effectively hidden from view.

Such work inevitably takes us into broader questions about the nature of information management in society by a variety of groups and institutions in conditions of unequal power, and therefore of unequal access to systems of information production and distribution. Given our present interest in the criminal justice system, our research necessarily centres upon the apparatuses of the state, which do enjoy privileged access to the media. However, this does not mean that we should ignore the activities of other types of source, as this unnecessarily deprives us of empirical knowledge of how the battle for access is conducted in the contemporary public sphere. For those who might consider this concern an arid exercise in micro-politics, we can only observe that the conditions of

[76] Ericson *et al.*, *Negotiating Control*, 259.

survival of alternatives are crucial to the survival of any public sphere at all. Indeed, we would argue that our findings have macro-political implications.

I
Sources in Action

Introduction to Part I

THE wider political public sphere may be conceived of as divided into specific arenas in which competition for public attention and resources takes place between political actors.[1] Gaining media coverage—a scarce resource—may be a major objective of political action in a given public arena. In the present case, that arena is the criminal justice system.

News sources' material and symbolic advantages are unequally distributed. We have argued that although official bodies undoubtedly dominate institutional news coverage, questions about differently endowed groups struggling to build and modify 'media agendas' are not thereby rendered irrelevant.[2] 'Media agendas' may be defined as consisting of 'those issues, actors, events, images and viewpoints that receive time or space in publications or broadcasts that are available to given audiences'.[3] As we shall demonstrate, in order to make an effective intervention in the media agenda—or to intervene at all—strategies and tactics must be pursued.

Media agendas may in turn be related in a variety of ways to 'policy agendas', namely 'the list of items which decision-markers have formally accepted for serious consideration'.[4] The struggle to influence the policy agenda involves a range of different actors. For instance, to name three possibilities, decisions could be restricted to a circle of government insiders, they could involve state consultation

---

[1] See Hilgartner, S. and Bosk, C. L., 'The Rise and Fall of Social Problems: A Public Arenas Model', *American Journal of Sociology*, 94 (1988), 53–78.

[2] See Lang, G. E., and Lang, K., *The Battle for Public Opinion: The President, the Press, and the Polls during Watergate* (New York: Columbia University Press, 1983). They observe (on pp. 58–9): 'Agenda building—a more apt term than agenda setting—is a collective process in which media, government and the citizenry reciprocally influence one another in at least some respects.'

[3] See Manheim, J. B., 'A Model of Agenda Dynamics', in M. L. McLaughlin (ed.), *Communication Yearbook 10* (London: Sage, 1987), 500.

[4] This is broadly in line with the notion of a 'formal agenda' taken up by political élites, which is distinguished from the wider 'public agenda' of potential issues from which the narrow range of policy matters is actually selected. See Cobb, R., Ross, J.-K., and Ross, M. H., 'Agenda-Building as a Comparative Political Process', *American Political Science Review*, 70 (1976), 126–38, citation from p. 126.

with interest groups, or they could be the outcome of pressures on political institutions deriving from popular mobilization. Our main concern here is with the second of these.

As we show, the institutional arena of the criminal justice process acts as a focus for the competing activities of official and non-official bodies in pursuit of their political objectives. The complex and various types of interconnection between the Home Office, criminal justice and law-enforcement professionals, pressure groups, and journalists seems aptly characterized as a 'policy network'.[5] In this framework of action, news sources may be seen as political entrepreneurs who are willing to invest their resources to attain their goals.[6] The aim of such political entrepreneurship is to affect the various audiences concerned with the policy process by means of influencing the media agenda. Often this entails working behind the scenes, rather than in public, to shape the interpretation of current issues by acting as a credible source, and, routinely, by building up a positive public image.

In Chapters 2 and 3 our aim is to offer some insights into aspects of the agenda-building process in the crime and criminal justice field, without in any way claiming to offer a comprehensive account of the working through of given issues. Rather, the objective is to draw the outlines of the arena in which conflicts over given agendas occur as a preliminary to more detailed work.[7] At the same time, in both of those chapters, and in Chapter 4 too, we also wish to show that in order to operate effectively in a highly mediatized political system, news sources have had to rationalize their activities. The growth in sophistication of media-using expertise is part of what is now routinely required for effective political action.

An ideal type of a news source's goals would involve at least the following conditions:

[5] For discussion of current conceptual debates see Marsh, D. and Rhodes, R. A. W. (eds.), *Policy Networks in British Government* (Oxford: Clarendon Press, 1992), esp. chs. 1 and 11.

[6] See Padioleau, J.-G., *L'État au concret* (Paris: Presses Universitaires de France, 1982), 23–31. For the more narrowly defined notion of a 'policy entrepreneur' see Kingdon, J. W., *Agendas, Alternatives and Public Policies* (Boston, Toronto: Little Brown & Co., 1984), 214.

[7] Given the findings of our fieldwork, we are principally concerned here with what Cobb *et al.*, 'Agenda-Building', 132 call the 'outside initiative' approach, where non-governmental groups attempt to gain attention for their claims and interests.

(1) that the source has a well-defined message to communicate, framed in optimal terms capable of satisfying news values;

(2) that the optimal locations for placing that particular message have been identified, as have the target audiences of the media outlets concerned;

(3) that the preconditions for communicative 'success' have been assured so far as possible by, for instance, cultivating a sympathetic contact or fine-tuning the timing of a leak;

(4) that the anticipated strategies of others (which may include support as much as opposition) are incorporated into ongoing media strategies. Support may be harnessed by coalition-building. Opposition may, for instance, be countered by astute timing or discrediting its credibility;

(5) that means exist for monitoring and evaluating the impact of a given strategy or tactic and for adjusting future action in the light of what is reflexively learned;

(6) that some messages may be as much intended for private as public communication, thus operating on at least two levels.

As we shall see in the chapters that follow, although these ideal conditions are rarely, if ever, all simultaneously realized in practice, taken together they do offer a key to understanding how news sources act. Such action is conditioned by the resources available.[8]

First, there is the extent to which any given source is institutionalized. The most advantageous locations in the crime and criminal justice arena are occupied by the apparatuses of the state such as the Home Office and the Metropolitan Police. These are locuses of permanent activity for which the routine dissemination of official information is important. Within the same institutional field defined by the criminal justice system, in competition for space in the media, and for legitimacy and credibility, are criminal justice and law-enforcement professionals and mainstream pressure groups. At the other end of the continuum are the least institutionalized actors, consisting of *ad hoc* issue-oriented groups or groups whose base of support is narrow and weak.

A clear distinction between the official and non-official worlds is difficult to draw because criminal justice and law-enforcement professionals are often taken by the media to have a quasi-official

---

[8] For a recent overview of planning in communication see Windahl, S. and Signitzer, B., with Olson, J. T., *Using Communication Theory: An Introduction to Planned Communication* (London: Sage, 1992).

status, and also because of the existence of state-funded, but relatively autonomous, pressure groups. For instance, some groups in the field of prison reform (such as the National Association for the Care and Resettlement of Offenders, NACRO) are directly funded by the Home Office and are sometimes expected to take up positions at variance with current policy. How is this kind of source to be characterized? Whilst coming partially within the orbit of the state, it retains substantial autonomy and it would be unduly reductive to assimilate it to a single, overarching category of official primary definer. Similar problems arise when the organized activities of state employees in the field, such as those of the Police Federation or the Prison Officers' Association, are considered. In some circumstances, such groups often behave just like other trade unions attempting to improve their bargaining positions. Once again, whilst recognizing their proximity to the state apparatus proper, it is reductive to obliterate distinctive positions over current policy.

A second resource issue is the level of investment a given actor is prepared to make in media relations. As media strategies have become increasingly perceived as important to political actors, the surplus within an organization directed towards symbolic and media-oriented action has become a crucial test of adaptation to the contemporary realities of a promotional and mediatized culture.

In this context, as we shall see, competition for media attention may become quite complex. However, strategies of co-operation also become salient: where political goals coincide (as, for instance, in relation to a piece of legislation) a combination of several groups may occur in respect both of lobbying and media strategy.[9]

Third, a further resource derives from the location a source has in the institutional arena. Perceived credibility, legitimacy, and authoritativeness condition the evaluation of sources within the media and the rules of thumb of handling them. Official sources may not always have to be believed, but they do generally have to be taken seriously. Non-official sources therefore have to acquire their credibility, legitimacy, and authoritativeness by dint of quite

---

[9] This point has also been made in relation to the study of social movements. See Zald, M. and McCarthy, J. C., 'Social Movement Industries: Competition and Cooperation among Movement Organizations', in Kriesberg, L. (ed.), *Research in Social Movements, Conflict and Change: A Research Annual* (Greenwich, Conn.: JAI Press Inc., 1980), 1—20.

developed media strategies, in which the aura of expertise is plainly important. Once acquired, this may then function as a kind of 'cultural capital', in the French sociologist Pierre Bourdieu's phrase, to be negotiated against future recognition in the battle for access to media coverage.[10]

[10] See Bourdieu, P., *Distinction: A Social Critique of the Judgement of Taste* (London and New York: Routledge & Kegan Paul, 1986).

2

Policy-Makers and Professionals

As in other areas of political, economic, and cultural life, the entire field of crime and criminal justice has been conditioned by the requirement to become more sophisticated in public relations and image-building techniques. The various actors that attempt to influence media coverage of particular events or policy issues have not been able to escape from these imperatives. Much of what we have to say here bears out Oscar Gandy's general contention that 'the primary role of public relations is one of purposeful, self-interested communication. . . . Public relations is seen as an instrumental resource that is regularly called into play by actors seeking to influence the outcome of a policy debate.'[1]

In this chapter, and the next, we analyse the triangular set of relations involving the Home Office, the news media, and the professional, occupational, and pressure groups whose work, in various ways, is centred on crime and criminal justice. Thus we shall examine both state and private-sector organizations. So far as the latter are concerned, astonishingly, this is the first time such an exercise has been undertaken in any British study of crime and the media. That is because the activities of non-official news sources have been largely ignored or discounted as unimportant because they are not seen as 'primary definers'. Moreover, there has been an almost exclusive focus on how sources are seen from the journalist's standpoint without looking reciprocally at how news sources think about journalists. To study news sources in this aspect is essential for any understanding of how the wider public arena operates as a locus of competition and co-operation. Whilst it is difficult to judge the overall effects of interest and pressure group activity, there is evidence from our interviews that relations

[1] Gandy, O., 'Public Relations and Public Policy: The Structuration of Dominance in the Information Age', in E. L. Toth and R. L. Heath (eds.), *Rhetorical and Critical Approaches to Public Relations* (Hilldale, NJ: Lawrence Earlbaum Associates, 1992), 137.

with the Home Office, and with the media, do affect the presentation of issues and condition not only governmental media strategies but also how reporters cover the news. Here we show how various organizations have established and developed their publicity aims and techniques, how they try to achieve them, and the extent to which they assess their own effectiveness.

The Home Office and Media Relations

The Home Office is the major source of official national news about policy and political developments in the crime and criminal justice system. At the time of our research the Home Office had developed an Information Division with some forty personnel, run by a Head of Information with a background in advertising, putting it on a par with several other major Departments of State.[2] Most senior personnel had come into the Home Office from the communication industry, although there was an increasing tendency for recruitment from inside the Civil Service, with about one-third of Information Division staff recruited internally. The Information Division was divided into two main branches. The Paid Publicity Section ran advertising campaigns and distributed printed matter of a 'non-controversial' kind, subject to Parliamentary approval on lines generally adopted by the Government Information Service. Typical issues were campaigns in favour of crime prevention, or fire prevention and safety, against Television Licence evasion, for the recruitment of personnel to the police, prisons, or probation service, and advice on civil defence. Of much more central interest to the present research is the second branch, the Home Office Press Office, directly run by the Deputy Head of Information, in effect acting as the head of news.

The Press Office's activities were broken down into competences that largely fitted the briefs of the department's junior ministers, such as police, prisons, criminal justice, and immigration and nationality. The then Head of Information, Brian Mower, regarded himself as the Home Secretary's press secretary and had the crucial role of advising the Secretary of State on how to handle the

---

[2] Such as the Northern Ireland Office (47 staff), the Department of the Environment (47 staff), and the Department of Education and Science (38 staff). See Golding, P., 'Political Communication and Citizenship', in M. Ferguson, *Public Communication*, 95, table 6.

media.[3] According to Mower, the Press Office's main function was to ensure an 'accurate portrayal of Home Office events in the press', and the media relations effort was seen as mixing both proactive and reactive modes. It has been observed that most government public relations officers 'consider media relations, specifically the provision of information and assistance to the mass media, as their single most important function'.[4]

The Press Office's activities are directed towards both specialist and generalist forms of journalism. In common with press offices everywhere, general enquiries from the media about issues in the news or about the Home Office's work are routinely fielded. Depending on the issue, the Home Office may at times hold general press conferences. However, it was stressed that cultivating links with specialists based on 'trust'—a continuing process—was regarded as of particular importance. Such journalists had direct access to the Deputy Head of Information and occasionally would contact the Head himself. As Brian Mower put it:

You must try to get into a position of trust with all the journalists you work with, because if you're not in a position of trust then you'll devalue them. That means to say that you never tell a lie to a journalist, that you do one of a few things. You say to a journalist either 'Well, OK, I know about that story but I'm absolutely not going to talk to you about it at all, because it's not at the point where I want to talk about it.' Or 'Well, I wouldn't have chosen to talk to you about it, but since you've got so much of it as it is, I might as well point out to you this, that, and the other'. Or, 'Yes, I'm perfectly prepared to talk to you about it.'

Much of the British government–media relations system works on the lobby principle. In the case of the Home Office, although attempting to influence in the usual official British way is an inherent part of departmental media relations, there is no formal lobby structure as such. That is because of the broad spread of the Home Office's work and the consequent fragmentation of relevant journalistic specialisms (described later in Chapter 5) which makes organizing the preferred system of privileged off-the-record briefings rather difficult. This diversity has meant that there is no

[3] Mower, who died in May 1993, enjoyed the confidence of Mrs Thatcher, and was a trusted aide of Bernard Ingham, the Prime Minister's press secretary and head of the Government Information Service. See Ingham, B., 'Brian Mower', obituary, the *Guardian*, 14 May 1993, p. 14.

[4] VanSlyke Turk, J. and Franklin, B., 'Information Subsidies: Agenda-Setting Tradition', *Public Relations Review*, 12 (1986), 33.

formal system of accreditation to the Home Office nor, as in the Foreign Office and other departments of state, any overall daily briefing for specialist reporters.

From the perspective of the Home Office, specialist journalists divide into various groupings. Crime correspondents are seen as mainly focused on individual police operations and therefore, on the whole, as directing their attention elsewhere. Sometimes, however, a major event such as the 'Hungerford Massacre' of August 1987, when a rogue gunman shot dead sixteen people before committing suicide, will transcend the usual category of murder and raise policy questions—in that case, about the availability of automatic weapons to members of the public. In such circumstances, crime correspondents will seek statements and briefings from the Home Office as well as from the police. A distinction was also drawn between home affairs correspondents, with a remit to look at the broad range of Home Office activities, and legal affairs correspondents (based only in the quality press and the BBC), who tended to focus upon detailed aspects of current legislation. In addition, in the highly sensitive political field of 'law and order', there was also awareness of the distinctive requirements of political journalists, who might come into the frame when a Home Office story became a matter of party political controversy, such as, for instance, over immigration policy. In general, in acknowledgement of its political sensitivity, where a Home Office bill is passing through the House of Commons it is normal practice to have a press officer available there with briefing notes on all of the clauses, ready to advise political correspondents.

The Home Office's information policy, we were told, is to 'call in the appropriate people for an appropriate subject'. This particular tactic of news management was reserved for major bills and was part of a broader strategy of cultivating specialist journalists, described by Brian Mower as follows:

It means to say that the issues of the week are being explained in some detail at the beginning of the week. And so (a) they [the journalists] can't complain that they haven't been fully briefed about it, and (b) if they subsequently receive other information of interest *at least they've got the background of the briefing against which to test those other ideas that are being put before them.* [emphasis added]

This shows a sense of overall strategic calculation in news management: the aim of establishing the Home Office's own perspective amongst journalists as a baseline for testing others' competing views gives the regular briefing of specialists its rationale. An illuminating instance of how government ministers may make use of their institutional base came to light. During his first period at the Home Office as Minister for Home Affairs, David Mellor, MP, held a series of briefings every week on the Criminal Justice Bill (1988) for legal affairs correspondents. According to the journalists, this form of regularized briefing was a new departure. It had not been organized during the passage of the previous major piece of contentious law reform, the Police and Criminal Evidence Act (1984). Joshua Rozenberg, Legal Affairs correspondent of the BBC, told us that every week Mr Mellor would say what would be coming up:

It was while the Bill was going through committee in the Commons. And he [Mellor] thought this was wonderful from his point of view because he got quite a reasonable amount of publicity and coverage out of it both on radio and television . . . If one is told 'David Mellor would be very pleased if you would come round and sit in his room and have a chat on a regular basis on a Monday afternoon, and he will tell you what is coming up,' and when he tells you it is something reasonably newsworthy, then you do so and it gets covered.

All the legal affairs journalists to whom we spoke believed that Mellor had arranged these briefings partly for personal publicity, as well as seeking to promote the government's arguments. As one commented:

First of all he's fighting a fairly marginal seat; secondly, he's very ambitious; thirdly, he is well aware that the Prime Minister listens to the *Today* programme and is thus desperately keen to be on it because he needs to make progress in his own field; fourthly, he is one of those approachable members of the government despite being reasonably wet in political terms . . . he realizes the value to him of journalists in general and broadcasting in particular . . . he does not take the view that he must not tell the press anything ever.

Another aspect of such preparedness for external reactions lies in the routine monitoring of the media. Every morning the Information Division prepares sets of newspaper cuttings based upon a comprehensive search through the national dailies and produces a press summary that is widely circulated. If individuals so wish, they can request particular cuttings to be made available, and newspapers are stored in the Home Office basement. The Press Association tape is routinely monitored. At the time of our research, the Home Office had begun to computerize its press cuttings data base so that as particular cases recurred this would facilitate searches to see what had been said before.[5] The daily bulletin was also entered into the computer's memory so that the official line on a given occasion was available for retrieval.

This system for press data was considered to be a 'Rolls Royce' inside the Home Office when compared with the 'old banger' of a service devised for broadcast coverage. There had been ministerial pressure to conduct a regular and comprehensive monitoring of broadcasting to match that of the press. However, this had run into both practical and resource problems. The sheer volume and frequency of broadcast output could not be as easily handled as that of the press, which both published within limited periods of time and, because of its physical form, lent itself to easier and more rapid analysis. The Information Division recorded all the main television news bulletins and current affairs programmes which, unless otherwise specified, were kept for three weeks. There was a wish to transcribe the content but this was felt to be beyond the Home Office's resources, although occasionally transcripts were bought on a commercial basis from outside organizations. Television was considered sufficiently important for a duty press officer to be assigned the task of viewing the main evening news and current affairs programmes when possible. If a matter of particular interest to the Home Office was broadcast, a brief summary had to be written up for the following day's press summary.

The Information Division holds a routine morning meeting with ministers to consider the known events of the day, parliamentary affairs, media coverage, and major issues that might need a quick reaction. This was described as getting a 'policy/political feel' for things. Aside from such routine meetings there are those held specifically to consider major policy developments about to be launched by the Home Secretary, or those specially called to handle the publicity aspects of major events. These meetings are minuted and circulated to interested parties so that key changes or developments will rapidly be known about.

The Press Office is also organized to ensure that ministers are

---

[5] The case of Myra Hindley, one of the two notorious 'Moors Murderers', was mentioned in this connection.

supported during their official functions. As noted, each of the junior ministers has a press officer assigned to assist in media relations. The Head of Information manages the Home Secretary's dealings with the media. In particular, careful attention is paid to the management of media appearances and interviews, and the bargaining over the conditions under which these should take place. The kinds of calculation involved were spelled out by Brian Mower:

If it were them wanting to televise him to be slotted into a programme, part of the conditions, in my opinion entirely reasonably, might be that they don't film for half an hour and use thirty seconds of it. Not only because it's a waste of his time, an unacceptable waste of his time, but also I simply do not believe that they should be given that degree of editorial liberty in what they choose to use out of a whole range of things he says. And consequently they should try to focus the area. It's not an attempt at censorship of the questions they can ask. It's to get them to focus their mind on the questions they want to ask him and then say, 'OK, you've got to allow us a bit of margin for cutting here and there, and there might be some repetition. But by and large we are going to use the sort of things we ask you.' I think that's an entirely reasonable point of view to take; sometimes editors will agree and sometimes they won't.

Such stipulations on the part of senior government figures are quite common.[6] A related calculation concerns how to respond to—or to anticipate—the alternative and opposing views put out by other political actors. These are taken seriously, as they may be given attention in the media. Although some views might be seen as ill-informed propaganda that could not be compared to the claimed objectivity of the Government Information Service, they could also not be simply pooh-poohed and dismissed. Thus, as Brian Mower put it:

We spend a great deal of time, a great deal of time, as any government department will do, in responding to whatever's come out of the interest group and trying to get it right from our point of view. . . . The classic, of course, would be when the Police and Criminal Evidence Bill was going through and almost every interest group was coming out . . . with their own version of this or that. . . . It almost at one stage became like a parasitic body, a host for parasites. I don't mean that in a denigratory way. I

[6] For a thorough account *inter alia* of prime ministerial management of television interviews, see Cockerell, M., *Live From Number 10: The Inside Story of Prime Ministers and Television* (London: Faber & Faber, 1988).

just mean that everybody seemed to be attacking the Police and Criminal Evidence Bill and therefore almost every other group felt they could join in and get a bite out of it. . . . Even the most respectable of those groups will give partial information because they're in the business of getting their point of view across. . . . Even a group that do not have [. . .] respectability can be taken seriously by the media and we may have to spend an awful lot of time dealing with a story that they've put round that is thoroughly misleading.

This does suggest considerable sensitivity to the contestation that occurs through the media and it was precisely at this point that the trust established with journalists was felt to come into its own, because it was possible to use established relationships to assist in achieving the deniability of a given story. We now turn to an analysis of how other political actors organize their media relations in a framework in which the Home Office is an obligatory point of reference.

Professional Associations and Trades Unions

Our survey of professional associations and trade unions sheds light on this. Broadly speaking, the rise to power of Mrs Thatcher after the unprecedented political marketing of the 1979 General Election constituted a kind of watershed: a new threshhold of sophistication in managing the media became *de rigueur* in the 1980s. There was widespread recognition of the value of being able to offer 'information subsidies' to the media. Internal and external communications were consciously improved, and where they could be afforded, design consultants and public relations experts were hired to build new images and help in presentational skills and in targeting media.

We conducted interviews with seven groups: the Law Society, the Bar Council, the National Association of Probation Officers (NAPO), the Prison Officers' Association (POA), the Police Federation, the Association of Prison Governors, and the Magistrates' Association. These organizations were set up in order to represent the professional and occupational interests of their members. For present purposes we shall treat them collectively as criminal justice professionals, although clearly only the lawyers constitute a fully fledged profession in the traditional sense. In this respect they differ from the pressure groups that we shall examine later. However, both types of organization have regular contact with the media concerning specific campaigns and law reforms.

What is noteworthy about these legal and law-enforcement occupations and professions from our perspective is their changed approach both to internal communications and to external relations with the media. Of late, a shared concern and major priority in all cases has been to develop a positive public image. For instance, the Bar Council, prison officers, prison governors, and probation officers have all been very active in changing their approach both to internal communication and to the media. The Bar Council began to use a public relations firm to deal with journalists' enquiries and for putting out press releases. Barristers were concerned about their image and there was a certain pique at the higher profile of the Law Society, which represents the interests of solicitors. The Prison Officers' Association had worried for some time about their image with the general public and made a conscious policy decision to promote it by engaging an advertising agency.[7] But this was only part of it. Officers of the association began carefully nurturing relationships with journalists, issuing more press releases, being more accessible to the media, and accepting more invitations to appear on television and radio. They not only aimed to change their image but also to raise their profile.

The change in attitude from diffidence and reclusiveness, a kind of fear and loathing of the media, to one of access and availability—in the over-used phrase of the late 1980s, of 'glasnost'—had evidently brought results. By providing journalists with information the groups acquired more of the kind of publicity desired. They had recognized the value of 'information subsidies', where speaking

---

[7] In the March 1987 edition of *Gatelodge*, official journal of the POA, the entire front page was devoted to derogatory quotes about prison officers headlined 'It's time we put the record straight.' The means, a piece inside explained, was to use 'the undisputed power of advertising'. It went on: 'By the time a union is in crisis it's too late for advertising. We need public support and understanding before we reach that point. The Conservative Party were the first political party to use advertising and the media properly. Leaving politics aside and whether you like it or not, they conducted a highly successful campaign. We could do the same given your support'. An advert was also used to ram home the point: 'Sadly, it cost each miner £9000 per head to strike. Unfortunately they couldn't control the media and their case was distorted. They failed to get public support behind them and the Government walked over them. They didn't plan first. They didn't put the record straight. They lost out.'

to the media and providing background material saves the journalist from having to engage in extensive research.

NAPO, for instance, completely revamped both their internal and external communications. In 1985, they appointed an assistant general secretary to run this area and a rapid change resulted in the association's media relations: press releases were produced, briefings occurred, and articles were written for journals and magazines, as well as appearances being achieved on television and radio. A communications working party was set up to examine in detail and substantially improve NAPO's external and internal channels of communication.[8] Amongst the recommendations put forward were 'the re-organization of NAPO's publications and "house-style"' to present it as 'a vital organization central to criminal justice issues', and the appointment of an information manager to provide expertise in information collection and storage and communications systems.

Media and Public Relations Strategies

There has been a noteworthy turning to outside agencies for help in media relations. Media training, so much part of the political and corporate scene, has also become a more general practice. The prison officers, for example, bought in a media course on self-presentation techniques which is now included on training courses for branch officials. There were also visiting lectures and demonstrations from Trades Union Congress officials involved in handling the media. For their part, the prison governors—in their capacity as civil servants—attended training courses run by a public relations consultancy organized and paid for by the Home Office.

The Police Federation has used designers, corporate video, and other communications professionals to help change its image. It became a major campaigner on law and order issues in the mid-1970s, initially picking up techniques from liberal pressure groups.[9]

---

[8] The Summer 1987 edition of the *NAPO Journal* stated: 'NAPO urgently needs an overall development plan which, within the limited resources available, seeks to streamline its internal machinery, provide a more compelling public profile and make use of the advantages to be gained from the investment in new information technology.'

[9] On the Police Federation's earlier proximity to Conservative policy see Reiner, R., *The Politics of the Police*, 2nd edn. (Hemel Hempstead: Harvester Wheatsheaf, 1992), 92–4.

Its annual conference, like those of corporations and political parties, has become a matter of professional design. With the conference held in May, specialists are brought in as early as February to ensure the right look for its visual presentation, with the television cameras in mind. Corporate videos have also been produced for the membership on topics such as the induction of new police officers, AIDS, and police pensions.

The main in-house publication for the Police Federation is the monthly journal, *Police*, which, according to Leslie Curtis, then the Federation's chairman, is the public relations channel for conveying their thoughts to the general public, and widely circulated. The Federation's entire membership is said to have access to a copy each month. Like the Bar Council's and other internal magazines, it is circulated to the press and may often be quoted by the media. The Federation will send out between twenty and thirty press releases annually, usually in relation to a set-piece speech, or in reaction to some event judged as needing a comment. The press release is usually drafted by the press officer, who generally consults the chairman of the Police Federation.

The Police Federation is frequently called on by journalists. As in the Prison Officers' Association, local branches are free to talk to the media and there are no specific guidelines from the centre, the proviso being that the main office be contacted for at least some guidance on the Federation's thinking. This contrasts with the police service itself, which has to follow internal guidelines about talking to the press, issued in each force by the chief constable. Again, like other organizations, the Police Federation have changed their media strategy over the last few years. Leslie Curtis's perception of the change in police attitudes towards publicity mirrored that of the police officers whose views are expressed below, in Chapter 4. Routinely offering 'no comment' had not been a viable approach for quite some time. Looking back some fifteen to twenty years, he argued, media reporting had then tended not to ask whether the police were doing their job correctly. As part of the changed context, he noted the rise of investigative programmes such as BBC Television's *Rough Justice*, which raised questions about prisoners' guilt years after the event. Curtis said he believed that much coverage during the miners' strike was unduly critical of the police, and also thought that the media had contributed to unwarranted fear of crime, which had harmed the police because they were perceived by the public as not doing enough to maintain law and order. Given this sense of being under siege from unsustainable demands, taking a sophisticated approach to media coverage was hardly surprising:

I think about ten or twelve years ago we in the Police Federation certainly saw that the media was a growing thing, it was becoming the eyes and the mouth. . . . They had a job to do and we could use the media to our own advantage . . . because we have always been ready to respond day and night to a media question . . . we've found by reacting there, and being there ready to answer, and answering then, our profile with the press has grown considerably. . . . The chief constables' organisation, for instance, has realized the use of this high profile contact with the press, not just on things operational when there's a big job going on in the force they're in, but general reaction. But at the end of the day, it comes down very much to the willingness and the ability of the people that have got the responsibility of talking, to actually do it and be prepared to do it. Now I am, I believe, I've always believed, that my role with the press is to let the people know what we think. And, of course, the other good example of that is Jimmy Anderton, who is at this moment in time the President of ACPO [Association of Chief Police Officers], who believes in the same thing. I know some of the things he says worry people, but that's beside the point. Certainly I believe that people are much more aware of ACPO because you have an individual there who is good on his feet with words and is willing to speak.

Apart from developing an ability to offer a 'sound bite' on request and being perceived as a usable personality, frequent exposure of this kind results in the development of broader media performance skills. David Evans of the POA said that he thrived on the confrontational approach often favoured by current affairs programmes. He believed that he had more expertise in the questions than anyone with whom he could be confronted, and that taking a confrontational style appealed to programme-makers' values:

They are not going to change that because it's good media coverage. That's the way they like it because it gets the viewers in, and to be honest we have to learn to live with it and play the game. . . . We can't change that, and if we can't change it we'd better learn to live with it, and do the trick on that particular format. . . . No, I think you have to adjust to the needs of the media, to learn to try and play the game better than they can, better than the people who want to criticize us can.

The likelihood of confrontation was also recognized by Leslie Curtis. In his position, he argued, you had to be ready to debate a controversial subject, such as community policing, or it might mean an argument with a politician, of whom he gave two left-wing examples, Bernie Grant, a London Labour MP, and Paul Boateng, then chairman of the Greater London Council's police committee (and now a London Labour MP). Curtis said that he was always careful to learn what the programme was about and to be prepared. He demonstrated the sense of tactics that comes with experience when he observed that the only time that he would not respond immediately was if there were 'a lot of unknowns'. He cited as an example the shooting of a black woman by a police inspector which had led to riots in Brixton: 'By reacting to a request to come on the media that would perhaps make it more difficult certainly for the officer because I was totally ignorant of the facts and had no ability of finding out the facts. So then yes, it's sometimes astute not to open your mouth every time.'[10]

Frequency of use by the media translates itself into frequency of contact with particular journalists or programme teams. Curtis spoke of his close relationship with people in broadcasting, particularly radio:

I mean, let's take radio first, Radio 4, especially the *Today* and *PM* programmes which of course is really the programme you want to be with. I wouldn't say that I do one a week, but sometimes it could average out like that. So that's the sort of relationship. And of course they're always the same people, so we're on a first-name basis, so the relationship is clearly established.

Curtis had also developed relationships with journalists in TV-am and stressed his availability to them at any time. He recognized that being in London offered specific advantages in securing coverage. Furthermore, he also had close links with journalists on certain unspecified papers whom he would call and tip off about forthcoming developments. He could also rely on a reciprocal flow of information from such journalistic sources.

Operating on a much more modest level, the Bar Council had hired a public relations company for reasons outlined by the chairman of its public affairs committee, Mark Potter. He said that for a long time the Bar Council had not given attention to its relationship with the press or television, nor even thought that it needed to develop one. This was rooted in the ethic 'instilled into every

---

[10] This case, Inspector Lovelock's shooting of Mrs Groce, is the topic of Ch. 7.

barrister that in some way you don't give yourself personal publicity as it may be regarded as touting [for work]', which inhibited personal appearances in the media, or comments, for fear of arousing professional jealousies. However, increasingly now, this amateurism was recognized as unhelpful:

> In the last few years we've come to realize that one's got to make a lot of compromises in this respect and that it's an unduly restrictive view, and because there is an increased need for comment in the media on issues which develop, and in which the Bar may be being criticized, or may be having its view sought not for critical reasons but for reasons of information. We've really got to play our role.

Behind this need to respond to an increased demand for information on the law lie shifts in media reporting which we shall address later. For the most part, the Bar had felt that their public image had been broadly favourable, with perhaps the occasional exception of investigative journalism that might disclose some malpractice. However, external circumstances had changed and there was no possibility of remaining complacent, as Mark Potter noted:

> I think with the development of the Big Bang, the increased concern of the government to restrict the cost of legal aid, and for a host of other reasons, the focus has come on the law. Lawyers historically have never been popular, but on the other hand they haven't really been newsworthy either. Now I think they're not any more popular, but I think they are regarded as much more newsworthy, and so far as the Bar is concerned it seems that whenever there's been comment it's often been hostile, and based on misconception. It's often been comment of the sort simply that barristers live in ivory towers and won't communicate with the public, so they mustn't be surprised if they have an adverse image. For all these reasons we thought it was high time we played a more positive role in the media, deal with the issues as they arrive, and make our voice heard.

Issues that were of particular concern were how solicitors and barristers could improve their practices and the cutting of legal fees by the government. The Bar were concerned to convey their views in a debate that involved them, the solicitors, and the government, and to be able to influence the findings of an inquiry into the structure of the legal profession. The context was seen as one of competition where 'there are a lot of papers circulating from legal pressure groups about this which either get leaked or released to the press. Consequently, there's a running series of stories one way or another about both sides of the profession, and in those circumstances it's as well to have professional advice about the best way of getting one's voice heard.'

The public relations company employed by the Bar Council has a brief to cover both parliamentary and press relations, and there is a consultant for each of these distinct areas. They have a close working relationship with the chairmen of the four committees of the Bar Council as well as the Council's secretariat. The PR consultants also field telephone calls from the media and are well briefed on whom they should put in contact with journalists.

Parliamentary proceedings are monitored in order to see when legislation might affect the workings or income of the Bar. In Mark Potter's words: 'From a trade union point of view we've realised the importance of knowing what's going on so that we can be alerted to it and if we have things to say about it we can say them, either through an MP, or by a quick word with the government department, or something of that sort.' The parliamentary consultant is also required to advise on how best to lobby MPs. The press consultant monitors press coverage, providing relevant cuttings that may require comment, and also prepares press releases and statements targeted at those newspapers most likely to print them, namely, *The Times*, *Telegraph*, *Guardian*, and *Independent*.

Mark Potter gave an example of how the relationship with the consultants operated:

I would say I'm on the telephone two or three times a week to our press officer for advice about this and that. And if, for instance, a hostile article has appeared in one of the leading newspapers about some Bar practice, or an inaccurate article—for example, the other day an article was published on an old theme, the image of the Bar—it's out of date, totally untechnologized, etc., when the truth of the matter is that about two-thirds of chambers in the Temple have fax machines, telexes, and are computerized for fees, which is probably rather more than the same number of offices in the solicitors' profession. When this appeared to suggest that this wasn't so, I rang them to say 'What's the best way of dealing with this? I or the chairman to write a letter to *The Times* and take the risk they won't publish? Or reissue a press statement? Or what shall we do?' He tells us what's the best thing to do, and then if a letter is wanted I will either tell him the lines of what I think ought to be said and say, 'Do me a draft and fax it to me and I'll approve it and then you get on with it.' Or he may tell me a particular way of doing it and I make myself responsible for the draft. But it's all very informal and we can now work very quickly and within 24 hours we'll get out whatever form of action we want to get out on that issue.

Because the Bar Council is a small operation its officers believed that they would not be able to attract a top press officer. So, although it was slightly more expensive, they decided it would be of more benefit to work though a public relations firm willing to supply other services, such as parliamentary relations, than to have an in-house press officer with limited expertise. The professionalization of public relations was simply one aspect of the change. There was also a drive to attain a higher media profile by way of complete approachability. The traditional reserve about public appearances had now been overcome and most barristers were prepared to represent the Bar's interests.

Walter Merricks of the Law Society saw his organization as making 'more perceptive and intelligent use' of opportunities available to it by maintaining 'as good and friendly relations as you can with the journalists who are in fact writing the stuff'. Indeed, as we have repeatedly found, such personal contacts cannot be over-stressed for their importance in helping sources to attain coverage. Merricks found that the Law Society's press releases were routinely picked up by the quality dailies. In part, he considered, this was due to a change in the quality end of the newspaper market provoked by the arrival of the *Independent*, which offered extensive legal affairs coverage:

The Times has deliberately set out to capture lawyers as a market and retain them. That's why they keep their law reports going, and they are very expensive to maintain, and why the *Independent* has started running law reports and why the *Telegraph* is going to start running them, because they're all out to catch lawyers. The *Guardian* has also started its law reports. Not just lawyers but also law-related occupations, justices' clerks, policemen, people in that field, I think, are seen as being a pretty important market, and therefore law is getting good space by all these papers.[11]

This was contrasted to a period three or four years earlier when the Law Society was receiving very bad publicity all the time. The loss of the conveyancing monopoly was instanced as producing some poor public relations, as well as a 'disastrous scandal surrounding the council member who was eventually struck off for over-charging. . . . A lawyer found doing something naughty is

[11] For further discussion of this issue, see Ch. 5.

always a headline.' Damaging issues such as cuts in legal aid, delays in conveyancing searches, in legal administration and finances, had all achieved prominent coverage in the main television news programmes.

Subsequently, however, publicity success had occurred during the Zeebrugge ferry disaster as a result of the growth in sophistication in handling media relations. The Law Society had warned survivors about avoiding approaches from claims assessors offering to settle their claim for a 50 per cent cut of the compensation. With astute news sense, Merricks, a former journalist himself, had recognized that news editors would be looking for another angle on the disaster and had served their news values, the public interest, and the interests of solicitors all at the same time.

The Law Society had also employed an advertising company when launching a campaign to inform the public about their right to see a solicitor at a police station, a new right under the Police and Criminal Evidence Act. The Law Society spent £50,000 on this campaign, directed at young people aged 15 to 23, those most likely to be arrested. Most of the money, therefore, was spent on advertisements in the *Sun* and the *Daily Mirror*. However, their agency also placed advertisements in youth pop magazines such as *Blitz* and *Sound* as well as Radio Luxembourg, all of which were seen as cost-effective media. According to Walter Merricks, this was a multi-targeted campaign, so other sites chosen were the *New Statesman*, *Social Work*, *New Society*, and *Social Work Today*.

We wanted to get the message direct across to young people, we wanted to get also to their parents, youth leaders, teachers, social workers, probation officers, intermediaries, who are likely to tell them that they have the right and reinforce their confidence to ask for a solicitor. And we also wanted as an underlying more subtle operation to show to the general public and to opinion-formers that the Law Society was prepared to take up a public issue like this and we made quite a bit of play with the fact that the Home Office weren't spending any money on it, and that solicitors were not just money-grabbing people who take money off you. Even though they get paid for doing this work it's quite a social service to actually operate a 24-hour legal scheme and that solicitors do get their nights and weekends interrupted as a result of being on call.

Coupled with the advertising was a large media launch that also attracted publicity in its own right.

In contrast, the Magistrates' Association and the Association of

Prison Governors, much smaller organizations, had not yet fully developed press and public relations operations. Given mounting problems in the prisons, the prison governors had had to respond to changes, making them more open to the media. According to John Dovell of the Prison Governors' Association, they liked to think that they had a very good relationship with certain journalists and in 1987, for the first time, they had asked certain correspondents (from *The Times*, *Guardian*, and *Independent*) to be present at their annual general meeting. These papers were invited because they enjoyed a certain measure of trust and were expected to take a 'responsible line and reflect some of our views' on the questions of prison overcrowding and conditions for which the governors were seeking attention. This was felt to have been a successful move by contrast to the 'bitter experience' of having views 'twisted' by sections of the tabloid press.

The prison governors' relationship with certain journalists in the quality press had been developing for several years. John Dovell's predecessor had initiated these relationships and they had been extensively cultivated since. Developing a sympathetic hearing in the élite sections of the media was especially important given the desire to influence the Home Office's decision-making over the intensifying crisis in the prisons. In general, prison governors had to be careful what they said in their capacity as public servants; however, there had been a shift in Home Office policy on this. In John Dovell's words,

it goes back, I think, to the late 1970s when the governor of [Wormwood] Scrubs made his 'penal dustbin' speech and then the governor of Manchester [Strangeways] followed it up and since then local governors and deputy governors have been encouraged to speak to the press on matters of public interest in relation to their own establishment . . . but they wouldn't in fact speak generally regarding the prison service on, say, nationwide overcrowding or anything like that.

Lobbying Coalitions

Our research has disclosed co-operation and contact between associations and trades unions over given issues that extend beyond this group of organizations, at times, to embrace some of the pressure groups that also operate in the criminal justice policy arena, and are discussed in the chapter that follows. Lobbying is directed towards the Home Office and Parliament.

Many of the trades unions and associations have a lot of contact with the Home Office because of the nature of their work. The tactical use of media coverage may be of considerable importance in pursuing specific goals on both sides. For example, David Evans of the Prison Officers' Association told us that the Home Office's *Fresh Start in the Prison Service*, which proposed to restructure prison officers' pay and conditions, represented 'the most major proposal we have ever had in a hundred years'. He had been approached for a reaction whilst the document was still officially under wraps by home affairs journalists from the *Independent*, *The Times*, and the *Guardian* who, according to Evans, knew about it because the Prison Department had tipped them off, and had given them copies of the proposals in order to manage the news. As Evans said, 'It's all part of the game.' In similar vein, if the prison officers judge a leak to be to their advantage, they will make public submissions that they have made in confidence to the Home Office. The Home Office would then ask, 'How come this came out?', and, according to Evans, 'We would say the same to them: "How did this come out? Some indiscreet governor?"'

Leaks to the media are one possible tactic. Another possibility is to use lines of contact with the Home Office to try and secure a specific aim before ever resorting to publicity as a means of applying outside pressure. Walter Merricks of the Law Society outlined this kind of approach:

If we're engaged in something like the Criminal Justice Bill it is preferable to use our channels of communication with the Home Office first to see if we can get them to include it in the Bill before we start, and we are brought into consultations of that kind well before legislation is prepared usually. And we will often have talks because of the kind of organization we are, partly because we know about the law and partly because the Home Office now treat us with considerable respect, I think, because . . . during the passage of the Police and Criminal Evidence Act in '83/4, when we, the Law Society, in effect became the main source of informed opposition that the government were prepared to treat seriously. We fed MPs with a lot of amendments and briefings and memoranda and MPs were happier to take up our cause . . . or happier to take up amendments we'd promoted and use our name, to say the Law Society thinks that this should be amended because there really ought to be pressure on the government in that way rather than, say, take up a similar or identical amendment proposed by NCCL, who are a rather more tainted organization as far as the Home Office is concerned. And so, I think the Home

Office learnt their lesson on that bill and this time in the Criminal Justice Bill that's now going through, they took us into their confidence right from the start, and even though we haven't got our way on everything it's been very interesting to note their use of the media in countering anything that we say almost immediately. We put out a press release in the very early stages of the bill about the powers of the Serious Fraud Office and we said there were going to be overweening powers and too draconian and that sort of thing, and within a very short space of time the Home Office had put out a great big statement countering all this.

This is a very revealing account of how a group acquires credibility and comes to achieve 'insider' status in the formative stages of the policy process. Such status allows a group to act as an expert—and 'respectable'—source for MPs in the modification of legislation and also might require a government department to develop its own media strategy to counter possible lines of attack. As is clear from the earlier discussion of the Home Office, precisely such second-guessing of alternative views and arguments to those of the government is a permanent part of the work of the departmental information machinery's work.

Lobbying coalitions may also at times include strange bedfellows. For instance, when the Police and Criminal Evidence Bill (1984) was going through Parliament, the Law Society worked together with the Police Federation and the National Council for Civil Liberties (NCCL, now called Liberty[12]) in what Walter Merricks described as 'an unholy alliance' over the reform of the police complaints system. According to Merricks, the Police Federation themselves had decided to back wholesale reform: 'They'd got fed up with so many accusations of policemen investigating the police they said, "Right, let's have somebody else do it," and they in a sense came to us and said, "Right, we'll join your bandwagon on this and the NCCL. We don't mind who we talk to," and we had a joint press conference about it.'

The co-operation during the passage of the Police and Criminal Evidence Bill between the Law Society and the Police Federation— resulting in a joint press statement—was quite unusual. In Leslie Curtis's words:

---

[12] In May 1990, this group renamed itself Liberty, but it was still called NCCL at the time of our research, and we have retained that use here. In any case, NCCL still remains the group's secondary designation.

It's somebody we're often in conflict with. We spend more time arguing with the Law Society than we do with most other people. They come up with some radical ideas sometimes about the way in which the law should be actually dealt with which wouldn't be enforceable as far as we're concerned. . . . Because of the large numbers of lawyers in the House, we went to them and said, "We want your support here", and they said, "We want a quid pro quo," and we had to give them support on something else. But we knew by that support we would enhance our chances of winning the argument on legal representation [for police officers involved in discipline cases]. And of course we did.

Alongside the lobbying coalition, the Police Federation also lobbied on their own, with representatives constantly in Parliament meeting MPs and Lords and also sitting in on the House of Commons Select Committee meetings. Moreover, the Federation also invested heavily in press advertising to secure legal representation in discipline cases, which was their main concern.

The Law Society co-ordinated and largely managed the coalition lobbying process. There was a major press conference and write-ups in the newspapers together with appearances on radio and television. In fact, the passage of the Police and Criminal Evidence Bill offers an especially good example of co-operation in the kind of private lobbying which often runs alongside the much more overt quest for media coverage. The existence of such lobbying coalitions remains largely unknown to the public. Harry Fletcher of NAPO described the process:

There were two forums existing that I attended. The first was the loose grouping around NCCL which included the Howard League, NACRO and ourselves. We discussed the Police Bill clause by clause. And then there was another grouping which occurred at Church House. It wasn't supposed to happen, really. It was called by the Church of England, basically, and we met on about four or five occasions and it consisted of bureaucrats who worked in Church House, the occasional bishop, the Law Society, the Bar Association. Very, very pukka. I mean, NCCL people weren't there. I can't remember who else was there, minutes weren't kept. It was much more of an establishment group and it discussed the Bill, means of influencing amendments, and that sort of thing, using the Lords and using contacts. And that met maybe three or four times.

Most of the time there were no joint releases or publicity, but joint behind the scenes lobbying was done. This is a largely invisible process which could not be reconstructed from the consumption of media coverage. David Evans of the prison officers described it as follows:

There were things that occurred during the course of the Bill where NCCL certainly said 'This statement is supported by . . .' and then gave a list. The same thing occurred with the Public Order Bill. Loose groupings, informal meetings occurred, and statements were made from time to time. All the groups agreed that the new offence of—in the Public Order Bill— causing a nuisance, making a fool of yourself in public became an offence, and there was a broad group of people who said that was not needed, that sufficient power already existed. But I would say most of the time the purpose of those groups was so that *A* knew what *B* was doing, and *C* and *D*, and people put out their own material.

Thus, while different organizations represent distinct interests, and may be in competition for resources, they may also coalesce for particular purposes—a point evident in other contexts from the literature on social movements and pressure groups.[13]

The kinds of relations that exist are various. Some are close and semi-permanent because of organic connections of interest, others much more fluctuating. For instance, the Prison Governors' Association has a very close relationship with NACRO and is represented on their standards committee. They attend one another's seminars, and as John Dovell of the governors told us:

There is a whole field in which we are fishing in the same pond. For instance, NACRO are quite adept at putting out press releases every so often. And they will come to me and say 'What are your views? Are they enough in accord with ours? Can we quote you?' With NACRO we would see a great deal of common interest and a great deal of mileage in having a fairly close relationship with them.

Apart from the coincidence of political view on passing issues, there is a clear economic logic underlying such coalition pressure politics: co-operation maximizes resources. At times, however, there may be a disincentive to doing this if one or other of the coalition partners has to carry a disproportionate amount of the financial burden. For instance, at the time of our research, the Prison Officers' Association had developed close relationships with pressure groups pursuing joint campaigns on minimum standards in

[13] See e.g. Zald, M. N., and McCarthy J. D., 'Social Movement Industries: Competition and Cooperation among Movement Organizations', in L. Kriesberg (ed.), *Research in Social Movements, Conflict and Change: A Research Annual* (Greenwich, Conn.: JAI Press Inc.), 1–20.

prisons and prisoners' rights. However, they did not organize media campaigns with pressure groups, not because of ideological differences but for financial reasons. David Evans of the POA said: 'Most of the pressure groups are poor and penniless and we have to pay for it all and if we're going to pay for it all I don't think our voters would stand for other people taking the limelight when we're having to cough up the ackers. That's how they would consider it.'

Media Monitoring and Evaluation

We have outlined some quite fundamental transformations in the approach taken to the media by professional associations and trades unions. Clearly, these would have not have been pursued had they not been thought of as producing benefits.

Our research showed that most associations and unions did little systematic media monitoring. For the most part, views on the effectiveness of media strategies' success or failure tended to be rather impressionistic. Basically, when an organization is gaining a higher profile than before in terms of volume of media coverage this does register with its officers and members.

It is notoriously difficult to measure success in news management with any certainty. The groups concerned did not have any systematic way of resolving this question. Clearly, favourable media coverage from their point of view offered one criterion, and positive feedback from members another. At one level, everybody has to play this game now, on the minimal assumption that it affords some benefits, and that to stand aside would simply be untenable. Harry Fletcher of NAPO, for example, was well aware of the problem of reaching a balanced conclusion on this question. His membership had no clear expectations of what developing a media and public relations strategy might bring about:

It's not very helpful to me, because when I ask they say, 'Yeah, fine, great, we never used to get in the paper at all before, we never got mentioned on TV documentaries and now we do.' . . . In terms of the kind of amount and quality in terms of sympathy then, yes, I'm pleased that all the press releases I've ever put out have got covered, but I don't think we put enough out, I don't think enough work has gone into it. . . . I think the amount of coverage as a percentage of what goes out is very high but as a percentage of other groups it's not good enough.

Thus, such evaluation as occurs may have a comparative dimension too, based upon a rather vague sense of how competing groups are doing. For instance, Stephen Shaw, Director of the Prison Reform Trust commented: 'NAPO's Assistant General Secretary, Harry Fletcher, is in my estimation the most effective user of the media since Des Wilson was at the height of his powers.'[14]

Examples of quite extensive investment in media monitoring came to light during our research. One was the Law Society, whose press office each day made cuttings mainly from the national press for internal use. A weekly 'In the papers' selection was circulated to the senior heads of departments, with a set also sent to the seventy council members, with an additional distribution of some 120 to other members. According to Walter Merricks: 'Most council members probably read only one or two papers and they would like to see the coverage, perhaps how something got covered in all the major newspapers rather than in just one or two. If they read the *FT* and the *Telegraph* they probably don't see how it was covered in *The Times* or the *Guardian*.'

There was also a more extensive operation, with a commercial agency cutting the local papers and providing items from periodicals that the Law Society itself might not have seen. As far as broadcasting was concerned, the Law Society had a monitoring agency which informed them of relevant coverage and also provided a transcript if required.

The POA received the monthly NACRO press briefings and monitored *The Times*, *Financial Times*, and the *Telegraph* every day, but not in a very systematic way. Other organizations, like the Police Federation, held their own press cuttings. At one time, they used to keep extensive video-recordings of appearances and programmes of interest, but this effort had become much more restricted in scope given the problem of viewing all this material. Similarly, the Magistrates' Association used to have a cuttings service but because of financial constraints decided to do it themselves. Material was sent to the four honorary officers of the Association.

Assessments of groups' corporate images, then, were largely

[14] See Shaw, S., 'Massaging the Media', *CJM: Criminal Justice Matters*, 11 (1993), 19. Des Wilson, a leading campaigner for a variety of causes codified his experience in Wilson, D., *Pressure: The A to Z of Campaigning in Britain* (London: Heinemann, 1985).

impressionistic. The sense of relative success or failure in media coverage was also substantially reinforced by the kinds of contact each group maintained with journalists.

Conclusion

The Home Office is the key player in terms of both news management resources and potential command over the media agenda. It is careful to cultivate relations with specialist journalists and also attempts to second-guess—and neutralize—criticism from outside.

The professionalization of media relations extends beyond government to embrace, in different measures, the major professional associations and trades unions representing the occupational interests of those who operate the criminal justice system. Although located in the private sector, because their members are mostly either fully or partially employed by the state, the criminal justice professionals' organizations may at times occupy a quasi-official status as news sources.

It is clear that none can now stand aloof from the competitive pressures of seeking media attention, and all have invested in developing both internal and external communications, with key personnel enhancing their media contacts and skills. At times, varied interests coalesce and pool their resources in campaigns intended to affect legislation and the wider policy process. Such campaigns may take two-track strategies, where what can be achieved by private lobbying is played off against seeking publicity, and vice versa. All engage in media monitoring to try and form an impression of their relative success or failure in the struggle for media attention, although this does not always seem to offer an unambiguous way of judging the effectiveness of media strategies.

3

Pressure Groups

APART from our survey of criminal justice professionals, we also conducted detailed interviews with twenty-five groups in the crime and criminal justice field. Of these, some have charitable status whereas others are straightforwardly political. Most have a campaigning role which is pursued in conjunction with their other work. The groups analysed fell into a number of categories: principally, they concerned themselves with prisoners and their families, with victims of crime, the administration of justice, reform of the criminal justice system, and also with the more specific interests of women, children, and ethnic minorities. In the present context, as we are purely concerned with how they organize their external relations in the political arena, we treat all as though they were pressure groups.

This chapter is based upon interviews conducted across the whole range of groups concerned. For the sake of clarity, however, we have drawn most of our examples from interviews with the larger groups that tend to dominate the field, namely the National Association for the Care and Resettlement of Offenders (NACRO), Liberty (the National Council for Civil Liberties, NCCL), the Prison Reform Trust (PRT), the National Association of Victim Support Schemes (NAVSS). Reference is also made to the jurists' organization, Justice, the British Section of the International Committee of Jurists, to the Joint Council for the Welfare of Immigrants (JCWI), the Howard League for Penal Reform, and to the Haldane Society of Socialist Lawyers, as these proved particularly useful in illustrating a number of points.

On investigation, it becomes clear that, as in the case of associations and trades unions, there is considerable overlap in the work undertaken by pressure groups and in the issues they take up.

Some are purely service organizations for their constituencies, whereas others both provide a service and campaign for reform. Apart from such variations there are also differences in how the groups are positioned within the policy arena. Some occupy a central 'respectable' locus whereas others comprise a more peripheral 'radical' fringe, positions relevant for understanding how media strategies are pursued and the differing relationships each type of organization has with the Home Office.

The new radicalism of the late 1960s and early 1970s resulted in a plethora of pressure groups, including those interested in criminal justice and the prison system. These were very different from the old-fashioned reformist, 'respectable' pressure groups which had been part of the policy arena for many years. In the field of penal reform, the best known of the prison groups emerging at that time was RAP, Radical Alternatives to Prison. This was not a prisoners' group as such but, rather, was involved in campaigning about prisons; it also questioned the whole nature of the law, the courts, the police, and official definitions of who is a criminal. In the same field of concern, another group that emerged was PROP, Preservation of the Rights of Prisoners. PROP was ignored by the authorities partly because of its ex-prisoner composition and also because of the manner in which it conducted itself in its early days. There was considerable antagonism between these new radicals and the older reformist pressure groups. Whereas the Howard League for Penal Reform was perceived in official circles as an 'acceptable' pressure group, others such as PROP and RAP were seen as much more radical both by government and the older groups.

The antagonism between the various groups had certainly subsided in the changed atmosphere of the 1980s. A group such as the Howard League, seen twenty years before as old-fashioned and respectable, and as never rocking any boats, had become just another part of the wider lobby. Groups such as PROP and RAP had shrunk both in size and importance. A further cohort of pressure groups emerged in the early 1980s. These tended to concentrate on highly specific causes: examples were Women in Prison, the Black Female Prisoners' Scheme, and Inquest, a collective of initially individual campaigns focused on people who died (suspected of being killed) in custody. In the 1980s, the growth of ex-prisoners' groups concerned with women's needs was particularly significant. Organizations such as those mentioned above were instances of new forms of self-organization by women.

Other less radical groups were also formed. The Prison Reform Trust, set up in 1981, was initially chaired by the industrialist, Sir Monty Finniston, and supported by an executive committee and council. This organization was praised for its work by the radical groups that we interviewed, and the quality of its information provision was appreciated by journalists involved in this study. It is an especially good example of a group able to straddle the gap between the older, reformist and newer, radical types without alienating either constituency.[1]

We uncovered substantial interchange amongst pressure groups, more markedly so than the patterns of co-operation found between associations and trades unions. In particular, there was considerable movement of personnel between the groups, and all the major actors knew each other.

The pressure group arena could be simply conceived of as having a centre and periphery. Perhaps most marginalized at the time of our study were the police-monitoring groups, most of which received funding from the Greater London Council.[2] Other groups, such as the Lesbian Policing Project, would not talk to researchers interested in their work, let alone to the media. These marginal groups neither received money from the Home Office, nor had liberal establishment backing in the form of trustees and patrons, nor any funding from concerned foundations and companies.

As with the professionals, the pressure activities of the groups are unavoidably centred upon the Home Office. One key distinction rests upon whether or not groups in this field receive state support for their work. At one end of the continuum are those that do have government funding, most of which comes from the Home Office. They may be given money for various projects and in some cases their work is actively encouraged by the government. In 1989/90, the National Association of Victim Support Schemes

[1] The Prison Reform Trust's purpose is to 'bring prisons and penal policy in general to the forefront of public debate . . . and to facilitate links between the community and the prisons' (*Prison Reform Trust First Annual Report, 1981/2*).

[2] This Labour-run authority was abolished under the Local Government Act, 1985 by the Conservative government. On the political background see Hillyard, P. and Percy-Smith, J., *The Coercive State: The Decline of Democracy in Britain* (London: Fontana, 1988), ch. 2.

(NAVSS), for instance, received £4 million of funding for its local schemes from the Home Office, which was anxious for such ventures to operate successfully. The Home Office also agreed to pay for public relations consultants to advise on profile-raising publicity and a fund-raising programme, and was keen to encourage public awareness of NAVSS's work with a view to attracting more resources from the private sector. At the other end of the continuum were groups such as Women in Prison, which would have refused any Home Office funding on grounds of principle for fear of compromising their ability to manœuvre. Chris Tchaikovsky of Women in Prison was quite adamant about never approaching the Home Office for funds:

No way. I have heard prison reform groups do get Home Office funds and I think that is outrageous. . . . I don't see how you can ever campaign freely when your money is dependent on the people you are campaigning against. It strikes me as fighting with your hands tied behind your back. . . . The Home Office has a way of swallowing up its adversaries. It always has. That is the reason that you don't ask for a Home Office pass to visit prison, for the very reason that once they give you something then they always have a hold over you and they can take it away again. . . . I think prisoners are very suspicious because the Home Office does swallow up so many people; it is so all-embracing. Prisoners would never trust us if the Home Office funded us, and rightly so.

What this quotation bespeaks is the quite distinctive status that the more radical groups have on the outer fringes of the policy community. Mick Ryan has outlined the differences between the reformist groups and the new radicals in the penal field.[3] For instance, groups such as RAP were refused permission by the Home Office to visit Holloway Prison as it was not normal departmental policy to admit groups of people from unofficial organizations to view Prison Department establishments. This was in contrast to those such as the Howard League which were allowed in.

Relations with the Home Office

In Chapter 1, we raised some questions about the extent to which official sources could be taken uncomplicatedly as 'primary

[3] Ryan, M., *The 'Acceptable' Pressure Group* (Aldershot: Saxon House, 1978).

definers' of political issues in the news. Our investigation has already suggested the negotiated character of certain policy initiatives. There are times when the Home Office might use groups to put over a position on a particular issue which it is itself either unable or unwilling to promote overtly. Paul Cavadino, press officer of NACRO, one of the largest groups in the field, offered an example of this process at work:

Sometimes the Home Office is under pressure to do something which it does not want to do and the more pressure that can be put on saying it should not do it, the better. For example, the judiciary might be putting on pressure, as they are at the moment, to have the possibility of imposing suspended sentences on young offenders . . . where at the moment it's only available for adults. The Home Office thinks it would do more harm than good and does not want to do it but there has been quite a lot of pressure from the Lord Chief Justice down to the judiciary. So the Home Office obviously decided that it ought to show willing and it put it in the White Paper [for the Criminal Justice Bill 1988]. It was quite clear from the Home Office officials that we spoke to that they thought it would be a bad idea and that comments coming in saying it would be a bad idea from different organizations would be helpful.

Such tacit collusion, according to our discussions, is not rare. It raises questions about what political compromises sometimes lie behind the official definitions that emerge as policy pronouncements and also brings out, at times, the negotiated character of the policy agenda.

Because the immediate political context is in continual flux, the attitude of the Home Office towards the various pressure groups is never constant. Stephen Shaw, director of the Prison Reform Trust, noted that the Home Office was not monolithic in nature and that over time his organization had experienced various shifts of attitude. He also tied the approaches taken towards his own pressure group to periodic shifts in media strategy by the Home Office and noted how using the media was part of a bid for extra resources for the Home Office's desired prison-building programme—not the only instance of such tactics, as we show later.[4] In order to achieve its ends, the Home Office had adopted a high-profile public relations strategy:

---

[4] HM Customs and Excise made use of precisely this technique, as is discussed below in Ch. 5.

Towards the end of the 1970s, the Home Office wanted to embark upon a new programme of prison construction. It saw one of the ways in which it could get the resources for that as being to put pressure on the Treasury, to open up the prisons to show just how decrepit they were. Hence the invitation to [the television documentary film-maker] Rex Bloomstein to carry out his brilliant *Strangeways* [Prison] series for television.[5] They [the Home Office] adopted a strategy of approaching journalists saying 'Please come and see how awful our prisons are.' Previously, the Home Office had always discouraged journalists, kept them out of establishments and would rarely tell them anything either on, or off, the record.

He characterized the Home Office's general media strategy as 'proactive' with 'off-the-record briefings and whispering in the ears providing material' and went on to observe that if the Home Office 'sees things in the papers it does not like it rings the journalists the next day and moans at them'.

The obverse of the strategy of publicity-seeking is that of secrecy or closure, a characteristic quite typical of British government.[6] Knowing that secrecy is desired may prove to be a weapon in negotiations with the Home Office, and groups may use that knowledge to secure a result that they want. Prison cases may offer such an instance, as Chris Tchaikovsky described:

The one weapon one does have against the Home Office is that they do not like publicity. All prison governors know, people in prison know, that you must not embarrass the minister, which means that they do not like getting in the papers. It is an effective weapon in that sense.

At times, pressure groups do not want to go to the media over particular issues or to seek publicity for certain cases because they are worried that if too much publicity is given, the Home Office may then see itself as embattled and react unfavourably. Even the more radical pressure groups will negotiate with the Home Office over a particular issue, knowing that publicity cannot help the particular cause.

Some of the journalists we interviewed also confirmed this broad picture of the interaction between Home Office and pressure groups and their competitive use of the media. However, it would

---

[5] *Strangeways* (BBC TV, 1982; prod. R. Bloomstein).

[6] Ericson, R. V., Baranek, P. M., and Chan, J. B. L., *Negotiating Control: A Study of News Sources* (Toronto: University of Toronto Press, 1989), ch. 1, argue that strategies of closure and disclosure are quite fundamental to source–media relations.

be wrong to assume that the relationship is purely antagonistic. Behind the scenes, discussions about particular cases take place all the time between various departments in the Home Office and pressure groups. So far as can be ascertained, sustaining a relationship with the Home Office does not seem to inhibit some groups from making criticisms of it, or other, government departments.

Leah Levin of Justice outlined her perception of this relationship:

Access to government departments is never a problem. It does not inhibit us in any way. We are totally outspoken about what we think are the failures on the part of the Home Office to deal with cases which are referred back, etc., to the Home Office from us. We are concerned with our cases but we are also concerned with the principle and the way that the Home Office deals with them and think it very unsatisfactory. The fact that we have ready access on the telephone or by letter or whatever, and the fact that we are usually given very reasonable consideration still does not inhibit us in any way of making our views known.

Justice, like other voluntary groups, is used by government departments to put over points of view with which they might sympathize but where it is politically advantageous to have them expressed at arm's length, as is often the case with reforms or changes to the law. Leah Levin outlined the kind of involvement that might occur:

They might be considering a White Paper on a particular aspect of law. I would not say that there might not be informal discussions or departmental discussions going on at various times just to get a sense of what the outside world thinks. I do not say that they would conclusively influence the position taken by the government, for they have their own political imperatives and so on. But that does not mean that there could not be informal discussion between members of an organization like this with individual members or even looking closely at our published material or anything like that. Then, of course, we would nearly always be asked for comments on interdepartmental working papers. That is preparation for anything that might follow.

The Home Office, of course, does not solicit opinions on every issue, but according to our informants, as a rule they would do so for something considered important. As part of this process of consultation it is common for groups to issue a press statement or, if journalists ring up, to give them a story about their own particular submission. This is even more so in the case of a White Paper. Because this is in the public domain, groups are free either to publish something themselves or to give a story to a journalist either at their own initiative or in response to a request.

With major pieces of legislation such as the Criminal Justice Bill (1988), the Home Office would make contact with various interests to find out what they thought should be in it. This consultative process mainly takes place after publication of the White Paper, according to NACRO's Paul Cavadino. For a group such as this, which receives extensive government funding from more than one department, the consultation process may also work in reverse when it discusses how to publicize one of its own projects with the government department concerned. In Paul Cavadino's words: 'If it's about something which NACRO is doing which involves them, then we would liaise with their press office before we put out the press release anyway.' However, there is a distinction between projects financed by government with which a given pressure group—which, after all, is the beneficiary—may be in full agreement and those issues that are a matter of contention. Paul Cavadino pointed out how this is so:

Where we are criticizing penal policy, obviously that is in a rather different sort of category in that normally we will be criticizing Home Office policy, not invariably, but normally we will be if we are arguing for change. There we always make sure that the Home Office press office know in advance what we are doing. We will make sure that they are aware of the press release we are putting out if it is attacking some aspect of Home Office policy because they are going to be contacted quite probably and asked what their reaction is to this criticism of government policy. So (a) it is only fair, and (b) it means that they are more likely to make a sensible comment if they know exactly what it is that we have said as distinct from being some garbled version second-hand by a journalist. It is fair to do this anyway if you are going to criticize people whom we work with on other things. They obviously want to know what you are saying in advance.

This suggests a rather delicate relationship in which the underlying dependency on the paymaster presses the group towards discretion and punctiliousness. That is not to say that any overt or crude pressure is necessarily exerted to block criticism, as we were assured that this was not the case. The above account also underlines a desire to convey one's organization's positions in one's own terms. By bypassing the media, as far as possible, an effort is made to ensure that misapprehensions introduced by incomplete reporting might be reduced. However—and this is the index of where power ultimately lies in these relationships—the Home Office does *not* reciprocate by giving advance notice of its intentions. Non-official actors in the policy network will receive a press release or ministerial statement from the Home Office at the same time as journalists and any other interested parties.

But there is a further twist to the tale, because external criticism may at times be of considerable use for internal bureaucratic struggles. For reasons of office politics, some individuals are quite happy to see given policies criticized, as Paul Cavadino pointed out:

The Prison Department does not like us criticizing aspects of prison policy but on the other hand, it would like to see fewer prisoners and it is quite happy for us to weigh in saying that the Home Office should do more to restrict the use of imprisonment by the courts. In so far as we are criticizing the Home Office policy, I'm sure that the Home Office would rather we did not on the whole. They have not wielded a big stick and we have not felt inhibited from saying things that we want to about penal policy because of the fact that we get funding from the Home Office.

Given the nature of our interviews, it has been impossible to establish whether or not the Home Office has, as a condition of funding, at times put pressure on groups not to say things that might bring unwelcome publicity. It is reasonable to suppose that its funding role does operate as a constraint. However, there is a further subtlety to the fact of receiving Home Office funding. Although it produces dependency, at the same time it may offer a certain scope for autonomy, because if the work that a group is undertaking enjoys confidence and esteem both inside government circles and without, 'acceptable' criticism is likely to be seen as both legitimate and credible. That is the view of a non-statutory body such as NACRO. However, this is not the only road to having criticism taken seriously. Groups such as the Prison Reform Trust or the Howard League may also feel they have credibility and legitimacy because of what they do and because they are perceived as backed up by the wider liberal establishment, which is a serious constituency in its own right.

The proximity to government of many actors in the policy arena, and the interchanges that occur, underline the fact that we should not see news sources in isolation from one another. Rather, they are heavily implicated in a web of exchange and negotiation—

although not, of course, one in which equal terms apply to each and all.

Media Strategies

It will be clear from the foregoing that a great deal of tactical media use is an inherent feature of the interrelations between component parts of the policy network. Such tactics, however, rarely fit into fully thought-through media strategies in the pressure group world. Whereas the experts in design have been at work amongst criminal justice officialdom and the professionals, such concentrated attention on image management is a rarity amongst pressure groups.

Target Audiences

NACRO was unusual in being able to articulate a media strategy with both clarity and concision. Not surprisingly, this was widely recognized and its sophistication made it a model others wished to emulate. Paul Cavadino identified two distinct aims. First, there was a public education goal:

On the general level we have got a duty to try where we can to get publicity for constructive approaches to dealing with crime, constructive approaches to dealing with offenders, and preventing crime as part of public education because the media, in any event, have a lot about crime all the time, much of which is sensational, distorted, negative, and unconstructive. If only to a small degree we can help to redress the balance by getting coverage of constructive ways of dealing with crime and offenders, then it is desirable to do that. On one level that is what we are aiming to do.

A second goal was to support NACRO's local action and gain support for this, although this was based upon quite a cautious view of the likely impact of any publicity:

On a more specific level, if you've got a scheme in a local area, particularly the sort of scheme that we run, and if they get a steady flow of reasonably good, sympathetic publicity for the work they are doing, then that obviously helps to build up good will in the area. . . . I think that you can change attitudes but you should not be unrealistic about what you can achieve by the way of press publicity and changing attitudes.

Most of the coverage achieved and the bulk of contact with the media by pressure groups is with the quality press and with television current affairs and documentaries. This inevitably means that the audience is a relatively small one. In that sense, it is possible to think of much of the debate within the policy arena as somewhat enclosed and of the main target audience as élites able to influence policy formation and implementation. Getting the message across to the wider public is much more problematic. Stephen Shaw, director of the Prison Reform Trust, spelled out a typical perspective on media-targeting, but also, like Paul Cavadino, underlined the need to attain a wider appeal:

Our aim is to get in the quality morning papers, some of the journals, and if we are lucky, on the *Today* programme and other morning radio shows. It is unusual for us to put out one of our reports that does not get on LBC [radio] for example. . . . If we had a written statement we would ring the Press Association, the *Guardian* and *The Times* and these days the *Independent* as well, and read it over. . . . The principal determinant of what we do is that most of our stuff is of its nature not visual and you are therefore interested in getting into the papers that the majority of our clients, people we are trying to get at, are reading, or the radio programmes that they are listening to. Like all pressure groups we are trying to inform the policy-makers, the opinion-makers, influencing people, say, in the POA executive, in the Home Office, politicians, *Guardian* and *Times* readers, and also we obviously have a wider brief in terms of the great British public. It is easy to get seduced into that first group and forget about the wider one.

A similar line of argument came from Sarah Spencer, general secretary of NCCL, who said that she tended to place high importance on BBC Radio 4 because 'We're trying to influence policy-makers and MPs. That's because of our strategy. We are not a grassroots organization. We try to influence policy-makers.' This reinforces the point made above about the pre-eminent lines of contact being with the élite media. However, like others, Sarah Spencer recognized the need to speak to a wider public, and observed:

It may be however that we ought to concentrate on, you know, Radio 2, and try for a bit more public pressure. We also concentrate on the quality press partly because in most of the tabloids we get a pretty unfavourable hearing. It's much more difficult to get in except on things like sterilization and you tend not to get the sort of coverage that you value. It tends to be 'The general secretary of NCCL said this was appalling'.

For the most part, then, the media relations effort is targeted towards influencing the élite via the quality press and current affairs radio and television journalism. Some groups, however, do aspire to break out of this context and win wider influence. Stephen Shaw, director of the Prison Reform Trust, said that reaching tabloids such as the *Daily Mirror* was desirable, but at the moment unattainable.[7] However, such experience as they had had of the popular press had resulted in 'greater distortion' of their message. He could understand why, since he felt that the amount of attention achieved by prisons was really quite surprising, given prevalent news values:

What is of interest to the popular papers and to radio and television is something out of the norm. Most prison life is incredibly boring and probably deteriorating in quality, but there is no news in that. The media are only going to report if someone holds a knife to a prison officer's throat, or there is a riot, or reports of drugs or AIDS. That distorts the reality of prison life and ignores what we would think of as critical in terms of prison policy—the long-term relationship between various grades of prison staff and the Home Office, the prison building programme, questions about grievance procedures, and disciplinary procedures within prisons. We think they are very important but they are not newsworthy. . . . What is more interesting is the way in which crime and criminals and prisoners, are presented more generally in the media. There is an interest in crime and criminals especially the most grave and unusual sorts of crimes and in a small number of infamous criminals, the Krays, the Moors Murderers, the Yorkshire Ripper, and so on. Have we a right to complain? The effect, no doubt, would distort people's impression of who is in prison. Most people seem to think from our public opinion survey that the prisons are full of violent criminals, but most are just burglars and thieves. This thought is inflamed by the media approach. This is nothing new and has gone on since the eighteenth century.

These comments show an acute recognition of the obstacles to sympathetic wider public attention for minority causes that is based upon a strong sense of how popular news values construct crime stories. Thus, on this analysis, highly goal-oriented targeting of policy-makers and influentials via élite media is an entirely

---

[7] Stephen Shaw instanced the Child Poverty Action Group as a model worth following in this regard, which, according to him, had taken some fifteen years to break through to popular press attention. In this connection, he made reference to Frank Field's book. See Field, F., *The Inside Story of the CPAG Campaigns in the 1970s* (London: Heinemann, 1982).

rational strategy, as anything else would be a wasted effort. Very occasionally, where there are sufficient resources, it might be possible to publicize a view and altogether bypass the media by publishing it oneself. During the celebrated row over the BBC's *Secret Society* series, which has involved the seizure of materials from the corporation's offices by the Special Branch, NCCL had wanted to spell out the civil liberties implications and had produced 10,000 copies of its own pamphlet for cheap distribution.[8]

But this level of activity is rare and could only occur at the more highly resourced end of the spectrum. In sharp contrast, the Haldane Society, which has few resources, and is without charitable status because it wishes to remain politically committed, cannot pay full-time organizers and sees its contribution as one of informing other people on the Left. It mainly targets the more liberal quality press, such as the *Observer*, the *Guardian*, and the *Independent*. Other groups see their media strategy as part of a campaign to educate the public on crime and to counterbalance popular press irrationality. This was the line taken by Frances Crook of the Howard League:

You actually give information in a particular way to the public through the media because we don't have the resources to do it another way . . . to present a different side to the story, the humane side and the rational side, because a lot of the media coverage of crime is totally irrational, it's hysterical and punitive in evil ways. So I see the job as partly to counterbalance that.

Such a view, contrary to the realism about the public appeal of popular news values expressed above by Stephen Shaw, rests upon an implicit model of communication that presumes that some media, at least, are there for purposes of public education. Although something of an orthodoxy in the pressure group world, there were signs that some were thinking beyond this and beginning to consider how they might be able to develop a more elaborated strategy and break through to a wider audience, as Ann Owers, the then director of JCWI indicated:

One of the things that we have to do is to think of ways to appeal to the tabloid press that are not totally unsympathetic. I do not think that the *Daily Mirror* is totally unsympathetic to what we are doing. At times even

---

[8] Thornton, P., *The Civil Liberties of the Zircon Affair* (London: NCCL, 1987).

the *Daily Mail* isn't totally unsympathetic. We have to try and reach the parts that we are not reaching.

In general, whilst our informants said that publicity was not of crucial importance for their funders, they were much clearer that media coverage is seen as of value for their memberships, as a means of communicating a group's activities and also of relating to its own constituency. Public exposure is also a potential means of recruitment, as Frances Crook of the Howard League pointed out:

Members will say 'Oh yes, you seem to be doing a lot, I've seen your name in the paper again.' The higher profile we get, the more members we get, so that's for the organization. But also because we want to raise these issues and get them talked about sensibly, not like the *Sun* does.

This is really consonant with the dominant view amongst 'respectable' pressure groups. Most commonly, the principal goal is to appeal to an élite, to the policy-makers. At the same time, however, it is also sometimes recognized that there is value in appearing on popular programmes and in achieving coverage by local newspapers for given purposes. There is unquestionably—and particularly strongly in some quarters—an idea that 'public education' is needed. And in achieving this goal, recourse to the media is indispensable.

Professionalization in Media Relations

Thinking strategically is merely one level of working out an organization's media relations. There are various supporting tactics to be employed in order to attain the overall goals set. These rely upon learnable knowledges and skills concerning how the media actually work, and it is to the growth of these amongst pressure groups that we now turn.

The trend to 'professionalization' in public relations was evident in many quarters. Researching this field in the mid- to late 1980s, it was impossible not to connect this emergent awareness with the changes taking place in how the Labour Party was now marketing itself.[9] For the 1987 General Election, Labour, which had had to

[9] For a critical account of the background to Labour's communication policy, which continued into the subsequent General Election, see Philo, G., 'Political Advertising, Popular Belief, and the 1992 British General Election', *Media, Culture and Society*, 15 (1993), 407–18. One of the best accounts of the background to Thatcher's political marketing remains Cockerell, M., Hennessy, P., and Walker, D.,

adjust to the marketization of politics embodied in the successful Thatcher campaigns from 1979 onwards, produced a slick and well-packaged campaign, although it still lost. Most of the pressure groups in the field are left-oriented and appeared to be influenced by the new Labour orientation towards publicity and the media.

The groups cited as having the best publicity machines were those with more substantial funding. The smaller groups often mentioned the coverage attained by NACRO, NCCL, the Prison Reform Trust, and JCWI. What they saw was the end product in the newspapers or on television, and this acted as a spur to emulation. However, they were not able to do so effectively because of resource constraints. With a high staff turnover, insecure, and often very short-term funding, coupled with an inability to invest in PR development or to hire media relations specialists, marginality was simply too difficult to overcome.

NACRO brought a rational calculation into its media relations. This meant targeting different media for different purposes—with a clear sense of what was likely to pay off in the local media and what would appeal to the national press. This also meant avoiding investments of time and energy regarded as inefficient, as Paul Cavadino pointed out. He had given up organizing press conferences for the most part, since he found good press releases much more cost-effective. Where relevant these would be targeted at local media where there might be interest in a local scheme. When the organization campaigned on penal policy it was this that was likely to attract national attention for relatively little effort.

For national coverage, NACRO first sends news releases to the main national newspapers' newsdesks, their home affairs and legal correspondents, and in some cases, the crime correspondents. Releases are also sent to the Press Association, to some of the larger regional papers such as the *Birmingham Post* and the *Yorkshire Post*, and also to specialist journals read by social workers, magistrates, and probation officers. Ethnic minority journals are also included, as are the newsdesks and specialist correspondents of the BBC and ITV. Local broadcast news stations are assumed to pick up any material from the Press Association, but the London radio stations are treated as if they were national.

Not surprisingly, in the light of this evident strategic sense, in

Sources Close to the Prime Minister: Inside the Hidden World of the News Manipulators (London: Macmillan, 1984).

many of the interviews which we conducted both NACRO and the PRT were most often cited, by other groups, as role models for their media strategies. As the director of one group commented;

I see Prison Reform Trust everywhere and I think they have really got their act together . . . they work very hard on it and they see it as part of their job. We have never actually seen it as part of our job. It is, and it should be. You have come to see us at a point where we are weighing up how much we are a welfare organization and how much we are a campaigning organization.

This perception connects with the PRT's self-conscious policy of targeting. In Stephen Shaw's words, 'what matters most is the coverage we receive in the *The Times, Guardian*, and *Independent*. . . . Best of all is coverage on Radio 4's *Today* programme, a programme listened to by just about every significant policy-maker in the land.'[10]

Groups such as NACRO constantly assess the coverage they receive. Such 'reflexivity', as the sociologist Anthony Giddens terms it, has become implanted as a permanent feature of the media relations approaches of the larger and more sophisticated actors such as the police, the Home Office, and some of the major associations and pressure groups.[11] Paul Cavadino spelled out in some detail how media monitoring was approached:

We do assess what we are doing, changing our strategy if it seems that a certain type of approach would be more effective than others for getting publicity. We have changed a lot of the way we do things—ranging from detailed issues such as whether you put embargoes at noon, or just after midnight, or certain times of the day, or what is more likely to give you better publicity because it will not clash with other things, trying to put out things on Bank Holidays because there is not much news around and you can get a lot of coverage that way. Practical things of that sort through to how much detail to put in a press release as opposed to putting it in a report, what kind of journals tend to cover our stuff, and what kind do not, where it is worth sending things, which individual journalists seem to be taking an interest in our area of policy that we have not come

[10] Shaw, S., 'Massaging the Media', *CJM: Criminal Justice Matters*, 11 (1993), 19.

[11] We may speculate that these developments in media are part of the emergent features of modernity, to which the media make their own contribution. The growth of rationalized media and public relations may well be part of an intensifying dynamic of seeking control in contemporary society. On 'institutional reflexivity' see Giddens, A., *Modernity and Self-Identity: Self and Society in the Late Modern Age* (Cambridge: Polity, 1991).

across before, and that we ought to make contact with and put on our press list, and so on.

This is not so much about strategy as basic competence in news management techniques, skills which can certainly be taught as they now are on public relations courses, or which are picked up by experience and sensitivity to what actually works. Thinking strategically will not produce results without this basic level of competence.[12]

The increasing professionalization of media relations is reflected in the monitoring that groups undertake to gauge the amount and type of coverage both they, and the area in general, receive. Television and radio are not systematically monitored whereas, by contrast, the press receives much more scrutiny. This was in keeping with what we had found elsewhere. Some of the groups subscribe to press cuttings agencies whereas others operate their own services for the benefit of officials and members.

NACRO is more thorough than any other in its monitoring and collects newspaper cuttings but as a general rule does not monitor television or radio. Brief television transcripts of news items are sought very occasionally. For example, during November and December 1986, they bought three transcripts that gave the BBC's and ITN's figures indicating the overcrowding in prisons. The main reason for not monitoring television and radio closely is the cost involved, a sentiment echoed by many of the other groups. NACRO obtain their newspaper cuttings from two main sources: a professional cuttings service that clips out any press items mentioning NACRO, overwhelmingly from the local press; and there are also items taken from the range of national newspapers clipped by NACRO themselves. Most cuttings concern stories and reports about the prison system, criminal justice generally, the operation of NACRO, and the schemes, activities, and policies of the Manpower Services Commission, one of the organization's main funders.

Cuttings are made every day and passed on to the press section of the organization by the information department and thence to certain key figures, such as the director, the press officer, and the section heads. When NACRO considers itself to be misrepresented, a press release will be written in order to correct the item. An

[12] For instances of this kind of literature see MacShane, D., *Using the Media*, 2nd edn. (London: Pluto, 1983); Bland, M. and Mondesir, S., *Promoting Yourself on Television and Radio* (London: Kogan Page, 1991).

example given was the *Guardian*'s coverage of a report by NACRO on the probation service, which was felt to be distorted and therefore of concern because of the damage that it might cause relations with probation officers. A press release was issued and contacts in the probation service alerted.

This level of investment in media monitoring was quite exceptional. Other larger groups, such as NCCL, receive agency cuttings but do not systematically monitor the effectiveness of their own work. Sarah Spencer told us that she herself would know what was in the *Guardian*, the *Independent*, *The Times*, and the *Observer* because she read those newspapers. Other groups could not even afford to have a press cuttings service. Frances Crook of the Howard League told us that she made her own press cuttings and these were quite rudimentary: 'I buy the *Guardian*, and if I speak to a journalist that day and he's from the *Daily Mail*, I'll buy the *Mail* the next day to see what he's written.'[13]

In the Law Centres Federation and the Haldane Society, attempts had been made to enlist journalists to help with ideas on media strategy and to organize training sessions. Solly Osmond, press officer of the Law Centres Federation, was trying to persuade his organization to take up training in public relations and seek help from 'sympathetic' journalists with 'nuts and bolts questions such as how to issue press releases and to cultivate links'. Beverley Lang of the Haldane Society commented in similar vein: 'What we are planning is to get some journalists in to give us some training in how best to use them. Like in any business, there's a right and a wrong way to go about it and since none of us are journalists we're almost certainly going about it the wrong way.'

In NCCL some of the staff had been on media relations and also management courses. When selecting personnel, NCCL would take into consideration a candidate's articulacy in putting across civil liberties issues. This was connected with the overall image that the organization itself projected, as Sarah Spencer noted:

My feeling is that the less radical you look, the more radical you can be and that we've too long relied on getting the argument right and forgetting

[13] One group, the Police Monitoring Unit, now defunct, at one time provided a cuttings service for others, but it had a very limited circulation. Tony Bunyan described it as 'a two-weekly cuttings service, which is roughly sixty sides every fortnight with key cuttings, and this goes to the local borough chairs, the leaders, London MPs, and some members of the media, because we only produce a small number, a hundred and thirty copies'.

to present it in a way that actually the public relate to. I don't say that we don't present it articulately but I think we need to give more attention to the physical presentation of literature, making it attractive, professional looking, not too rich and wealthy so that you look like you don't need any more money, but actually looking efficient and organized and approachable. We've been thinking about the image we have and sat down and discussed what image ought we to have, and it was a mixture of radical, responsible, caring, democratic and so on. And the friends in advertising are about to go through all of our literature and advise us on what image we are creating and advise us how to change it in order to create a different image.

Larger groups such as NCCL, NACRO, and the Prison Reform Trust showed particular awareness of image politics and could devote at least some organizational resources and energy to developing this area of their campaigning. Some of the smaller groups lacked the resources needed in order to work out a particularly strong or recognizable approach. As we shall later see, such differences of investment were reflected in journalists' views. What they tended to like were groups with stable staff members with the required information at their fingertips who knew what the media wanted and how they are organized. In line with the 'information subsidy' argument, this simplifies the journalist's job. As we shall also see, when we turn to the journalists' perspectives in Chapter 5, this kind of investment may be cost-effective because it also establishes source 'credibility' over time.

The relative disadvantage of the smaller groups in achieving news coverage in their own right means that they tend to allow the bigger organizations to take up certain issues. For instance, financially insecure groups like the New Bridge will tend to rely upon NACRO to publicize the big issues. Small organizations may send out press releases only four or five times a year, whereas NACRO issues them at least once a week, sometimes more. The Haldane Society also lacks resources. Despite having 'some distinguished people in our membership, people who are always in those big cases and are quite media-type figures', the problem, according to Beverley Lang, is that 'we haven't got an office' and 'there's no easy system of getting hold of anyone. . . . Because barristers particularly are always out of court we just don't get publicity in the way that NCCL and the Legal Action Group do.'

Pressure groups, like social movements, face an inherent tension between co-operation and competition with others in their chosen field of activity. As with capitalist enterprises seeking to establish their corporate images and market their products, a clear identity is also important to each pressure group for marketing purposes, and consequent recognition by the public. NCCL is particularly aware of its public image. This is partly because it encompasses such a diversity of issues in its work whereas other groups are much narrower in their focus, but it also depends on with whom they are competing. Sarah Spencer of NCCL observed of the furore during the banning of the BBC's *Secret Society* series in 1987: 'On certain stories, certainly, you're in competition with other people to get your viewpoint in. On Zircon, for instance, because so many worthy people were saying the right thing on it, it was actually quite difficult for NCCL to get coverage, because, I suppose, what we were saying was more predictable.' Asked whether she would feel worried if NCCL did not get the coverage that it ought to, she said:

I have to feel worried. In general political terms . . . the most important thing is that people with power say the right things. But as an organization that survives on membership income and publicity you actually can't afford to be too magnanimous about your press coverage. And that can be a problem. For instance, if you're working in an umbrella group with other organizations you can't afford to be subsumed into some other order of things because then you can spend hours and hours at work and you might achieve something politically. But if you don't get any recognition for it as an organization you couldn't survive like that.

Having a clear identity is especially important for a group such as NCCL because of its heavy reliance upon a membership subscription base and donations. Where finance is received from more secure sources, a constant high profile might not be as crucial.

Some groups have had to make decisions about the kind of profile and media coverage that they want. The National Association of Victim Support Schemes offered an example of a dispute about the kind of publicity and public relations to be used that was linked to notions of what constituted 'success'. Helen Reeves outlined the issues in question:

Some of our key funders introduced us to a public relations consultant because they thought that we should be promoting ourselves much more. All of those people, people in PR and money, advised us that we should not be putting all our eggs in one basket getting public money. We should be going out to the public and private industry, and so on, and that we should be playing our two trump cards. These are: 'Look at these poor, fragile old victims.' And we were saying victims are anybody, there is nothing poor, tragic, or pathetic about being a victim, it can happen to any of us. It is quite a different philosophy. The other one was: 'Look how much money is spent on crooks in comparison.' So that you actually end up with a competitive lobby. We did not think that was particularly helpful either. It would have polarized the criminal justice issues and that was not what we were after. It would have been very destructive to us.

The NAVSS council refused to play this game and the public relations advisers apparently left, proclaiming imminent failure. This account identifies quite distinctive criteria for what was success and what failure. Helen Reeves continued, noting that the public relations advisers had suggested that

if we played our cards properly, people would identify with victims of crime. You tap into the fear, you ought to play up children being abused and old people being abused because that would make people put their hands in their pockets. We were saying (a) it rather goes against the philosophy of the organization which is about reducing the effects of crime rather than increasing the effects of crime, and (b) we would lose an enormous amount of our support. People are actively on committees like churches and probation services, and good voluntary organizations. We would have lost an enormous amount of field support, not to mention the staff.

This debate crystallized a fundamental difference of opinion about the nature of the organization as represented through publicity. In this instance, those in day-to-day control were actually very clear about how they might best position themselves in the field.

Relations with Journalists

Most pressure groups had contact with the home affairs and legal affairs correspondents, but there was little connection with the crime correspondents. That is because most groups were concerned with prison reform or helping prisoners, so the journalistic division of labour meant that crime correspondents were largely irrelevant to them, although, exceptionally, some concerned with victims did have such connections.

As noted, the key emphasis is on targeting the quality press and in particular the *Guardian*, the *Independent*, *The Times*, and to a lesser extent, the *Daily Telegraph*. The *Observer*, and in some cases, the *Sunday Times*, also figured on the map. The advent of the *Independent* had certainly been a gain as far as the groups that we interviewed were concerned: the paper's distinctive interest in prisons was seen as valuable, with the then home affairs correspondent, Sarah Helm, frequently cited as writing good stories.[14] Stephen Shaw, however, has commented less than approvingly more recently that although 'The *Independent* has been particularly strong on penal policy issues since its launch . . . its editorial line—like that of *The Times*—has been in favour of privatization of the prison system'.[15]

Cultivating journalists—in a form that parallels the development of such relations by other actors in the policy arena—was also widely seen as crucial amongst pressure groups. As one group director pointed out:

We are well aware that if a journalist rings up on a story they are doing, it is part of our job to supply information for them, but we are also aware that either we will get quoted this time or next time, because it is a two-way process. There is that sense of collusion between journalists and all their sources—not that there is anything unusual about us or penal pressure groups, but we are aware of that. The only time we are irritated by it is when we are continually providing information, usually for television, and we are not getting any return for it.

The sense that exchanges did not always pay off occurred much more frequently with television than the press. Moreover, there was some resentment that the groups were being used as research assistants by journalists, but essentially most viewed this as a necessary trade-off for publicity. It was pointed out that television

[14] At the time of our research, the *Guardian*, which had traditionally been the journalistic home for pressure groups, had begun to reconsider its approach in this regard. To have a story about a relevant issue published in the *Guardian* typically also meant to have the price and date of publication included at the end of the article. Peter Preston, the paper's editor, reflected on the value to his newspaper of servicing the interests of small pressure groups, observing 'if you then step back and say wait a minute, how many people are there in this group and how many people apart from the three top dogs who are constantly complimenting the editor on the tremendous service that is being provided are actually reading it? And you may come up with different answers.' He went on to say, 'That doesn't mean to say that the *Guardian* is in any way changing except that it obviously has, over the last ten years, constantly looked to make sure that it isn't the outlet for a number of well-targeted pressure groups.' See Jenkins, J., 'Who Guards the *Guardian*?', *New Statesman*, 12 Feb. 1988, pp. 16–17.

[15] Shaw, 'Massaging the Media', 19.

researchers came and went rapidly, whereas, in the words of the PRT's Stephen Shaw, 'We have influence over newspaper journalists who use us a lot because we are helping to substantiate their stories and feeding them other stories and providing them with copy every couple of weeks.' Another group director commented: 'We could do two things. First we would not feed them stories we do not want our name attached to. That would hurt them. We just give them to another paper. Or we would say we are not going to send you press releases for three weeks or three months.' Because relationships with newspaper journalists are much closer than those with television, and built on trust, if expectations of fair treatment are confounded this is viewed much more seriously.

Not all groups necessarily seek high-profile publicity. For instance, Justice—given the highly specialist nature of its operation—is somewhat low-key, according to its director, Leah Levin:

We would naturally be in touch with the various legal correspondents, then we would do a broad mailing to a rather wider press sector to inform them. Then each of [our] committees would have specialist lists of people who might be interested. . . . Then we would also from time to time have an informal chat with legal correspondents in the media, people in television that we have good relations with. . . . We would certainly want every report that we produced to be made public and to try and create some public interest in whatever report we produced.

Justice, like all the other pressure groups and criminal justice professionals, has journalists ringing up for information and comments. The initiative comes from both sides. This relationship principally exists with legal affairs journalists and is 'on a very "responsible" footing', with no off-the-cuff quotations provided. This is another mode of calculating the costs and benefits of publicity, in which breadth of coverage is traded off against trying to achieve a serious understanding:

We are very mindful to try and develop not only good relations but reliable relationships with the press. We are not always what they are looking for, the sensational press certainly not, because we are never prepared to go for sensational publicity, that is absolutely out. . . . So resulting from that, and that all our reports have to be approved by [our] council, that also builds up a body of policy so if anything happens and we are phoned by the press and they say, 'What does Justice think of that?' . . . then I am in a position to say that these are the positions we have taken, those are the recommendations we make . . . But assuming that it is an event of the day—a verdict of a case which we had nothing to do with. They say 'What do you think of the verdict?' I would say that I don't have any views on it. That is where they do not get much out of us if they are looking for a quote just to hang something on.

Others, too, might at times regard such background briefings as more important than attributed publicity. Ann Owers of JCWI noted that if her organization did not from time to time appear in the press, journalists would not know that it existed and would not call for their views. However, at quite a different level, having those views enter into the public domain even in unattributed form was also regarded as important, for it could condition current debate:

For example, a lot of the reporting recently on the Tamils [refugees]—I don't think we were mentioned at all, but I had spent a lot of time talking to journalists, and if what I say is reflected in some way in the report they write or the questions that they ask Ministers, then that is my aim, it actually gets over a point of view, it gets an argument put, it gets the policy issues ventilated, and I think that is the important thing. It is much more important too than publicity for individual cases—we rarely seek publicity for individual cases.[16]

There is, then, a distinction to be drawn between achieving publicity that enhances the profile of a group and finding means that will ensure that the case, issue, or campaign achieves an airing.

Lobbying

Coalitions

Relations between the various pressure groups exist at both formal and informal levels.[17] Many of the personnel have worked for more than one organization and sit on the committees and councils of others.[18] Formal links manifest themselves primarily in the

[16] For a study of the 'Tamil panic' in the press see van Dijk, T. A., *News Analysis: Case Studies of International News in the Press* (Hilldale, NJ: Lawrence Erlbaum Associates, 1988).

[17] All are based in London, and at the time of our research in one part of South London there was a little ghetto comprising the Howard League, APEX, SOVA, NACRO, the Victim Support Schemes, Black Female Prisoners Scheme, and PROP.

[18] e.g. members of the Haldane Society may be on the executive of NCCL while members of the Haldane committee might work in the Legal Action Group (LAG). There has also been movement of personnel, for instance between NAVSS and the Howard League, and between JCWI and Justice. So although there may not be

shape of joint press releases, joint lobbying, and in writing for each other's journals and publications. Informally there is considerable help in liaison and sharing information. Apart from NCCL, which differs from other groups interviewed because its interests are broad, there is much close co-operation, although some differences of approach exist, as Stephen Shaw commented:

There is some competition for resources, but both the formal and informal links with all those organizations, and the more radical ones like PROP and RAP, are very close indeed. . . . The thing to remember is that penal policy is rather a small field, it tends to attract young, cuddly, left, people who of necessity are going to the same meetings and are involved in the same work in one way or another. They share largely an identity of outlook, often an identity of age and background. I think that is as important as anything else.

Co-operation often takes the form of lobbying and suggesting amendments to proposed legislation. It is important to note that achieving media coverage is only one part of the lobbying process, and as was shown in the previous chapter, behind-the-scenes efforts to achieve changes in legislation, for instance, may be viewed as much more important than going public. At other times, seeking media attention may be coupled with backstairs lobbying. The overall picture that emerged from our discussions with pressure groups was that whereas there might be quite extensive co-ordination over, say, the detailed laying-down of amendments to a particular piece of legislation, on the whole this was much less prevalent when it came to seeking media coverage.

In diverse situations, different organizations might take a leading role, although it was noteworthy that the larger pressure groups normally tended to take on the task of co-ordination. Lobbying might concern particular pieces of legislation or given cases. Some illustrations follow.

An example of NACRO's co-ordinating and campaigning role occurred during an attempt to bring back capital punishment in March–April 1987. A backbench Conservative MP was putting forward a Private Member's Bill calling for the reintroduction of hanging. A response was required fairly swiftly, and NACRO co-ordinated this. The initial idea came from the Association of

---

formal relationships of co-operation, the informal ones are very close, not least because of this dynamic of staff interchange.

Chiefs of Probation, which contacted NACRO with a proposal for a joint statement. NACRO wrote the first draft and circulated this to various groups, asking for changes. Other organizations were canvassed for support and the whole exercise was completed in a week. A press statement titled 'Death Penalty Would Damage the Penal System' was issued and began, 'The reintroduction of capital punishment would be a damaging blow to the whole penal system, six organisations concerned with the treatment of offenders warn in a joint statement issued today' (31 March 1987). The statement was set to coincide with the House of Commons debate on the subject and signed by NACRO, the Association of Chiefs of Probation, the Prison Governors, the National Association of Probation Officers, the Howard League, and the Prison Reform Trust. Further lobbying was also organized by the groups on an individual basis. Paul Cavadino commented that the response was effective at that moment because it both carried weight and was well-timed.

Another relevant example occurred during lobbying to amend the Criminal Justice Bill after its publication in November 1986 following an earlier White Paper.[19] On that occasion, NCCL organized a meeting attended by many groups, where participants outlined their interests, divided the tasks, and agreed to liaise. Liaison over certain clauses in the Criminal Justice Bill overlapped with already established areas of co-operation. On this occasion, for instance, as NACRO informed us, there was a consensus amongst those involved that an enforceable code of minimum standards for prisoners was needed and that relevant amendments to the Bill should be tabled. NACRO took on the task of issuing a press statement and briefing paper on behalf of a coalition that included, amongst others, the PRT, the Howard League, Justice, the Prison Governors, the POA, and the Association of Members of Boards of Visitors. As Paul Cavadino explained:

The briefing paper among other things will mention the fact that all those organizations support the case for this [the code] and quote from things which the POA and Governors have said, but it will be a NACRO paper. The other organizations will also put out their own documents at different times arguing the same case. We go to great lengths to ensure that they know what we are doing and we ask them what they are doing.

[19] Because of the 1987 General Election, the Bill was dropped and then reintroduced in the new House of Commons.

Frances Crook of the Howard League outlined an instance of
how such co-operation had worked when a woman prisoner's baby
had died in Holloway Prison:

There was an inquest and NCCL was representing the mother, who was
released by the Home Secretary. NCCL, Women in Prison, and the
Howard League held a joint press conference on the issue. NCCL handled
the legal side, Women in Prison handled what happens to mothers and
babies and what the problems are, and we handled what should be done
about it. So there was that. Also I organized a series of fringe meetings;
we had NCCL, Prison Reform Trust, Women in Prison, and MIND sent a
representative, an all-women platform, and they were joint meetings. So
there are formal things, actions, that we do together as well as a lot of
informal contact.

This desire to articulate the different inputs into common action
is an inherent part of the coalition process, and smaller groups
might subordinate their contributions to the needs of the wider
cause. As Beverley Lang of the Haldane Society underlined in relation to the Criminal Justice Bill lobby:

Our first objective would be to ensure that we don't act in a way which is
counter-productive to NCCL or is anything other than complementary. So
what we've decided is instead of doing our own briefings and sending our
own people to sit during the committee stages in the Commons we will
offer our services to NCCL and will treat them as the umbrella group.
Our criminal law sub-committee will sit down and go through the bill,
work out proposed amendments, do all that sort of stuff, and in this particular instance we're going to channel it through NCCL.

At other times, one group might organize a public meeting
whilst the others would be carrying on with parliamentary lobbying. On some occasions, too, there is a co-ordinated media campaign. This is quite typical of pressure group politics, as the
experienced campaigner, Des Wilson has pointed out.[20] Whether
the media relations aspect is highlighted or not is simply a matter
of pragmatic judgement. Paul Cavadino summarized the approach
taken by his organization to the Criminal Justice Bill: 'You can
make as much noise as you like in the media only if . . . you have
not got MPs and peers who at the time the legislation is going

[20] He noted, for instance, that various campaigns combined 'detailed negotiations
with Whitehall and Westminster with exploitation of the media to force politicians
to take them seriously'. Wilson, D., *Pressure: The A to Z of Campaigning in Britain*
(London: Heinemann, 1985), 18.

through are putting down the necessary amendments to change it.'
Seeking media attention might then be a supplementary activity at
key stages of the Bill's passage. Comments would be short and
pithy so that they could easily be slotted into a story, and journalists would be contacted to try and ensure coverage in such circumstances. Such individualizing of the publicity effort—despite
co-operation over the behind-the-scenes lobbying—is, as already
pointed out, closely linked to the need of pressure groups to
market themselves.

The process of co-ordination outlined here operates continuously
and the publication of a White Paper, and later of a Bill, merely
heightens the level of activity. Typically, for White Papers, groups
will submit comments to the Home Office and also sometimes
issue press releases. With the publication of the Bill itself the lobbying of Ministers and MPs by some groups increases, as does the
media campaign. On some occasions the objectives sought may be
achieved through lobbying alone.

Solo Lobbying

Some of the groups believe that their energies are best served by
putting pressure on government and feeding information to sympathetic MPs. Such relationships may be very close and might involve
helping to draft amendments and also preparing parts of speeches,
as Leah Levin of Justice illustrated:

Any amendment that we propose is not just written down on a piece of
paper—it has a rationale behind it so there is an argument attached to it.
If further information is required then we provide further information. I
think that we have reached a stage when we would get calls from Peers or
MPs saying, 'We have not seen your comments on this circular. Will you
let us have it?' It has developed into something that they almost expect.

In terms that echo Leah Levin, Sarah Spencer underlined the particular importance for opposition MPs, who enjoy few back-up
research resources, of such information subsidies:

We have an influence on MPs because of the quality of information we
provide . . . because the opposition MPs have so few research resources.
We provide a service that they desperately need and it gives us an enormous amount of influence because we give them something that they can't
do without. For instance, they haven't got the resources to draft amendments to bills. If an organization comes along that is competent at drafting

amendments, is discreet so that it's not going to go around shouting out that this particular party refused to put an amendment on that, provides them with amendments and briefings to back them up, then you're obviously in a position to influence.

Just as information subsidies flow from sources to journalists, so too do they flow from pressure groups to legislators. This process may be linked to the credibility that a given group has achieved with politicians over a period of time. It is credibility and reliability that make such briefings acceptable and usable in parliamentary debate. By using political contacts, lobbying can often be a more effective strategy than using the media, although, as noted, they are often combined. For example, Helen Reeves, director of the National Association of Victim Support Schemes, was successful in achieving some of her aims by lobbying the Parliamentary All-Party Penal Affairs Group, inside which she had contacts. This body produced a report on victims of crime and their needs and the NAVSS provided them with relevant information. Because this was part of a wider contacts network it resulted in a number of positive developments. Helen Reeves described the process in detail:

There was a bit of old-school tie. . . . I knew the Labour people who very quickly became front-bench home affairs people, much to my amazement. I did not know that I knew important people, it just happened, and by going along to the all-party group I met people from the other parties who were very helpful and interesting. They produced a first report called 'A New Deal for Victims'. . . . We managed to get a section put into that document on victim support and compensation. . . . Then the Home Affairs Select Committee picked it up and did a report on what is going on in victims. In the normal way they wrote to all the relevant organizations to ask for information and we submitted a big chunk of stuff and so did all the other bodies. All of them were very supportive of victim support so we got called in to give verbal evidence as well. That was a major triumph, the Home Affairs Select Committee report, because their primary recommendation was improved funding for victim support schemes. That is what has happened.

An exploration of information subsidies from pressure groups to politicians opens up further interesting questions about the process of 'primary definition'. We have pointed out that *behind* the so-called primary definition may lie a prior process of definitional struggle or negotiation. Empirical support for this argument derives from the nature of the interrelations between pressure groups and politicians with access to the forum of Parliament and thus to broader publicity. How issues are defined may at times be heavily dependent upon other sources than those that make the official utterance.[21]

Publicizing Cases

Using the Media

Relationships with specific journalists really pay off when they initiate campaigns over specific cases. This exchange benefits both the group and the journalist: the group achieves publicity that may help to solve a problem, whereas from the journalist's point of view a good case can produce a human interest story that may also be used as a peg for a comment on the wider issues involved.

A number of instances of extensive coverage were cited by our informants. Tony Bunyan of the Police Monitoring Group succeeded in enlisting the *Guardian*'s David Pallister to write about the police's brutal behaviour towards student demonstrators at Manchester University during a visit by the then Home Secretary, Leon Brittan.[22] The paper had devoted a full page to the story, which, because of its prominence, had sparked off follow-ups by other media. This had a much more far-reaching impact than earlier, quite modest, attempts to achieve publicity.

In the majority of cases, contact is usually with journalists working on the *Guardian*, the *Independent*, the *Observer*, and *The Times*. Occasionally, however, relationships develop with some of the tabloids. Solly Osmond, the press officer for the Law Centres Federation, gave an example:

I had a client two years ago who served in the Second World War and was awarded the Burma Star medal. He was granted an exempt visa to come and settle here in error and the Home Office were trying to deport him and I was surprised that papers like the *Daily Mail* and the *Daily Express* took up the story. 'War Hero Faces Deportation'—that sort of angle. It wasn't too long after the Falklands [campaign of 1982], so with that sort of thing I will certainly go for the populars.

[21] Clearly, our material is illustrative of this point rather than conclusive evidence. However, it does open up a potentially fruitful area of investigation.

[22] Murphy, D., *The Stalker Affair and the Press* (London: Unwin Hyman, 1991), 41.

According to Osmond, the man concerned, a Pakistani national, had been erroneously led to believe that he would be permitted to stay in Britain by the Foreign Office. But on arrival he had been refused leave to remain. He went on: 'I thought this was something which especially the popular press would love to report. Television took it up, *South East at Six*, I think the BBC, and it did something like a 5-minute interview, which was not bad.' Then, according to Osmond, sections of the ethnic minority press picked up the story as well. The outcome of the campaign was that the national dailies covered it, with columns in the *Guardian*, *The Times*, the *Daily Telegraph*, and the *Daily Mail*. The Burma Star Association also became involved. 'Meanwhile the deportation appeal was allowed by the adjudicator. Remember, when the press picks it up they keep on asking the Home Office for a response and if that continues for a period of time I think psychologically it's a pressure on them to come clean and say, "OK, we admit that we made an error," and that puts them in an embarrassing position.' Had the case been lost, the next stage would have been to have a very supportive senior Conservative MP meet the Home Secretary and take up the issue with him. Contacts in the House of Lords would also have been alerted.

The man was allowed to stay. The group had successfully used the media and publicity to win the case. However, there are occasions where publicity can be detrimental and may make the Home Office completely intransigent when under pressure. According to Solly Osmond, in most immigration cases his group would not use the press, as the client's consent needs to be sought; usually they will turn to the press when all legal remedies have been exhausted and all that remains is campaigning pressure. The media are then the only recourse, but unless the deportation story has journalistic value their interest is hard to arouse.

Others concurred that publicity was not always desirable. In the words of Ann Owers:

Publicity is a double-edged weapon. First of all, there are situations in which if you expose the Home Office publicly they find it much more difficult to retreat gracefully, and I think there have been immigration cases which have actually led to the deportation of the person concerned because of the way the campaign has been carried out.

In addition, she pointed out, certain deportation cases might win public support but there was also the concomitant risk of stirring up 'the other sort of publicity—you get the "Keep them out!" publicity. The "We are being swamped" publicity every time one of these stories comes out. The individual cases . . . are not the real issue—the real issue is to get a good policy. . . . You do not get it by that sort of press coverage at all.' She knew of cases where the political principle of fighting immigration control had overwhelmed the pragmatic need 'to go through the usual channels, which is to say, "Please, Minister, out of the goodness of your heart will you let this dear sweet lady stay here?" Whatever your views about the awful convolutions you have to go through with the Minister's office if you want him to be nice to somebody, the important person is the client, and you have to keep that very clearly in your head.'

Being Used by the Media

The demand for publicity in specific cases may also come from the media. Many groups said that they were constantly being asked by television producers and researchers to provide 'bodies' for their programmes. However, pressure groups working in this area were concerned that such vulnerable people could be exploited, as Anne Owers of JCWI explained:

The problem for us comes when the media have got a story they want to run and they want a body. I think that is much the most difficult issue or certainly one of the most difficult issues that we have got. You want a point to be covered. You need for a policy reason a discussion to happen and the press and particularly television will say to you: 'In order to make this a story we have got to have a real person.' You then have to ring around people who are already victimized by the system, who are already under enormous pressure and ask them to make their lives public to other people.

It is quite common, especially for television and radio programmes, to contact pressure groups and ask for an ex-prisoner, or a member of a prisoner's family—usually a wife—to comment on a prison riot, or a legal issue that affects prisoners. Another typical request is for the victims of particularly brutal crimes. At times, the pressure to provide such services can be extreme, and the protective attitude of the pressure groups may not be understood, as is graphically illustrated by this account of an approach to Helen Reeves of the NAVSS by one reporter, who had said to her:

We want to run a series on battered old ladies, mugging of ladies. Would you be able to produce a new case for us every day and you would get lots of publicity out of it yourself? We would give the line, 'Well, actually, of course, that is not a typical crime. It causes alarm and stresses lots of other old ladies unnecessarily.' They would say: 'That's all very interesting and very responsible of you—but it is not what our readers want to read.' That is an actual quote—the journalist actually said that.

Thus, most of the time, deciding on whether or not to use publicity is subordinated to the interests of those whose case is being pursued, unless, of course, the media already have some of the facts and can use these as leverage to prise out more.

Access to publicity, we have suggested, is highly dependent upon the relative institutionalization of a source and its credibility. We can shed some further light on the question of access to publicity by considering differences between the established or respectable core of pressure groups and the radical fringe. The larger, more 'acceptable' groups tend to take the lead in co-ordinating lobbying and media campaigning. At one level, we have suggested, this emergent leadership is a result of inequalities of resources. However, there are also other forces at work. As the novelty value of small, newly emergent groups diminishes, so does the level of media attention they are likely to achieve. Geoff Coggan of PROP described the shift from an initial 'honeymoon period' with the media to relative indifference by reference to the experience both of his own organization and also that of Women in Prison:

When Women in Prison started up the media were so excited. They had a real honeymoon period. . . . Now the media is finding increasingly that they can do without Women in Prison and goes to NACRO and to the Howard League. That really is exactly what happened to us—that is, PROP. I don't even know if Women in Prison recognize this, or even want to, but I can see them following the same sort of path. In a way it is not criticism of them or of us. That happened because what is a pressure group there for if it is not to stir people up into doing things? If, because of that, we have managed to stir NACRO and the Howard League and the Prison Reform Trust into acting in a far more radical way than they would have been doing before, then that is fine. I don't think that there would have been a Prison Reform Trust, frankly, if it had not been for the sort of pressure that we and other people have put in. They have done magnificent work, they have done just the sort of things that we would have done in a lot of cases—all this stuff on body belts and restraints— and of course they have been able to do it with that air of respectability that we've never had. In a sense, the more successful you are the more you are going to cut yourself down. If we were totally successful there would not be any need for us whatsoever.

In some respects, this is an instance of what the political scientist Anthony Downs has termed the 'issue-attention cycle'. He argues that for a given major issue there is a 'systematic cycle of heightening public interest and then increasing boredom'.[23] Here, the loss of novelty for the media by small groups means that the advantage passes to larger ones, better able to offer information subsidies over the longer term because of their broader and deeper resource bases. In addition to this, we can observe a kind of displacement effect, in which the radical pace-making of the outer fringe is co-opted into the more 'respectable' institutionalized pressure politics of the centre.

Becoming a Media 'Expert'

As non-official groups acquire media visibility and credibility, there is a tendency for their leading personalities or officers to become media spokespeople.[24] For official bodies, although visibility inheres in their institutional position, as we have seen, credibility still has to be cultivated. In general, in line with what has already been argued, it is the larger and better-known pressure groups that are contacted most frequently. Stephen Shaw has emphasized that the major penal reform groups' success with the press is based on three factors: 'the authority of our research and information; the regularity with which we pepper the papers with stories and press releases; and, finally, the speed with which we respond to initiatives and statements emerging from the Home Office'. Journalistic mistrust of the Home Office Press Office, he went on to suggest, meant that major penal reform groups ended up as 'the preferred source'.[25]

The media are quite selective about whom they want to speak to inside organizations regarded as useful. Having 'expertise' means providing quotes and making appearances on television and radio

[23] Downs, A., 'Up and Down with Ecology: The Issue Attention Cycle', *Public Interest*, 28 (1972), 38–50, citation from p. 39. Downs's example is that of 'ecological' concern in the USA, but there is no reason why this cannot be applied to specific issues in the field of 'law and order'.

[24] Gitlin, T., *The Whole World is Watching: Mass Media in the Making and Unmaking of the New Left* (Berkeley, Calif.: University of California Press, 1980) remains the best-documented study of this process.

[25] Shaw, 'Massaging the Media', 19.

discussion programmes and in broadcast documentaries. It also means becoming adept at structuring what one has to say to fit in with the needs of different media and avoiding comments that might be used either against one's own organization or to stir up undesired complications with a government body. At times, a member of a particular pressure group, not necessarily a full-time worker, might be used because he or she has a well-known name. For example, although the Haldane Society is not particularly well known, some of its lawyer members are and may be used to comment on legal matters; they are, in effect, speakers provided by the Society but not speaking for it.

The attribution of expertise may also come about in less easily anticipated ways. PROP's spokespeople rapidly acquired high credibility with the media as a result of the Hull prison riots of 1976, when the organization set up a public inquiry into how they were handled. This achieved a great deal of coverage, and put PROP on the media map for some time afterwards.

The more appearances a spokesperson makes, the more he or she becomes known as an expert. Expertise in this sense is a role that develops over time. Paul Cavadino, press officer of NACRO, commented in terms that precisely sum up how expertise is connected to the marketing of an image. Usually, he said, NACRO's director would speak for reasons of status: 'Provided that the person concerned is reasonably good on the media there is a great advantage in building up credibility of a brand name, but obviously if she can't do it then sometimes other people would do it. It depends whether they are willing to have somebody other than the director.' Becoming a 'good performer' in media terms means that one is likely to be asked to repeat the performance, as Frances Crook of the Howard League pointed out: 'I even get asked by other groups to do them. NCCL have asked me to do a radio interview on capital punishment for them because I've worked here for years and years. Actually I turned that one down, I turned it down because they wanted me to do it with NCCL and I said no, I'd only do it for the Howard League.' Another aspect of such expertise is to learn to judge whether or not a particular interview or appearance is likely to pay off in terms of the kind and scale of publicity it generates. For groups in high demand by the media, such as NCCL, there was a continuous attempt to balance their officers' time against the likely benefit to be secured, as Sarah Spencer stressed:

For instance, yesterday I went on Thames' *Daytime*. . . . It took a couple of hours and I was thinking, 'Is this a good use of my time?' Then I discovered that their audience rating is over 3 million. Just the fact that NCCL's name is mentioned actually to 3 million people, and assuming I say something that makes them think we're a good thing, that makes it worthwhile.

In one group, 'expertise' in the shape of virtual consultancy to a television programme became completely institutionalized for a time. Justice worked very closely with the BBC programme, *Rough Justice*, which specializes in exposing miscarriages of justice. The cases that *Rough Justice* pursued were for the most part those on which Justice had done a great deal of preparatory work. As Leah Levin explained:

Very often, we have cases which have merit. We've done all the initial investigation, we know the whole framework of law which relates to the case, but we are not in a position to do the additional bit of investigation that is required in terms of on-site investigation, interviewing witnesses, foot-slogging, perhaps going to other parts of the world. It has been very useful co-operation because we have the expertise and they've got the pounds and also the journalistic expertise to do the kind of investigation when we cannot pursue it. Then we would look to the Home Office when we have new information.

However, the terms under which expertise may be provided are not those usually stipulated by the pressure groups, and the spaces opened up by the media for this kind of expert contribution may often be regarded as inappropriate. Many of the groups were very critical of popular 'reality' programmes such as the BBC's *Kilroy* because their formats, with a constant shifting of attention and high-profile 'personality' presentation, were felt to be too superficial to get a reasoned case across. In keeping with the orientation towards the quality press already identified—which conforms to a largely implicit model of a rational public sphere *à la* Habermas—there was a strong preference for interviews on Radio 4 news programmes, and for some Channel 4 documentaries.

Conclusion

As with the criminal justice professionals' organizations, pressure group activity in the criminal justice field is substantially centred upon the Home Office and Parliament. From an official perspective, groups are rather loosely thought of as 'respectable' or as 'radical', and these perceptions affect their access both to the policy-making apparatus and most of the media. Although most pressure groups are in the 'private sector', matters are not really quite so clear-cut, as some groups, although non-official, do receive government funding. This has implications, that merit further investigation, for what we think of as an 'official source'. Furthermore, although much of this sector may be thought of as relatively 'resource-poor', that description also tends to over-simplify somewhat, given the varied range of groups concerned.

Media strategies by pressure groups are worked out in relation to a quite specific, if implicit, conception of the public sphere. This is strongly centred on élite media both as educative vehicles and as means of communication with opinion-formers. The quality press and public service broadcasting figure pre-eminently here as the key media to be targeted. The evidence suggests that this approach would seem to be well founded. So far as crime-related items in the press are concerned, the quality papers carry twice as many views or comments from experts, élites, and members of pressure groups as the popular papers, and about 25 per cent more than the mid-market press.[26] This restricted conception of the media that count—which excludes the popular press as largely resistant to policy discourse—is coupled with a strong awareness of the need to lobby through the parliamentary process in order to influence policy formation. As with the professionals, media strategies resulting in publicity and private lobbying are thus seen as complementary to one another. They may be played off against each other, according to the advantages perceived of one, or other, course of action at any given time. In both arenas, public and private, there is evidence of co-operation and competition over specific issues. The routine incorporation in official circles of arguments and proposals deriving from the professionals and the pressure groups raises questions about official news sources as 'primary definers' of the news agenda. Media research needs to move increasingly behind public positions, for hidden processes of negotiation often lie behind these, and make the media merely a starting-point for further investigation.

[26] See Schlesinger, P., Tumber, H., and Murdock, G., 'The Media Politics of Crime and Criminal Justice', *British Journal of Sociology*, 42 (1991), figures cited from p. 413, table III.

The growth of sophistication in media relations already noted in official bodies and amongst the criminal justice professionals is also evident—to varying degrees—amongst the pressure groups. This is shown by how specific media are targeted and monitored, expertise in promotion and presentation has been acquired, and relations with journalists cultivated in the clear awareness of the value of 'information subsidies'.

In short, the findings of this chapter and the previous one show that in the criminal justice policy arena, the mediatization of political action is fully entrenched and irreversible. It is a characteristic and inescapable feature of the contemporary public sphere and cannot be ignored by any who wish to command attention in the public domain. That, too, is the message of the next chapter, as we shall see.

4

Promoting the Police

In England and Wales, as we have seen, the government department dealing with questions of crime and criminal justice is the Home Office. Given its exceedingly wide remit, this is a major source of news about developments in policing, prisons, the judicial system, immigration, and many other areas. However, as far as routine news about crime is concerned, it is the police who are looked to most by journalists.[1] England and Wales have forty-three separate police forces, and these enjoy considerable autonomy in their dealings with the news media.[2] One important area in which the Home Office retains explicit discretion to intervene in media relations is in cases of terrorism. In general, however, the evolution of media relations in Britain's police forces, although broadly inspired by developments in the country's largest force, London's Metropolitan Police (the Met.), has been quite varied.

In the past two decades, the police have come into increasing prominence for a variety of reasons, including their deployment by government in public order policing, notorious cases of rigging of evidence, concern about racism and sexism in the force, and the rise of armed policing. In short, the very function of policing has become highly contentious and exposed in an increasingly conflict-

---

[1] This is by no means specific to Britain. One US researcher has observed that 'Crime news is primarily news about the actions of the police and the courts, and only secondarily is it news about criminal activities.' See Fishman, M., *Manufacturing the News* (Austin: University of Texas Press, 1980), 76.

[2] At this time of writing, discussion prompted by the publication on 28 June 1993 of the Conservative government's White Paper on police reform suggests that the number of forces will be reduced by amalgamations. See *Police Reform: A Police Service for the Twenty-First Century. The Government's Proposals for the Police Service in England and Wales*, sponsored by the Home Office, Cm 2281 (London: HMSO, 28 June 1993). It remains to be seen how the forthcoming restructuring of the police will affect the practices analysed here. See Sheehy, Sir P., chairman, *Inquiry into Police Responsibility and Rewards*, vol. i, Report; vol. ii, Appendices, Cm 2280 (London: HMSO, 30 June 1993).

ual society.[3] Policing has always been a staple of crime-reporting, and the police are inherently an object of more general reporting interest given their symbolic position as the everyday representatives of law and order.

The police are not exempt from the general tendency to 'promotion' outlined above. Their very exposure to the public gaze, and to political conflict about their role in society, has led them increasingly to develop means of image management. This tendency first began to be consciously developed, notably in the Metropolitan Police, from the early 1970s onwards, but it really came into its own during the Thatcher years (after 1979) with the wholesale marketing of political life and the related governmental and corporate advertising campaigns associated with the massive privatization of public sector bodies. Neither the police, nor the wider criminal justice system, have remained immune from these privatizing trends.[4]

These developments are not restricted to Britain alone. As Ericson *et al.* have noted in comparable research into the Toronto metropolitan police, there has been a shift from a defensive and secretive posture to 'being proactive in making their public image'. They also suggest that from the police's point of view the news media are perceived as '*part of* the policing apparatus of society'.[5]

The police are a major public sector organization and thus quite different from private corporations that try to position themselves in the market in order to enhance the sale of their products. Such corporations, however, do also go in for more generalized promotion of their images, and the public sector, too, more and more participates in this kind of activity.[6] The police have quite specific

[3] For the complex background to this see Reiner, R., *Chief Constables* (Oxford: Oxford University Press, 1991) 2nd edn. (Hemel Hempstead: Harvester Wheatsheaf, 1992); Waddington, D., *Contemporary Issues in Public Disorder* (London: Routledge, 1992) and *Calling the Police: The Interpretation of, and Response to, Calls for Assistance from the Public* (Aldershot: Avebury, 1993).

[4] For recent articles on privatization and criminal justice see Matthews, R. (ed.), *Privatising Criminal Justice* (London: Sage, 1989); Johnston, L., 'Privatisation and the Police Function: From "New Police" to "New Policing"', in R. Reiner and M. Cross (eds.), *Beyond Law and Order: Criminal Justice Policy and Politics into the 1990s* (Basingstoke: Macmillan, 1991).

[5] Ericson, R. V., Baranek, P. M., and Chan, J. B. L., *Negotiating Control: A Study of News Sources* (Toronto: University of Toronto Press, 1989), 93; original emphasis.

[6] For relevant discussions see ibid.; Tumber, H., '"Selling Scandal": Business and the Media', *Media, Culture and Society*, 15 (1993), 345–61, and Tilson, D., 'The

problems in presenting themselves, as the expert in corporate design and public relations, Wally Olins, has pointed out:

A police force is perhaps the ultimate service activity . . . each contact that we have with a police force largely depends on the behaviour of each police officer. A police force depends for its success largely on how the individuals who belong to it behave in a multitude of encounters—many of which, in the nature of things, are likely to be stressful. . . . It offers a large spectrum of services, ranging from giving directions to tourists to controlling riots. It also allows its junior officers a degree of discretion that is probably greater than any other organization.[7]

Precisely because there is such scope for damage to their image, the police, in Olins's terms have been highly concerned with their 'corporate identity', with how they present themselves and are perceived by a variety of publics. Olins's comments relate closely to recommendations made by his design consultancy, Wolff Olins, to Britain's most publicized force, the Metropolitan Police.

In 1988, in a move aimed at boosting support for the Metropolitan Police, the then Commissioner, Sir Peter Imbert (appointed in 1987) hired Wolff Olins, at a cost of £150,000, to make a design audit of internal and external attitudes towards the force. The Met., by its own recognition, was suffering from a 'corporate identity crisis' and very concerned about its relations with the public, government, and the media. In particular, adverse media comment was perceived inside the force as causing frustration, low morale, and a lack of confidence in management by the staff. The poor public image was seen, moreover, as contributing to problems in recruitment.

A Force for Change, the eventual consultants' report, was 'primarily concerned with identity, with what the organization stands for, how it does things and how it is perceived'. It recommended the need for cultural changes within the Met. to support the planned organizational changes, and argued for the establishment of a clear collective vision. Such change, the report stated, should be comprised of a series of developments, many already taking place, affecting management systems, behaviour, attitudes, commu-

Shaping of "Eco-nuclear" Publicity: The Use of Visitors' Centres in Public Relations', *Media, Culture and Society*, 15 (1993), 419–35.

[7] Olins, W., *Corporate Identity: Making Business Strategy Visible through Design* (London: Thames and Hudson, 1989), 34.

nication, and visual identity.[8] The designers advocated such changes in the belief that they would produce more favourable public opinion towards the police.

Again, it is worth noting that this kind of process has been paralleled elsewhere. In Toronto, a similar consultation took place in the early 1980s, when the management consultancy Hickling and Johnson were brought in to evaluate the police's public affairs activities. As a result, these were thoroughly reorganized and civilian staff with journalistic and public relations experience were hired.[9]

The Met.'s response to *A Force for Change* was *The Plus Programme*, a continuing series of measures drawn up by Deputy Assistant Commissioner Charles Pollard and Commander Alec Marnoch, under the guidance of the Commissioner. The question of communications was assigned to a marketing group, one of whose remits was to examine how the Met. communicated with the public, both directly and via the media.[10] The strategy has been to regard the public as consumers, as the customers and paymasters of policing, not as potential criminals and trouble-makers. Sir Peter Imbert summed up the new line thus: 'The Metropolitan Police has a strong tradition of service to the public and our common purpose must now be to make the quality of that service even better.'[11] He further wrote, 'it is about changing the emphasis from a "Force" to a "Service" ethos.'[12]

The general approach has been endorsed by Imbert's successor as Commissioner, Paul Condon (appointed in 1993), who has embodied it in what is significantly titled the Metropolitan Police *Service*'s corporate strategy to 1997/8:

We have changed the ethos of the organisation from one of rigid enforcement to that of service delivery; good service delivery is essential if we are to retain public approbation. This shift in philosophy presented the

[8] Wolff Olins, *A Force for Change* (London: Wolff Olins, 1988), 3.

[9] Ericson *et al.*, *Negotiating Control*, 94.

[10] Brooking, T., 'What is PLUS?', *Police Requirements Support Unit Bulletin*, 39 (1991), 52–3.

[11] *The Plus Programme: Making it Happen* (London: Metropolitan Police, 1989), n.p. For an analysis see Kirby, T., 'How Police Force Plans to be Reborn as a Service', *Independent*, 27 Nov. 1989, p. 6, and for an account of its implementation see Campbell, D., 'Keeping Pace with the Force of Change', *Guardian*, 4 Sept. 1991, p. 19.

[12] *Report of the Commissioner of Police of the Metropolis for the Year Ended 1989*, Cm 1070 (London: HMSO, 1990), p. xiii.

workforce with a major cultural challenge and has led to improved communication both internally and externally.[13]

Although it is too early to judge definitively what the impact is, the implementation of *The Plus Programme* has resulted in some new media- and public-relations-oriented initiatives. Undoubtedly, a substantial investment has been made in promoting a corporate image, on the lines adopted by commercial companies and privatized former nationalized bodies, with £1.2 million spent in 1992 by the Met. on posters and full-page advertisements in the national press. The London force is the only one with the resources to undertake this kind of approach. It has been commended for its slick campaigning, and at one point employed the leading photographer Don McCullin. The Met. also ran an award-winning recruitment campaign for ethnic minorities (an area of long-standing weakness and contention) using the Collett Dickenson Pearce agency. Other advertising has concentrated on social issues such as domestic violence and homelessness, marking a new publicly proclaimed departure in the Met.'s priorities.[14] A series of local free newspapers has been produced and distributed in the ten Metropolitan Police Divisions of North and East London. Each appears under the title *The Beat*, but has specific local content, and comprises some thirty-two pages, divided between editorial and advertising content. The estimated potential readership is 1.25 million people. Major aims are to inform the public directly about policing and police policies, to encourage co-operation in crime prevention, and to reduce fear of crime. This publication is quite expressly seen as countering the 'over-dramatization of crime stories' in the media and misunderstandings of police work believed to be fuelled by the popular ITV series, *The Bill*.[15]

Changing Media Relations

Of late, the police's relationship with the media has changed considerably. As the sociologist Steve Chibnall has pointed out, this

[13] Condon, P. L., *Corporate Strategy, 1993/94 to 1997/98* (London: Metropolitan Police Service, 1993), 5.

[14] Humphrey, M., 'Police PR: A Force for Change', *PR Week*, 20 Feb. 1992, pp. 10–11; Beatt, A., 'The Image Builders', *Police Review*, 18 Dec. 1992, pp. 2342–3.

[15] Wrigly, A. E., '"The Beat"—Series of Newspapers', *Police Requirements Support Unit Bulletin*, 42 (1992), 30–1.

tendency first began to be developed in the Metropolitan Police in the late 1960s, when, in response to growing complexity, and a breakdown in the previously cosy relationship with crime reporters, a new head of public relations 'immediately set about a task of image reconstruction', bringing in people with experience of the press and public relations.[16]

In 1972, when Sir Robert Mark became Commissioner of the Metropolitan Police, he fully initiated a new approach.[17] He effected what the criminologist Robert Reiner has dubbed the 'Marksist revolution at Scotland Yard' by deciding that his force should be more accessible to journalists, keeping back information 'subject only to *judicial restrictions, the right to individual privacy*, and the *security of the state*'.[18] The Metropolitan Police and the London-based national media agreed upon the new terms of reference, and the Home Office ratified them. Mark's objective, as he later observed in a general memorandum issued to his force on 24 May 1973, was to improve the police's relationship with the media and consequently to produce 'a better understanding on their part and that of the public of the force's problems and policies'.[19] That said, it should be noted that Mark was far from dewy-eyed about the police's relationships with the media. Speaking to the Institute of Journalists on 30 November 1971, he described these relations as 'an enduring if not ecstatically happy marriage'. He later complained to the London Press Club in 1974 that the police were 'Without doubt the most abused, the most unfairly criticized and the most silent majority in this country'.[20] Mark's new 'openness' was coupled with a determined effort to secure a measure of control over journalists. The general memorandum referred to a new press identity card. This enabled the police to identify as accredited journalists those who held the card, and to select out those deemed to be unhelpful, in particular, members of the radical press. Efforts

---

[16] Chibnall, S., *Law-and-Order News: An Analysis of Crime Reporting in the British Press* (London: Tavistock Publishing, 1977), 72.

[17] As Chibnall points out, he had taken an interest in media relations since the mid-1960s. See *Law-and-Order News*, 175.

[18] Mark, Sir R., 'The Case of Great Britain', in *Terrorism and the Media* (London: International Press Institute, 1980), n.p., emphases in original. Also see Reiner, *The Politics of the Police*, 92.

[19] Mark, Sir R., *Policing a Perplexed Society* (London: Allen & Unwin, 1977), 123–9.

[20] Cited in Reiner, *The Politics of the Police*, 173, 177.

by the National Union of Journalists to ensure that its card alone would constitute acceptable accreditation proved unsuccessful.[21]

For the most part, Sir Robert Mark's thinking has been endorsed by successive Commissioners. His immediate replacement in 1977, Sir Robert McNee, was really the exception. As Robert Reiner comments, in his term 'relations with the media seemed to become more abrasive. A number of incidents led to harsh criticism of the media, especially the BBC.' This, he suggests, was 'not so much a consequence of personalities, of McNee being a less adroit media manipulator than Mark. It was a symptom of the politicized state of policing.'[22] As, after a high-profile period in national politics during the late 1970s and early 1980s, the police retreated from the political front line, and sought to distance themselves from their strong identification with the Conservative government and its version of law and order policies, subsequent commissioners staked out new ground, presenting themselves differently to the media.[23]

We have already seen how Imbert initiated a far-reaching pro- gramme of image and cultural change, still being implemented. Sir Kenneth Newman (Commissioner from 1982 to 1987), whose sensi- bilities concerning communication had been tried and tested in the counter-insurgency war in Northern Ireland, on a number of occa- sions during his time at New Scotland Yard stressed the need for a good relationship between media and police and also tried to 'cul- tivate legitimacy'. Although they all used the selfsame rhetoric of 'openness', both these later commissioners tried to move away from the politicized approach to the media adopted by Mark, in Imbert's case with greater success.[24]

Speaking at a conference on the media and the police, Newman told his audience, 'In a democracy like ours, the media performs a very valuable role in correcting any tendency on the part of officialdom towards corruption and towards arbitrary or unfair behaviour.' He said that he was trying to instil the need for good

---

[21] Ericson et al., Negotiating Control, 104–14 note that the media's relations with the police in Toronto are divided into a favourable 'inner circle' and a more critical 'outer circle', broadly along the lines of popular and quality outlets. The same clear-cut conditions do not apply in London.

[22] Reiner, The Politics of the Police, 179.

[23] This view was shared by the majority of chief officers by the later 1980s. See Reiner, Chief Constables, 216–17.

[24] Ibid. 181.

televisual qualities to be built into police operations and observed, 'A policy of openness is vital. Balance and understanding in the media depends on it.'[25] In the Police Foundation Lecture 1986, Newman presented the problem as a more general one of police–public relations at a time of rapid change, noting that 'relations with the police can be improved by publicity. The public can be brought to understand better the demands upon police, the interplay of causes that seems to indicate a continued increase in crime in the future for reasons largely beyond the control of the police, and the sort of role the police are called upon to play, with its occasional contradictions.'[26]

For his part, Sir Peter Imbert, speaking to the International Police Exhibition and Conference in September 1989, sounded a new note when he said, 'Openness must be central to the policing of a democratic and pluralist society.'[27] Mark's terminology was beginning to be filled with a different content.

The Metropolitan Police have merely offered the best-known example of the need to manage media and public relations. The problem, however, extends to all forces around the country. The police recognize that without public confidence in their ability to deal with crime, or in their professionalism and integrity, they will not receive public co-operation, and will encounter political difficulties. In recent years, there has been a feeling within the police that the public and the media have overlooked the good work that they do. The emphasis in the media, it is believed, has been on bad news and rising crime, with the implication that the police are unable to contain it. This has been injurious to morale and has also fostered the siege mentality noted, for instance, by the Wolff Olins report, which observed that the 'attitude of the Met. towards the world in which it works can best be described as

[25] Reported in 'The Media and the Police', a St Catharine's Conference held at Cumberland Lodge, 4–6 Apr. 1986, n.p.

[26] Newman, Sir K., 'Police–Public Relations: The Pace of Change', Police Foundation Lecture, 28 July 1986, pp. 14–15.

[27] The similarity of words, however, concealed differences of thinking between Newman and Imbert, respectively more authoritarian and more liberal in orientation. See Rose, D., 'An Astonishing Shift of Power' and 'An Opening at the Met', *Guardian*, 8 Nov. 1989, p. 25. Imbert has been seen by journalists as having the best credentials, given his decision to allow the documentary-maker Roger Graef access to make his warts-and-all series *Police* during his time as Chief Constable of Thames Valley Police.

wary. Many policemen and women feel beleaguered and misunder-stood.'[28]

It is not surprising, then, that like the Met., forces around the country have also been alive to the need for change, given that there is more debate about the functions and nature of the police. Some chief constables, particularly in the larger forces, have con-sciously changed their public relations approaches and tried to pro-mote a positive image. This marks a significant shift in a relatively short period: as recently as 1982 the seasoned observer Ben Whitaker could comment that outside London 'in many other forces "public relations" are still regarded as dirty words'.[29] However, there is no uniformity in how various forces have gone about developing a public relations capacity. Nor, whilst growing centralist trends may well change this, is there presently any overall national media and public relations policy for the police in the United Kingdom that has been made publicly available. It is known, however, that in its confidential *Public Order Manual*, the Association of Chief Police Officers (ACPO) does have guidelines dealing with 'information management' which offer 'eighteen rec-ommended options for the management of rumours in times of tension'. Amongst these are the establishment of a 'media rumour clinic' in a suitably vetted local news organization and the use of counter-information strategies against those deemed to be hostile.[30] The journalist Gerry Northam, has commented that 'Press relations are presented as another "tactic" to be used for specific police pur-poses, and to be handled with care or, more usually, with suspi-cion.' None of the customary lip-service to 'openness' is apparent, and the management of media relations to the advantage of the police is stressed.[31]

Contact with the Home Office in respect of news management is usually confined to cases of terrorism or major incidents that might have political implications in which the Home Secretary is called to account. The Home Office does take a view about the best way to proceed in such instances, but offers advice pragmatically and also stresses that intervention is exceptional. Brian Mower, then Head

---

[28] Wolff Olins, *A Force for Change*, 11.

[29] Whitaker, B., *The Police in Society* (London: Sinclair Browne, 1982), 298.

[30] Northam, G., *Shooting in the Dark* (London: Faber & Faber, 1989), 75–6. This document was prepared in 1983 and has 'restricted' status.

[31] Ibid. 123. On the background to ACPO see Reiner, *Chief Constables*, 270–85 and appendix C, pp. 362–7.

of the Information Division at the Home Office, spelled out current thinking in some detail:

Just occasionally media questions creep into guidelines we have at the Home Office, and the one I am thinking of, which goes back a few years now, are the studies that were done after the [Yorkshire] Ripper cases, where there was criticism of the way the police, when they got hold of Sutcliffe, briefed the press. And in the various guideline things we put out following that case, which mainly concerned how the police had operated and handled computer records, there were some guidelines about the handling of the media. That's rare, but that's that.

He went on to say that so far as hostage-taking cases went, the Metropolitan Police had an understanding of their own with the media and that ACPO had tried to develop a national understanding. However, this had come up against the resistance of the provincial press, who were not prepared to give up their editorial control. However, he did single out 'terrorist hostage situations' as those meriting a more interventionist approach:

Now, in those situations first of all the chief constable is the man in charge and that is certainly the formal constitutional position and it's the *de facto* position except that where you have got very considerable political and international overtones obviously Ministers are going to want to push their point of view forward into whatever is going on. You will be aware of the existence of the Cabinet Office briefing room that opens up on these occasions, and relevant officials man that from whichever departments are concerned. I would normally be there and Ministers will come in from time to time and meetings will be called in a formal way and there will be a Home Office liaison team out of sight of the incident and there will be communications between that liaison team and the police. So there is a connection in those kind of situations. And this is a huge exception to the normal police operation thing where there is no question of any kind of connection. This is because you are almost inevitably going to get international political overtones to any kind of terrorist thing. And so in that situation again the chief constable on the spot is entirely responsible for handling media relations. We have sought to engage the general sympathies of the broadcast media in this and chief constables obviously are aware of what we have done, so that if you have a situation where the broadcast of certain information, assuming that the terrorists have access to a radio, possibly even a television in some cases, could be prejudicial to people's lives being held hostage, then we will try to speak to the media concerned and say 'Look, please can you lay off,' or whatever. So that is a sort of possible direct media involvement in these situations. It could be the chief constable doing it, it could be me doing it. It's never happened in my experience, but that's the sort of thing that can actually happen and I only give you that, not because it's in any way typical at all, but because it is an exception to the rule which is that just as all police operations are the responsibility of the chief constable so will be the media handling of those operations.

Much of this picture was confirmed by the then Chief Constable of Merseyside, Kenneth Oxford, who said that in the event of a terrorist action he would call the Home Office Press and Information Branch and ask them to send one of their people up to help him. According to him, however—in contradiction to Brian Mower—the Home Office *had* issued guidelines in that area. So far as the rationale for such intervention went, though, there was no disparity in the accounts offered. In Oxford's words:

I would say 'I want you up here because of the international aspect and the central government aspect and I want you here to advise me.' It would be up to me as to how we should be handling it. We're OK in this country when you're dealing with the home-grown press. When the world's press are here you've got no—dare I use the word?—control over them at all, because they're here today and gone tomorrow—so they've got a licence to kill. I think there is a disciplinary factor with the national and local press. They've got to live with us tomorrow.

Apart from intervening in such rare cases, Mower went on to say, the Home Office would not seek to interfere in how police operations were presented to the public via the media unless political consequences were likely for the Secretary of State:

There is absolutely no possibility of my picking up the phone to a chief constable somewhere and saying you're really making a balls-up, or whatever. My only interest in these things is being kept informed in case there are ramifications for the Home Secretary. There might be direct policy repercussions like [in a] shooting. . . . The Home Secretary has got an overall responsibility for the law and order of the country so if the crime is big enough and the Home Secretary will be asked about it in the House, if nowhere else, and so we will have to have a report on it and I will certainly need to know what's going on too.

Given, then, that the Home Office currently operates a broadly permissive policy, the solution to the problems that police–media relations pose have had to be worked out by each individual force. By common assent, the Metropolitan Police has led the way in pioneering new methods for the management of publicity.

Public Affairs in the Metropolitan Police

At the Metropolitan Police headquarters at Scotland Yard, the Directorate of Public Affairs and Internal Communication is headed by a Director of Public Affairs, backed up by a Deputy Director, both civilians.[32] Scotland Yard first opened a press office in 1919, Robert Reiner notes, 'largely because of fears of unauthorized leaks produced by reporters bribing officers'. He goes on to remark that relations with the media have fluctuated considerably since then, with different tactics pursued on each side either to try and extract, or to control, information. It was the Mark reforms that had led to the system in place at the time of our research.[33]

In 1992, there were some 145 staff in the Directorate, which has four branches: News, Publicity and Advertising, the Secretariat, and the Briefing and Planning Unit, which includes a press library. Whereas in 1986/7 the Directorate spent just over £2 million, by 1992 the operational budget was £12.5 million.

The News Branch has a head of news and is in turn divided into three sections consisting of a Press Bureau, a News Group, and an Area Liaison Unit. The News Branch deals with media contacts and briefings, media facilities for the press and broadcasting, press conferences and requests for interviews. The main function of the branch is to react to various stories that arise, and there has been criticism within the force that it tends to be too reactive and does not always facilitate good public relations. Officers in the News Branch are encouraged to develop contacts within the news media. Their aims include putting out material which reflects credit on the force by portraying what they would regard as an accurate and positive picture of the police and their problems. The Branch also seeks to develop the public's understanding and sympathy for the police and its awareness of crime.

Within the News Branch, the News Group monitors radio and television programmes and is intended to respond to the increasing demand for information from the media, with priority given to those outlets with high audience figures. In 1989, more than 35,000 'news items on policing matters from London and suburban newspapers

---

[32] At the time of our study these were, respectively, Robin Goodfellow and John Stubbs.

[33] Reiner, *The Politics of the Police*, 178.

and magazines were identified'.[34] The News Group is supposed to work 'proactively' and pursue news initiatives. The News Branch also organizes the monthly briefings between the Commissioner and selected reporters. These operate as a lobby system, with only certain crime specialists invited. The aim is to develop better contacts between the police and journalists and to inform them about the police's perspective on various activities and problems.

The Press Bureau is the force's press office. Journalists can telephone press officers in the Bureau, which also produces the Yard's 24-hour tape-recorded information outlet. First introduced in 1988, by the following year this had received 106,234 calls. In the same period Press Bureau staff were reported to have dealt with 10,150 incidents or policy issues.[35] The Bureau provides facilities for journalists working on their stories and allows them to make telephone calls. However, as we shall see in Chapter 5, these facilities are now less used than once was the case, due to changes in the nature of crime journalism.

The third department in the News Group is Area Liaison, which has a co-ordinating function. The force is divided into eight geographical areas, each with their own information officers whom the press can approach directly. The number of people working in these areas has increased, as has the amount of proactive work towards the media. In 1989, for instance, 'press officers based on the eight areas and at New Scotland Yard arranged 1,560 interviews and briefings for journalists'.[36]

The second branch in the Directorate of Public Affairs is Publicity and Advertising, responsible for advertising campaigns, exhibitions and displays, printed literature, films, audio-visual aids and broadcast training. This department produces 'start-up' publicity material for neighbourhood watch schemes, and also runs campaigns against car theft, and other types of crime prevention. Publicity and Advertising also provides booklets to the public. One such example was *Positive Steps*, which offered advice to women about what to do in the event of rape and other violent assaults. At the time of our interviews an accompanying videotape was being produced. This branch also develops public education packages designed to help the police and other agencies in direct contact with the young, such as, for example, to discredit the carrying

---

[34] *Report of the Commissioner, 1989,* 6.   [35] Ibid.   [36] Ibid.

of knives. The department is also responsible for recruitment advertising and for co-ordinating publicity and communication material and for broadcast training, the last of which is seen as increasingly needed within the force.

The Directorate of Public Affairs' third branch is the Secretariat, which provides a general administrative service. It is responsible for clerical support in the other branches and responds to enquiries either by letter or telephone call from the public. It also makes the arrangements for official visits, attachments from other forces or government departments, guided tours of Metropolitan Police premises, and is responsible for the police museums.

The fourth and last branch is the Briefing Unit. Its main remit, which came into effect in 1986, is to identify emergent trends in the media and to alert and brief senior officers of likely areas of interest for police action. Apart from monitoring the media and scanning Parliamentary Questions files, the unit is responsible for preparing the Commissioner's annual report, senior officers' CVs, and briefing notes for the force's top-level Policy Committee, which in the post-Imbert era is described as its 'board of directors'. The unit also engages in speech-writing for senior officers, the production of newspaper articles, preparation of the Metropolitan Police Fact Sheets on various topics, and general briefing notes. The speeches in question are usually written for the Commissioner and Deputy Commissioner. Newspaper articles normally tend to be written at the request of particular newspapers, often under the by-line of the Commissioner.

The monitoring service is very thorough and goes through all the newspapers, political weeklies, and magazines, teletext, and the Press Association's news files. It provides a weekly note called *Policing Issues in the Press* based upon a review of the national newspapers, which are evaluated in terms of whether they have been 'positive' or 'negative' towards the police. This is primarily intended for use by the Directorate of Public Affairs, but also goes to the Commissioner.

Media Relations Innovators

In the course of our interviews at the Met. and the Greater Manchester, Merseyside, and West Midlands forces, it became evident that the restructuring of media relations was part of a wider innovatory current, and that those who implemented such change saw themselves as modernizers. It is the larger forces that are particularly concerned with how they handle their media and public relations, because frequently they have to be concerned with the national media as well as the local and regional. By contrast, it is much more common for smaller forces to be primarily concerned with their local press, and consequently these do not need such developed media and public relations operations. The larger forces have made considerable changes in this aspect of their operations, adapting ideas and practices from the Met. Some chief constables and other senior officers who have worked at the Met. have been an important direct route for transmitting change to provincial forces.

Precisely how such innovation was introduced and managed may be illustrated by considering some examples arising from our interviews.

Geoffrey Dear, then Chief Constable of the West Midlands Police (and appointed one of HM Inspectors of Constabulary in December 1989) had served in the Met. as an Assistant Commissioner before taking up his position. This evidently affected how he went about reorganizing his force's press and public relations operation—in his view, for the better. A central purpose of developing good media relations was to establish a relationship of trust with the press and broadcasting organizations. According to Chief Constable Dear, where his force went 'off the record' it was now believed, as the information was found to be accurate. Favourable media coverage was a major goal because of the impact that it could have on morale, and he had found that secrecy under the previous chief constable had led to misreporting and a consequent poor image.

He drew a sharp contrast between himself and what he termed the 'old regime' of his predecessor, Sir Philip Knights:

When I came, the force was very wary of its relationship to the media and had been bitten several times. They had had a lot of bad publicity. On the whole the force was not forthcoming, certainly the Chief Constable was not forthcoming. That goes largely to the personalities between me and my predecessor, a man with a very distinguished background who had been here for a very long time but just because of the way he was made did not feel happy, or as happy as I did. I have always had a very warm relationship with the media and brought that in. So my thrust in the two or three years that I've been here has been solidly to be as open as we possibly can with the media generally, and I'm talking about all branches of the media whether it's news on radio and television, or Fleet Street, or local newspapers, or the more relaxed media, and people doing articles for publication in magazines or books.

In order to cope with this change of orientation he had had to make resources available for the growth in the force's press office, which had to be enhanced by increasing both the staffing allocated and the hours it stayed open. At first, Dear noted, the force had been very reluctant to adjust to the new order and wanted to assess the impact of the policy. The new arrangements, which anticipated events requiring what public relations practitioners call 'crisis management', were soon put to the test, as Dear went on to observe:

We had three months with very big incidents in the first few months which, strangely enough, provided a showcase. We had the death of a 5-year-old boy shot by a police officer, the Shorthouse case.[37] We had a riot at Birmingham City football ground. The Handsworth riots which went on for two or three days in September. Two or three very large drug raids—all vehicles for a very intense national media interest. And we started responding where this force had never responded before. We used to set up press conferences almost at the drop of a hat and service the media.

The development of media relations was carried further by putting it under the supervision of a senior officer. Superintendent Martin Burton, whose thinking was based on some substantial research into the practices of a number of different forces and news organizations:

So consequently, having satisfied myself that the police force in this country had little to offer by way of a model, I did go to America, to New York, to have a look at their Public Information Department. In many ways that was very, very useful but the whole thing was tinged with their Freedom of Information legislation and an attitude towards the media in its broadest sense including newspapers, radio, TV, books, magazines, the lot. [It] was quite a different approach. It is generally accepted in this country that police lines are listened to by the media, although they would never, ever admit it, for obvious reasons. In America the openness is such that they are legally tuned in to police lines all the time and as a result of

---

[37] Issues raised by police shootings are considered in Ch. 7 below.

that they have got residential journalists, cameramen, radiomen in the police plaza in New York twenty-four hours a day, seven days a week. Scotland Yard has one or two crime reporters, one or two national news-papers, but nothing of the order that they've got in New York. The man-ner in which they handle the media in New York was very useful. It's a sort of more direct and positive way which is perhaps typical, having in mind the attitude of New York people, but it was a very, very professional relationship. There was very little, if at all, by way of socializing, which is quite a feature of police–media relations in this country.

In New York, then, the police–media relationship was perceived as being far more formal than in Britain. The journalists often knew more about a crime than the police themselves, and would chase the police for further details before they were even aware of the situation. Part of the police headquarters was specifically desig-nated for journalists, with major media outlets having their own facilities there. This visit abroad, therefore, provided a contrast case, by yielding positive lessons about police 'professionalism' in relation to the media, but at the same time underlining differences in the culture of police–media relations between Britain and the USA. A similar trip was made to Copenhagen to gain a 'European' perspective. In addition, as part of this research, various British forces (including the Met.) were visited, extended attachments to Central Television and the BBC undertaken, and visits were made to local and national newspapers and radio stations.

Burton's views as Public Relations Officer were grounded in his Chief Constable's broad approach, which distinguished between 'proactive' and 'responsive' approaches to media relations. In Dear's words:

In the very best sense of the word we try and use the media. I don't mean manipulate because that would be wrong and they wouldn't allow it to happen anyway. By 'use' I mean we're in the business to inform the pub-lic, to create a position where the public are better informed about what we're doing, to ask questions of the public through the media, and to use the media in the sense of running a story.

Initially, the change of style at the top led to continual demand for Dear to appear as the exclusive spokesman for his force. This occurred at a time when several chief constables had acquired national media standing and were identified with political and moral stances. The names of John Alderson and James Anderton, for instance, were variously associated with a liberal model of community policing in Devon and Cornwall and a moral crusade based upon Christian morality in Greater Manchester. As we have noted, this phase of high-profile intervention in political debate is now apparently in the past.[38] Dear had to accept what he considered to be over-exposure and the risk of becoming, in his words, a 'cult figure', because of his novelty value. His aim, however, had been to spread media relations expertise inside the force and gain acceptance for others to speak on its behalf, as he explained:

It's been a slow turning-down process where one has almost coached the media, saying the chief will only come on occasionally, not because he's Greta Garbo or a prima donna, but because there are some things he should be on and many others where others lower in the organization have got greater skills, greater knowledge, and they're the people you should be talking to.

Superintendent Burton, who had been assigned precisely the task of developing such media relations skills, above all believed that what distinguished the West Midlands force was its 'proactive' orientation.[39] Exceedingly sensitive to the need to cultivate and maintain relations with journalists, he used a revealing analogy:

Building up your collateral, your credibility with the media, is an exceedingly difficult prospect, because so often it's like policing a multi-racial area—you're only as good as your last job. It's that fickle . . . It's an ongoing thing, and invariably, if you balls something up and you get something wrong, they'll crucify you.

Whereas, he claimed, most other forces whose practices he had examined were continually responding to the *media*'s priorities, a fundamental goal in the West Midlands force was 'to pump out information about what's going on not only in terms of crime but in terms of current affairs', an approach which he considered to be unique at that time. In common with his chief, Superintendent Burton saw the change as a major break with traditionalism. The Metropolitan Police did offer an unavoidable point of reference, he acknowledged, but 'it's got its own peculiar relationship with the

[38] See Hall, S., *Drifting into a Law and Order Society* (London: Cobden Trust, 1979); Reiner, *Chief Constables*, 216–17.

[39] The force consciously set out to explore potential conflicts with senior journalists from the BBC, ITV, and the local press and radio at a police–media symposium also attended by members of the police authority. 'Openness is the Best Policy', *Beacon*, 102 (Apr. 1987), 1.

media in London, being seen as having a virtual national remit', and consequently 'as an overall strategy, it wasn't appropriate mainly because of its size'. By contrast, other police forces such as Kent, for example, had 'cosy little arrangements that were servicing two or three media outlets, a newspaper and perhaps one or two radio stations'. As the largest force outside London, the West Midlands force had to deal with a great deal of media attention, and needed to devise its own solutions. The outcome was a Public Relations Department divided into a News Bureau, Information and Publicity, and Administration. In 1992, now managed by Superintendent Ray Starkey, the Department consisted of fourteen full-time staff (including a head and deputy head of news), mostly ex-journalists. The department had been restructured to allow individual PR officers to be responsible for 'client handling' on a divisional basis.[40]

Another important provincial force which had consciously transformed its media relations was the Merseyside Police. Change came in 1974/5 when Kenneth Oxford arrived as chief constable. He had been at the Met. before, and had worked at Scotland Yard for some six years, mixing with Fleet Street crime reporters there. He often would have drinks and talk to journalists when off duty and was able to develop a sense of how to build up trust and to know what kinds of stories they were after. In 1978, he 'allowed the BBC freely to film the reality of police work'.[41] On arriving in Merseyside, it had seemed an obvious step to set up a public relations and press office:

Almost twenty years ago it was almost an indictable offence under the discipline code to talk to the media, which to me was counter-productive. And relating to my experiences in the operations field, I have always felt on balance that if you take the media along with you, you're going to overcome a lot of unnecessary hurdles. That doesn't mean to say that there are not the occasional problems because of over-enthusiastic journalists.

Oxford argued that openness—'a sort of populist approach'— and presenting the police's version of the facts produced 'a good PR spin-off' in terms of public perceptions of the police. He saw this as a matter not simply of media relations but also of the community relations aspects of policing, such as involvement with youth and the elderly. An outgoing policy towards communication,

---

[40] Humphrey, 'Police PR', 11.   [41] Whitaker, *The Police in Society*, 302.

he argued, enabled the Merseyside Police to convey messages about questions such as road safety, violent crime, and child abuse, as well as other aspects of law enforcement.

Merseyside Police's Public Relations Department is divided into three sections: Press, Youth and Community, and Publicity. At the time of our research there were ten staff in the department, headed by a superintendent whose deputy was a chief inspector in charge of Youth and Community Affairs. There was also one inspector for Youth and Community Affairs, and two press inspectors, one administration sergeant, one civilian publicity officer, one clerk, one higher clerical officer, and a constable on attachment. The press office was run by two inspectors who generally worked between 7.30 a.m. and 9.30 p.m., with an overlap of a couple of hours in the middle of the day. If the press inspectors felt they themselves could not respond to questions from the media, these were then redirected to the appropriate division or subdivision.

Apart from advocating a proactive approach parallel to that current in the West Midlands, Oxford noted that there had to be a responsive mode too:

Of course it's not all one-sided. We try to initiate that but similarly . . . the press will come in to us and say, 'Well, what's the Merseyside force policy on the law enforcement factor on seatbelt legislation?' The one thing that we try to avoid is getting into comparisons, or critical comparisons. Because I am involved nationally, internationally, and have a particular role to play in certain broad aspects of policing, I will get overtures: 'Kenneth Newman has said so-and-so, what's the view of Merseyside?' In that argument we say we haven't a view—you'd better get back to the press bureau in London and argue it with them. I would never get into voicing a view about the public statements or policies of other forces. We are so near to Manchester. Jim Anderton says some pretty pungent things at times and I might have a private view as to whether he should or shouldn't voice them in public, but there's no mileage gained on that.

Amongst other things, such concern with the susceptibilities of other chief officers recognizes that playing off senior police figures against one another could be a source of good copy, and ought to be avoided. This kind of open conflict had occurred in early 1981, for instance, when the Chief Constable of Devon and Cornwall, John Alderson, openly fell out with his ACPO colleagues over the drift towards paramilitary policing in Britain. A press interview and then conflicting press releases were the vehicles used on that occasion.[42]

Merseyside Police operates a policy which devolves the response to media enquiries either to departmental heads where appropriate, or, where a more senior voice is required, to the assistant chief constable on duty, or senior officer nearest in rank. In an extreme case, the chief constable himself would be contacted. But usually the enquiry is answered by an officer of sufficiently senior level to give it credibility. Chief Constable Oxford pointed out that because his officers in the field knew that the press office could deal with media queries, they would often avoid answering by referring journalists there.

The Merseyside Police, like other forces, will issue joint statements with government departments where the need arises. For example, they had conducted a joint operation with the Department of Transport and the Driver and Vehicle Licensing Centre against the abuse of road fund licences by setting up road checks. Oxford described the approach thus:

We've alerted the motoring public that last year Merseyside county as a contributor to the road tax showed a deficiency of £1.7 million, and I think you'll get the great lawful motoring public saying, 'Why should those people get away with it?' So there has been a lot of house-to-house billing and the press and the media have told the motoring public at large, 'You've got fourteen days to get your house in order and if you're caught thereafter you're in trouble.'

This was a good example of the police using the media to put over official policy and a warning in advance of launching a particular operation. Without the media's participation in this, it would not work, and the police would possibly have to advertise. There may at times be considerable co-operation between the police and the media over this kind of public interest issue.

In the course of our interviews with four major English forces, we found that in the Met., West Midlands, and Merseyside there was considerable concern about media relations and consequently an active policy of developing the force's corporate identity by this means. At the time of our research, however, Greater Manchester Police were taking a rather different line. Gwynfor James, Assistant Chief Constable, told us that in his view there was no formal pol-

---

[42] Northam, G., *Shooting in the Dark* (London: Faber & Faber, 1989), 47–50.

icy to develop a media relations system and that the system had developed over time in what he described as 'a rather topsy-turvey-like growth'. A review of media and public relations objectives and goals was under way, with particular interest in seeing what these ought to achieve, and how they might meet the needs of the force. Mr James was very reluctant to say much about what he was after in terms of his review, nor would he say where the force was looking in order to find what he called 'best practice'. At the time of our interview, the Greater Manchester Police's chief constable, James Anderton, was a particularly controversial figure, and the force was busy dealing with the fall-out from the celebrated Stalker affair.[43] As a result, the Greater Manchester Police had received a great deal of publicity in the national media. External pressures had produced both the need for change and a reluctance to talk about it.

Police Training

One response to the developing media relations requirement has been the growth of training in how to use the media. According to Robin Goodfellow, then Director of Public Affairs at the Metropolitan Police, Sir Robert Mark had given the original instruction that any police officer likely to have media exposure should have some training, a policy shift that has now come to encompass all aspects of information activities.[44]

In response to this move in priorities, the Police Staff College at Bramshill runs a number of specialized media courses for officers of different ranks. One-week intensive courses, open to all ranks from sergeant to chief superintendent, are available, and there are specialist courses for police press officers too.

The senior command course programme for future chief constables lasts for six months, with one week allocated for media training. Alan Davidson, Director of Television and Radio Training at

---

[43] Murphy, D., *The Stalker Affair and the Press* (London: Unwin Hyman, 1991) discusses in detail how the story was constructed. Greater Manchester's deputy chief constable had been suspended from duty in the wake of his investigation into shoot-to-kill allegations against the police in Northern Ireland. He faced allegations of misconduct. These were rejected by his police authority and Stalker was reinstated, subsequently retiring to write his memoirs.

[44] Ericson *et al.*, *Negotiating Control*, 103, note that virtually no training was available to the Toronto force they studied in the early 1980s.

Bramshill, would first assess the competences of each participant. For several years, Bramshill had made use of Thames Television's Teddington studios, where it ran its courses using journalist tutors, as Davidson described:

During that week, top management, top editors come down. We have a working lunch each day with the senior police. It also gives them the environment of a broadcast studio. We also have good studios at Bramshill. What we offer in that week, depending on their past knowledge, is location—what it's like to be on location, scenes of murder, everything that relates to a location interview, the editing that actually happens, and why people edit. All the team that come down are working journalists. . . . The worry of every policeman I've met is to be edited unfairly. My research tells me that most television journalists will not edit unfairly, but common parlance is to 'stitch up'. Editors have got to condense a 4 to 5-minute interview down to 50 seconds or a minute, and like all of us, the police worry that their best bit is left out.

The objective behind all the courses at Bramshill is to give senior policemen an intense practical training and the confidence to understand the demands of the media and how to deal with these. This is part of a conscious attempt to break down the traditional police hostility towards the media. Senior news executives are invited to explain the media's demands and problems when a big story breaks. As Davidson put it, describing a scenario that is acted out:

The police say, 'This is why we won't give you an interview. This is why we don't want you on the street.' It develops on the lines that television is going to be on the streets anyway. We also develop something which I'm trying to introduce into my practical training: live ENG [electronic news-gathering]. Toxteth, for instance: live cameras on the streets. Live cameras at the miners' strike. What do the police do about that? Direct broadcast satellite. What are the police going to do when a camera might be on the streets during a public disorder, when it's beamed to Europe, the world? . . . I think we've gone past the days when a hand was put against the camera.

At one level, then, media training is largely concerned with teaching interview techniques for the camera and the microphone to individual officers, and awareness of how to present oneself. The other side of media training deals with how the police force can interact with the media to its best advantage. Chief Inspector Mike Frost, Head of the Audio-Visual Aids Unit at Bramshill, and former head of press and public relations in the Essex police, believed that the police service ought frequently to be proactive towards the media, 'rather than, as is often the case, saying that we are going to be proactive and in fact being very reactive, if not to clam up altogether'. From 1988 onwards, every senior police officer in England and Wales has been required to go through Bramshill training, with a consequent diffusion of some media training by this means.

Apart from this national facility, some of the major city forces run their own courses. For instance, the Merseyside Police used their own studios to teach interview techniques and inter-personal skills. According to Kenneth Oxford, 'It's all-embracing, both in operational policing, in police management, and public relations, because any of my guys and girls could be called upon, and some people are good at it, some are not, but they could be called upon to give an instant comment.' Although the majority of the senior officers at Merseyside had been to the Police College on various command courses, for Inspector Bob Dugdale this was not always enough:

I think that's fairly obvious on *Crimewatch* at times. Some of the fellows that go on *Crimewatch* are brilliant. The trouble with *Crimewatch* is that they do like the officer running the case. I can understand that because it gets the personal bit. They don't want the same people turning up every time. They don't want the public to see the press officer from their force coming every time and talking. They want the officer in charge of the case. The trouble is, of course, that officer in charge . . . might be a brilliant detective, but it doesn't mean to say he's going to be good on television.[45]

In-force training was also undertaken in the West Midlands Police. Superintendent Martin Burton had lectured on various courses in his force, and instruction was also given by media representatives from radio, television, and the press. Scenarios were acted out using television and radio reporting, and there was also training in interview techniques and handling journalists. The force subsequently introduced one-week courses designed specifically for officers likely to face regular broadcast interviews.

---

[45] For a specialist television producer's view on variable police performances on a crime appeal programme, see Knox, B., 'Going on the Box', *Police Review*, 3 Nov. 1989, 2230–1.

Media Monitoring

Some form of monitoring was common in the forces studied, although it was not always systematic. At Merseyside Police, staff scanned a variety of publications for coverage relevant to the police, including aspects of the law and, on a broader level, political stories. Programmes deemed to be relevant were tape-recorded, and a daily press cuttings service was used for monitoring all the national and local newspapers, as well as the political weeklies. A compilation of cuttings was circulated to all senior managers on a daily basis. This facility was also made available to all police authority members. Monitoring was seen as a way of countering misrepresentation. An instance was given by Chief Constable Oxford:

Just recently there was a pretty horrendous presentation about violent crime in the inner city which annoyed me rather, because only seven days earlier I'd produced a report and spoken to my authority and given interviews to the press [saying that] contrary to the national pattern we'd seen a reduction in that crime. That excites people, and if two days later they're putting a totally different picture, you're contributing to almost a fear factor.[46]

For its part, the West Midlands force was in the process of developing its information resources and had expanded its cuttings service to include everything from Hansard, all newspapers, both local and national, as well as books and magazines containing material deemed relevant to the police. New Scotland Yard, with its far greater resources, is undoubtedly the most systematic at monitoring. As Robin Goodfellow remarked: 'We see everything. Where we may miss something is perhaps the odd radio news broadcast or something like that. But we even monitor all the local papers, and all the ethnic and minority press, and so forth, which is done at area level. So we know what's going on there.'

The 'Civilianization' of Public Relations

A major issue encountered in our research was whether or not the police's media and public relations should be handled by serving

---

[46] Similar concern about news coverage and fear of crime was evinced by Reiner's interviewees. See *Chief Constables*, 131–3. Also see Ch. 6 below.

officers or civilians. The Home Office's view is that 'the Home Secretary will not normally approve increases in establishment if police officers are occupying posts which could properly and more economically be filled by civilians'.[47] In 1992, civilians accounted for almost a quarter of police service personnel in England and Wales, and there was a trend for highly qualified professionals to move into specialist areas.[48] The Home Office's desire to cut costs has, in fact, inevitably led to the civilianization of posts in the public relations field. Brian Mower of the Home Office observed:

I don't view it as necessarily good or bad. What is important in any police force, as in any organization, is that public relations is taken seriously enough for the person who holds that post, whether he be a civilian or an officer to have access to whatever level of seniority is necessary to deal with a particular problem. The danger in any organization, police or elsewhere, is that the PR man is the recipient of the word passed down a long way from above and has to put it out in an unquestioning way to the public.

He went on to underline the fact that the pressure from the Home Office to 'civilianize' a wide range of activities in police forces was a general one and by no means limited to the public relations field alone. The Home Office ultimately authorized police establishments, and civilianization, said Mower, reduced the cost of posts by one-third. This economic logic was in line with long-standing government cost-cutting in the public sector. In keeping with this, the privatization of some prison functions—with questionable success—and plans by chief constables to generate additional revenues by selling services, both received considerable publicity in 1993, as did the further slimming-down of the police establishment proposed in the Sheehy report.

Despite pressures from the Home Office, decisions about the composition of media and public relations staff have remained a matter for the forces in question. There is also considerable variation in frameworks of accountability. In some forces, public relations officers are answerable to the person in charge of community affairs, in others to the deputy chief constable, and in others again, to the chief constable.

[47] Brown, J., 'Changing the Police Culture', *Policing*, 8 (1992), 311. This quotation resumes Home Office Circular 114/83, *Manpower Effectiveness and Efficiency in the Police Service*.
[48] Ibid. 317–18.

The debate on the question remains unresolved. At Bramshill, the Police Staff College, considerable thought had been given as to whether the head person should be a civilian or an officer with a civilian underneath him or her. Mike Frost, Head of the Audio-Visual Aids Unit, said:

I think if you look at police forces that have police officers at their head and no journalists, and you look at police forces that have journalists at their head and no police officers, and you look at the forces that have a combination, I think that, as a purely subjective opinion, the police forces that have both have the happier and more effective media relationships. I personally go for having a police officer at about the rank of chief inspector at the head of the press and public relations office.

Frost's reasons for favouring this structure lay in the fact that in most day-to-day dealings the officers concerned were likely to be inspectors or chief inspectors. It was only in cases of serious crime that the press office might routinely deal with superintendents or chief superintendents. Consequently, he argued, a chief inspector at the head of the department would have an understanding of police procedures coupled with an understanding of media relations. Back-up from 'a journalist of some repute', preferably with experience of local and national electronic media, was indispensable:

You don't expect a police officer to write a press release for the *Mirror* and for the *Telegraph*, which are two entirely different styles, and then to write a story for TV-am which is a different style again. But the journalist is able to do that and will get their story acceptable almost verbatim. If you look at what a journalist writes, the Press Association will take it down and disseminate it almost verbatim. A police officer tends to use jargon, tends to use three words where one would do, and what you get from the Press Association as often as not is a very much edited version of what you have actually said because you don't know how to phrase it for them. So if you've got the two running side by side in the press office you've got the best of both worlds.

Frost warned of the danger of over-identification with the police on the part of journalists coming into press and public relations, with the result that they might in six months or a year become 'more of a pseudo-policeman than a professional journalist and ending up both a pseudo-policeman and a pseudo-journalist, which is an unhappy situation'. By contrast, a police officer, rotated every two or three years, was not at risk in this kind of way and could help civilians concentrate on retaining their journalistic skills.

Alan Davidson, Director of Television and Radio Training at Bramshill, concurred that the ideal combination was for the senior press officer to be a policeman and the staff to be civilian. Once again, the relevant factor cited was 'credibility': 'If a policeman is the head of the PR unit he's got the credibility to go to the next rank and get decisions. A civilian press officer won't have that, a civilian press officer has got to go to the senior policeman to get permission for various aspects of information.'

Our research suggested that although, as yet, there was no standardization amongst forces, the civilianizing trend did seem to be in the ascendant. The lodestar force, the Metropolitan Police, had civilians in charge of press and public relations: the then Director of Public Affairs, Robin Goodfellow, and his deputy, John Stubbs, both civil servants, had come from other departments in the government.

In Greater Manchester the staff were civilianized. Robin Thornton, the press officer of the Greater Manchester Police, recognized the problem of being a civilian in a police service. Not having the rank, he accepted, could produce problems with serving officers, and it was very difficult to do anything more than strongly advise. He rationalized the difficulties of his role by thinking of himself as a 'mediator' between police and press—though clearly, his first loyalties lay with the police. His reflections did underline the rather closed and hierarchical nature of police culture:

A policeman will never know exactly what a pressman wants and a civilian pressman will never know for sure exactly how the police service works because he's not really part of it. Despite everyone saying 'Yes, you are', you never are because a policeman has to do what he's told, that's the bottom line. With a civilian there's always a little bit of something, a bit of the unknown if you like, to a policeman. . . . I'm a believer in working with the police rather than for the police, I want to have a relationship where I can help them and they can help me, who in turn helps the press. . . . We will never, ever, bridge that gulf between press, media, and the police, we never will. . . . But what we can do is move a way to getting a little closer in understanding and trusting. It's very important, vitally important to any flourishing relationship between the press and police. . . . So what we've got to do is just try and act as mediators. I look at my self as Jim'll Fix It [a reference to the television personality, Jimmy Savile], although I'm not as heavily paid as he is. I see myself as being the guy in the middle who knows what should happen and tries his best to fix it up to the satisfaction firstly of the police, because that's who pay my wages—I've got to look at it that way—and secondly, very close behind, to the satisfaction of the media. As long as they understand that we can't always give them what they want and as long as the police understand that we can't always co-operate from the media's point of view either.

In contrast to Greater Manchester, Merseyside Police operated with two inspectors in its press office. The advantage from their point of view was that they had been in the force for over twenty years, enabling them to respond easily, they said, to many questions. Glancing sideways at the neighbouring force in Manchester, Bob Dugdale, one of the inspectors in the press office, remarked:

They have eight civvies in Manchester Police's press office. We can ring up and say 'Who's dealing with such a job?' and they won't know. . . . The advantage being with only two of us is that we know basically everything that's going on. It has disadvantages. Civvies wouldn't do it, civvies would not do what we do up here. I've been here fourteen months now and I've never had my three-quarters of an hour meal break in that fourteen months. We have a sandwich sat here and get on with it. Civvies just wouldn't do it. It's all against their union rules.

The West Midlands Police were civilianizing their posts and also facing questions about to whom the press and public relations function was accountable. Superintendent Martin Burton told us that the chairman of the Police Authority, through the various personnel committees, had stipulated that the new PR person was to be accountable to him and not the chief constable. This proposal had been defeated. Burton gave a very clear account of why the police might want to retain as much control as possible over their public relations, given its intimate connection with the promotion of their corporate identity. Police Authority control over police PR, he maintained,

was seen widely, certainly within the media, as being another step, another attempt to have some element of political control over a police organization. And when you think about it, this particular department is certainly the most influential as far as the media is concerned and it's from there that the image and reputation of the force is tempered. So, therefore, if you have a political appointee in it, you see that you'll have a great degree of control over the reputation and confidence of the people in the police, simply by that appointment. I'm pleased to say that all that's gone now.

This underlined how over the years the police have been worried about the pressure for curbs on, and controls over, their work. By controlling sensitive PR appointments themselves the police see a means of being more effective in their media relations. The West Midlands plan drawn up by Burton and Dear envisaged civilianization of the main public relations post. In Burton's words:

Initially it was my intention, and still is my intention, that the office will be staffed by journalists. They won't be awfully highly qualified journalists, but they will be people embarking upon a journalistic career who will act as assistant press officers headed up by a head of news. The whole department, which I think will consist of about twenty to twenty-five people when we've finished, will include a publicity department as well as administrative support at the back of it.

However, making a point glossed over by Brian Mower, but also emphasized by other interviewees, Burton stressed that one problem with civilianization was the relationship that civilians had both with the police force and the media. According to him, many editors had already expressed their disquiet about a civilian appointee:

They're very happy to have a comparatively senior officer who they can refer to because they know that that senior officer has got clout within the organization and can get results, whereas, for example, a civilian hasn't got that clout. It will take an awful long time for him to get his credibility up to the level whereby when he talks people jump. It's going to be very difficult. And so for that reason you may well find a senior officer lurking somewhere in the day-to-day events of the department.

Amongst other forces at the time of our research, Staffordshire, for instance, had a civilian press officer, whereas both Suffolk and Surrey had civilian assistant press officers. In Lincolnshire, Tony Diggins, a former police officer himself, but now a civilian, was the public relations officer, with an inspector and a sergeant working for him. He stressed that police officers often did not like being controlled by a civilian; as an ex-policeman he was particularly sensitive to this issue, and thought that his insider knowledge had prevented problems from arising with his police colleagues.

Thus the trend towards civilianization is driven from the centre by a concern with cost-cutting. At the level of each force, however, this is translated into considerations defined by the police's desire to control sensitive appointments relating to their public image, and at the same time the wish to devise means of using civilians that will not create problems for their professional credibility with the media.

Conclusions

As is clear, there is as yet no uniform national system according to which police forces around the country operate their media and public relations. In particular, the balance between civilian and police inputs in this area still varies considerably, although the trend to civilianization and greater centralization of Home Office control may in the end produce greater uniformity. There has been an uneven, but quite definite growth of general expertise in the police in response to the perceived need for image-building and influencing public perceptions, the roots of which lie in the early 1970s. Today, competence in handling media is seen as an essential requirement for police officers at every level. It remains the case, though, that innovation in this area, the broad attitude taken towards the media, and the precise practices instituted locally for dealing with the press and broadcasting in any given force, depend considerably upon the vision of the chief officer. If the direction presently taken by the Met. is an indication of future trends, we may expect more efforts towards corporate identity-management by the police, with the concept of service rather than that of force as the key to public and media relations efforts in the remainder of the 1990s.

II
Making Crime News

Introduction to Part II

THE empirical sociology of journalism conventionally focuses on the practices of reporting. As is already clear, much research of this kind has tended to pinpoint a given institutional arena, and then go on to examine how journalists are organized to cover it. In Chapter 5, we begin this second part of the book by looking at the reciprocal face of the source–media relationship—the specialist organization of crime-reporting. This is the first such analysis to be conducted in Britain for some two decades. While new specialisms in home and legal affairs have developed since then, mainstream crime-reporting has also undergone some change, as well as retaining many of its traditional characteristics. As our objective was to investigate the interface between sources and journalists, we have left aside any analysis of the news organizations in which the specialists work, although it is clear that how these define their correspondents' briefs varies to some extent, and that there are differences of emphasis in the organization of reporting in different media markets.

Questions of story production both begin and end this part of the study, but how the stories are told occupies the space in between. The question of fear of crime is a leitmotiv explored in quite distinct ways in each of Chapters 6, 7, and 8. In Chapter 6, we examine the routine news-reporting of official crime statistics in one quarter of 1992 in the context of arguments that such coverage is (or may be) fear-producing. For the first time, to our knowledge, we have offered a qualitative overview of how the release of crime statistics was covered on one occasion by press and television. This allows us to pose some pertinent questions about whether such reporting can reasonably be seen as a major cause of fear of crime, or whether the periodic debate about crime statistics really concerns something quite different. Chapter 6 also connects with questions raised in Part I, as it demonstrates the use and limits of news management by a Home Office official source, and the widespread 'reflexive' recognition in sections of the media that this activity was taking place.

In Chapters 7 and 8 we address the question of fear rather differently. Of the totality of crime covered by the press and television in Britain, violent crime against the person is given disproportionate attention by all news outlets. Violent crime ranges from almost a quarter of crime items covered in the quality press, through some 39 per cent of those in the mid-market press, to almost 46 per cent in the popular press. On national television news bulletins, violent crime occupies 40 per cent of crime-related items and it occupies more than 63 per cent of such items on local bulletins. Moreover, in terms of news prominence, violent crimes against the person constitute as much as 22 per cent of front-page crime items in the quality press and 45 per cent of those in mid-market and popular papers. There is a strong case, therefore, for considering the representation of criminal violence to be of considerable importance, and especially so when it achieves major coverage.[1]

During the course of our fieldwork we sampled news coverage across the range of newspapers and television. In Chapters 7 and 8, we present qualitative analyses of two quite different cases of violence reported in one week in 1987 (both of which have lingered in the popular memory) that allow us to illustrate a number of crucial points. In the first, we look at alleged criminal violence by a police officer. This story, as will be seen, is about the excessive use of legitimate armed force, where the propriety of the action taken is questioned. Rather than fear of crime, we argue, this opens up the neglected issue of fear of authority; when officialdom abuses its powers this brings repair work in its train. Once again, a qualitative analysis of news coverage connects up with our arguments about news management, for, as we show, on this occasion Home Office and Metropolitan police media strategies seem to have been more effective in defining the news agenda. This intervention went almost entirely unreported, and was not, as in the case of the crime statistics, a subject of self-aware commentary.

Sexual offences also loom large in British news coverage, ranging from over 7 per cent of crime-related news in the quality press, through more than 9 per cent in the mid-market press, to over 11 per cent in the popular press. As a proportion of crime-related television news, it is somewhat less: over 5 per cent for national bul-

---

[1] See Schlesinger, P., Tumber, H., and Murdock, G., 'The Media Politics of Crime and Criminal Justice', *British Journal of Sociology*, 42 (1991), figures cited from tables, I, II, and IV on pp. 412–14.

letins and almost 9 for local ones. In terms of prominence, however, it is of major importance in the popular press, comprising 20
per cent of crime-related items on the front pages of mid-market
papers as well as almost 23 per cent of popular papers' front-page
crime news. By contrast, for the quality press, sexual crime constitutes less than 3 per cent of crime-related front-page news.[2]

This brings us to our second story of violence, that of a sexual
murder, given major treatment. Here, the issue of fear of crime
comes more directly into play again, on various levels. There are
some striking differences in modes of reporting, with some treatments raising the issues of sensationalism and voyeurism. In general, this story provokes questions about the representation of
sexuality in the context of crime and how this might articulate
with fear of crime, especially amongst women.

In our qualitative analyses of news coverage, we have aimed to
present as comprehensive an account as possible of one day's coverage in each case. This allows us to illustrate in detail some styles
of reporting across television and the press, and to point out market differences where apparent within each medium.[3] Such differences relate to different ways of addressing readers and viewers,
using different formats and evincing distinctive priorities in news
discourse. We have sought to illustrate such variations by presenting a related set of narratives in each case, with some telling detail
as appropriate, picking out the main themes covered in different
sectors of the market, and elaborating on their significance.[4]

Finally, we return to questions of production. Chapter 9—in a
distinctive way—takes up the question of crime-reporting, by
analysing aspects of production practice and thinking in the leading
British 'real crime' television programme, the BBC's *Crimewatch
UK*. This serves as an important contrast case to the account of

[2] Ibid.

[3] On market, medium, and format variations across radio, television, and the
press see Ericson, R. V., Baranek, P. M., and Chan, J. B. L., *Representing Order:
Crime, Law and Justice in the News Media* (Milton Keynes: Open University Press,
1991), ch. 2. Evidence of the growing polarization of the quality and popular press,
with mid-market papers losing readership to each of the other market sectors, is
provided in Sparks, C., 'Popular Journalism: Theories and Practice', in P. Dahlgren
and C. Sparks (eds.), *Journalism and Popular Culture* (London: Sage, 1992), 24–44.

[4] On the whole, this has meant sacrificing the finer-tuned methodologies of
analysis of language provided by discourse analysis and semiotics. For relevant
instances of such work see Fowler, R., *Language in the News: Discourse and
Ideology in the Press* (London: Routledge, 1991) and van Dijk, T. A., *News as
Discourse* (Hillsdale, NJ: Lawrence Erlbaum Associates Inc., 1988).

journalistic practice, because the use of dramatized crime reconstruction, and the entertainment orientation of 'real crime' programmes, suggests that there are both commonalities with
conventional journalism, and certain differences. Such programming does not operate within the normal conventions of broadcast
news and current affairs reporting, nor is it identified as such.
Crucially, it is explicitly tied to one source alone for its information—the police—and is openly promotional of social action
against criminals by the public. It differs significantly from the
news, which is formally required to be impartial and independent.
However, in the use of reconstructed real-life stories for entertain-
ment-based audience-building, *Crimewatch* transgresses the conventional borderline between fact and fiction; and by using
human-interest-based tales of misfortune, it has more than a little
in common with the staples of the popular press. Thus at the same
time it both differs from broadcast journalism and shares common
features with tabloid print journalism.[5] In addition, picking up the
theme of Chapters 6–8, our case study of *Crimewatch* once more
raises the moot issue of whether media coverage creates fear of
crime.

[5] For some considerations on journalism as popular culture see Dahlgren, P.,
'Introduction', in Dahlgren and Sparks, *Journalism and Popular Culture*, 1–23.

5
Crime-Reporting

JOURNALISTS covering the crime and criminal justice system can be divided into three groups: 'Crime', 'Home Affairs', and 'Legal Affairs'. Although these three categories encompass the whole field, not all the national newspapers or television organizations have separate correspondents covering each distinct area, as there is variation in the designation of personnel. Consequently, it is no simple matter to provide a cut-and-dried listing of correspondents that matches exactly the three areas now designated as crime or criminal justice specialisms. This chapter discusses our findings from interviews with the whole range of specialist correspondents working in the UK national press and television, but it should be understood that the boundaries are often blurred between subject-matters and that the personnel designated to cover them do not always easily fit into one or other category. In this respect, crime and criminal justice is no different from any other area of journalism, being subject to changing definitions over time as new agendas emerge in the public domain. The construction of journalistic specialisms is the outcome of a process of negotiation both within news organizations and between news organizations and their sources. Specialisms frequently tend to develop in line with institutional developments in the state.

A Changing Field

The nature of crime coverage has altered considerably over the years, and the type of journalist has also changed. Twenty-five years ago, reporting mainly concerned murder, jewel thefts, and petty crime. It now encompasses drugs, terrorism, child abuse, rape, mugging, fraud, football hooliganism, and also policy matters. George Hollingberry of the *Sun*, one of the veterans of the field, described it thus:

There is a multitude of stories which the crime reporter now has to cover. It is a very wide field indeed. . . . You have gone from smash-and-grabs and the odd murder story into this vast field of crime that's developed in the last twenty years. Where one thought in your last days of covering crime it would end up as a sinecure, you find that there is more and more crime to cover and many offices are increasing their coverage and their crime teams.

This sentiment was echoed by many of the crime correspondents. Geoff Edwards of the *Daily Star*, apart from pointing to developments in police work such as the use of computers and forensic science, also noted changes in the law with which correspondents now had to keep abreast. He observed: 'I would say that we are currently seeing a revival in interest in crime generally in British newspapers. In the mid-seventies I think it started to die off and that is because as the crime rate has increased and as extraordinary crimes become commonplace, they are devalued in interest. . . . Now there is a greater interest in law and order.'

A number of factors may be identified as contributing to the changing pattern of crime coverage. For example, the abolition of capital punishment in 1965 has had a significant effect on the news value of a murder, lessening its impact considerably. The former top *Daily Express* reporter, Alfred Draper, commented that 'The end of capital punishment may have been enlightened but it had knocked the drama out of murder.'[1] George Hollingberry concurred: 'In those early days . . . murder was a very dramatic affair because one knew that this was a capital offence and that you were looking for a killer who, when found and tried and convicted, was hanged. You usually followed the case through, beginning with the investigation, then the trial and then the grisly business of covering hanging.'

One correspondent thought that, in the days of capital punishment back in the 1950s and 1960s, murder cases had been the subject that sold newspapers. For an earlier generation of crime reporters, this was evidently a 'golden age', and a time when very close links between specialists and investigating officers prevailed.[2]

---

[1] Cited in Snoddy, R., *The Good, the Bad and the Unacceptable: The Hard News about the British Press* (London: Faber & Faber, 1992), 25.

[2] This period, and the early 1970s, are covered in Chibnall, S., *Law-and-Order News: An Analysis of Crime Reporting in the British Press* (London: Tavistock Publishing, 1977), ch. 3.

Despite its abolition, the public fascination with capital punishment has still remained, contributing to the success of feature films made about Ruth Ellis, the last woman to be hanged for murder in 1955, and Derek Bentley, hanged in 1953 for his part in the murder of a policeman.[3] Indeed, some play is frequently given by news organizations to murder stories from the USA where the perpetrator might end up in the electric chair, as well as, sometimes, to cases in other countries. There is a perceived public interest in the fate of those on death row. The amount of coverage given to the fate of British citizens under threat of the death sentence in Thailand for drug smuggling in the early 1990s is another example of this obsession.

George Hollingberry, like many of his colleagues, has suggested that the increase in crime has changed the reader's interest in crime stories. To warrant inclusion in the paper or on television news the story has to be unusual or bizarre, he believes, otherwise readers 'would be bored with it. . . . For instance, this morning, two security guards were ambushed and shot; I dare say it will make two paragraphs in some papers and nothing at all in others. It's a daily occurrence.' But the story still had to be checked out 'in case there is more in it than meets the eye. . . . If one of them dies and then it becomes a murder story. . . . But if it's just a straightforward shooting of two security guards I doubt whether it will make the paper now, whereas in the old days it would have been a splash story: "Two security guards shot." Front page; pictures plastered all over the papers.'

John Weekes of the *Daily Telegraph*, one of the most experienced correspondents interviewed, also believed that readers were 'fed up with the everyday murders', and that in order to get coverage a killing had to be of particular interest. Likewise with robbery: 'People are still interested in major robberies but now it's got to be a big bank robbery . . . or it's got to be a 10p robbery, or something horrendous, to make the paper in any length.'

Geoff Edwards of the *Daily Star* shared this sense of change:

When I first joined the *Evening News* in 1974, if there was a security van robbery and three people with stocking masks and baseball bats stole

[3] For Ruth Ellis see *Dance with a Stranger* (UK, 1985, dir. Mike Newell) and for Derek Bentley see *Let Him Have It* (UK, 1991, dir. Peter Medak). In July 1993, the Court of Appeal recommended that the Home Office should formally acknowledge that the death sentence had been unjust, given Bentley's diminished responsibility.

£5,000 from Securicor, they'd find a place for it on the front page some-where; four or five years later, if three or four men with guns attacked a security van, stole a quarter of million pounds and shot a guard in the leg, it would make half a dozen paragraphs inside somewhere.

Edwards believed the change in news values was due to the growth in the number of offences during the 1970s and that a crime was not worth reporting unless it was something very special. This emphasis on the special and dramatic accords with the general news values identified by previous research. The shifting percep-tions of veteran crime specialists point to broader cultural changes taking place over time. For whilst news values, viewed quite abstractly, may appear to remain constant—with an emphasis on drama, frequency, proximity, and other such structuring concepts seeming to be invariable through time—in actual fact, the identification of given events as newsworthy is time-bound. Murder, according to the crime correspondents interviewed, is no longer seen as 'important' in the way that it once was. Hence, some events—earlier the meat and drink of such journalism—now go unreported, although the preoccupation with violence generally, and the gruesome in particular remains. This sense of change is occasionally reflected upon in the media themselves. For instance, the *Independent on Sunday* on one occasion looked at murder trends in Britain under the headline 'Those we Forget'. The story noted how murder was now being viewed as commonplace and that the victims in the majority of cases were quickly forgotten or not even publicized at all.[4] As one of the crime correspondents remarked: 'Crime is not seen as such a big seller as it was. . . . Ten years ago if there was a teenager strangled you would have all the crime reporters staying at the spot. Now it rates a few paragraphs.'

'New' crimes become predominant in the news media until the level of saturation reaches a point where future events are deemed to be of no further interest to the public unless they exhibit some unusual characteristic. The label of 'new' crime presently refers either to offences concerning drugs or terrorism, which are fairly recent areas of running news interest, or to crimes such as child abuse and rape in marriage, which are far from new occurrences but have only recently been culturally identified as widespread crimes.

[4] *Independent on Sunday*, 12 Jan. 1992.

Rape has attracted wide media attention recently. In Britain, it has been noted, the volume of reporting of rape and other sexual crime has grown, and the 'popular daily newspapers are much more likely to carry such stories today than twenty years ago. However, the reports are typically sensational and titillating, rather than serious accounts of these crimes.'[5] Nor is it just rape in Britain that evidently fascinates: the Kennedy-Smith and Tyson trials in the USA in 1992 attracted extensive and detailed media attention in the UK. In those cases, it was because of the personalities involved, but often in the British newspapers, as many of the correspondents underlined, it is some unusual aspect of the case which gets the event covered.

Some correspondents were also aware of having to tackle their work rather differently than before. The public discourse about crime has shifted from predominantly offering descriptions of crimes and punishments to a wider one that now includes police accountability and government policy on law and order. John Weekes formulated it thus:

People are getting more intelligent these days and they like to read what the thinking is behind things more than they do current crime. . . . They are interested in what are the police doing about burglaries because it affects them personally, what they are doing about auto crime, are there going to be twenty policemen on the streets and are they armed? They want to know these things and so you tend to get more shows on that sort of story.

The growth in legal affairs journalism, particularly in the quality dailies and television, is one manifestation of the broadening-out of traditional crime-reporting. As a consequence of this growth in complexity some crime correspondents now specialize in particular sub-fields rather than attempting to cover the whole area.

The five national 'quality' newspapers (the *Guardian*, the *Independent*, *The Times*, the *Daily Telegraph*, and the *Financial Times*) all have legal affairs correspondents, who, together with their BBC counterparts, constitute a fairly cohesive group. At the time of this study, four of these journalists were, in fact, qualified lawyers. We have identified four main reasons for the growth in coverage of this specialism in the 1980s. First, the Conservative

[5] Soothill, K., and Walby, S., *Sex Crime in the News* (London: Routledge, 1991), 3.

government introduced several major pieces of legislation such as the Police and Criminal Evidence Act (1984) and the Criminal Justice Act (1988). Second, proposed changes in the legal system (for instance, giving solicitors the right of appearance in courts) served to focus the spotlight on this area. Third, the major prosecutions in the 1980s of Sarah Tisdall, Clive Ponting, and Peter Wright under official secrecy legislation meant that newspapers required specialists to handle these stories' legal ramifications and could not rely solely upon home affairs or general reporters to cover them. Fourth, with the launch of the *Independent* in October 1986, competition between the 'up-market' or 'quality' newspapers intensified, with battle joined for an audience that included solicitors, barristers, and others working in the legal profession.

As Robert Rice, legal affairs correspondent of the *Independent* told us: 'One of the reasons [that] we have a law correspondent is because we think that lawyers are a very good market within our ABC1 group which we are trying to attract to this new newspaper. And so we decided at a very early stage that we would have to have law reporters to try and compete with *The Times*.'

Journalists have also increased their reporting of the European Commission on Human Rights in Strasbourg and the legal implications of industrial relations stories. Here, the miners' strike of 1984–5 was of signal importance, given the complexity of its legal dimension. The BBC's Joshua Rozenberg observed that the strike 'was being fought in the courts just as much as on the picket line and people were interested in what is a sequestrator or would Arthur Scargill go to prison for contempt of court'.

Given that amongst other things it addresses an opinion-forming élite, the 'quality' press has found it necessary to adapt to the increase in information being made available in the criminal justice field, particularly by state institutions. Malcolm Dean of the *Guardian* pointed to one example of this change: 'It's very interesting what has happened to the Lord Chancellor's department: four years ago there was no press officer, you just called his private secretary. . . . They now have three press officers, a chief information officer and two junior officers.'

The brief of the home affairs correspondents is not as easily definable as that of the legal affairs or crime correspondents, as they cover a wide area shaped mainly by the remit of the Home Office, which includes police, civil defence, criminal law, penal policy, prisons, courts, gambling, immigration and nationality, community relations, voluntary services, data protection, the fire service, and electoral matters. Some home affairs correspondents cover all of these, others concentrate upon just one or two areas.

The scope of home affairs, then, varies across the press. Apart from being largely anchored in the activities of the Home Office, it may also at times depend on the individual news editor's categorization of a given story, with the previous experience and contacts of particular correspondents also playing a part in defining the brief. The interest of a correspondent or an editor in a particular subject inevitably produces more coverage, which in turn sets off a relatively enduring pattern. The *Independent* has taken an interest in prisons from the outset. According to Sarah Helm, then the newspaper's home affairs correspondent:

That was something that was pushed right from the top, that was the editor's interest. When we first started it seemed to be his personal issue . . . and it is a great social issue, I am very interested in it too but I would not have pushed it because on the whole it is not something that is easy to get people to read, it is not a very acceptable sort of subject. But it is all relative, it is very important and there is an endless wealth of material to write about in that area.

Traditionally, reform of the penal system has not been a subject at the top of the public agenda. The cynical view put forward by some of the pressure groups interviewed by us was that there were no votes to be gained by political parties or individual politicians by taking an interest in or championing reform. It has been viewed as having little audience or readership appeal. Hence, for a new 'quality' newspaper to be launched at a time when liberal and reformist views in Britain were under attack, and outlets for such views were perceived to be shrinking, was a boon for the voluntary and pressure groups working and campaigning in the criminal justice arena. For the paper to take an active interest in prison reform was even more of a welcome bonus.

Crime is one of the biggest and most competitive areas in journalism. National newspapers differ in the number of specialist crime correspondents and reporters they employ. The majority have one, some have as many as three. The reporting staff available significantly determines the number of stories and the amount of space devoted to crime. There are differences in personnel, in briefs and subject emphasis according to medium, markets, and formats. Differences exist between the press and television; between the daily papers and Sunday papers and between the popular, mid-market, and quality press.[6]

Although when consumed on an everyday basis, it would appear that the categorizations that make up the news are natural, in fact these are the product of cultural conventions that we have come to accept. The distinctive ways in which newspapers handle the broad field of crime-reporting illustrate this point rather well, as internal conventions, based on assumptions about the markets that are being addressed, and the type of medium involved, affect how the field is structured. The *Daily Telegraph*, for example, employs a crime correspondent, Neil Derbyshire, and a police correspondent, John Weekes. Weekes is technically responsible for policy matters, principally in the Metropolitan Police and the Home Office, but he also deals with chief constables and senior policy-making figures in other forces. Derbyshire's brief is more concerned with day-to-day crime and trends in the incidence of crime. As he put it: 'That sounds like a very grand distinction, and that is how it is meant to be, but the two areas overlap all the time.'

Chester Stern, crime correspondent of the *Mail on Sunday*, told us that his paper had no designated home affairs correspondent and that his own brief covered broadly the full range of law and order topics. Its scope had never been discussed in detail with the editor but was dictated

much more by the nature of the newspaper than the nature of the subject, [by] what the editor wants. We are a Sunday newspaper which is very middle of the market. . . . We do not go running news stories unless they happen on a Saturday or unless you are doing a more background piece to events earlier in the week. I am doing a wide range of material. I think you find on the Sunday newspapers there are more investigative pieces. I have got a fairly broad and wide-ranging brief and I can pick and choose to a certain extent the stories I go after myself.

Some crime correspondents are expected to have a specialized knowledge not only of current criminal investigations but also of

[6] For a detailed quantitative and qualitative exploration of how such differences affect news content in radio, television, and the press see Ericson, R. V., Baranek, P. M., and Chan, J. B. L., *Representing Order: Crime, Law, and Justice in the News Media* (Milton Keynes: Open University Press, 1991). For our own, qualitative, exploration of these differences, see below.

policy matters within the police and the Home Office and, as Geoff Edwards of the *Daily Star* noted, knowledge of 'changing trends in all aspects of policing, criminal detection, and crime prevention'. Edwards, a crime reporter for fifteen years, had also covered other types of news and believed that crime reporters were capable of doing most other assignments because the brief itself was so wide: 'I assisted on the King's Cross inquiry [into a serious fire in the London Underground] and they asked me to monitor the forensic approaches to it in case it should turn out to have been deliberately caused. There was a large-scale police involvement in the rescue operation—police officers were hurt. It is just another example of how, although it was not actually a crime story, they needed some input from me.'

Peter Archer of the Press Association, like most specialists with the UK home news agency, had a very wide brief. It included the Home Office beat and major crime stories including terrorism, drug-trafficking, and City fraud. Archer described one aspect of his job as dealing with 'Mission Impossible stories', where other reporters had difficulty in obtaining information: 'It's the same with a lot of specialists in Fleet Street. They are meant to have contacts who will give them information which is not officially available. . . . I could be called on to do any crime story, actually. I would probably object if they wanted me to go out and stand on doorsteps and interview eye-witnesses; I don't see that as my job. I am not being prima donna-ish, but really they pay me to do other things and to have a little bit of specialist knowledge.'

This sentiment was shared by other crime correspondents with whom we spoke. Sylvia Jones of the *Daily Mirror* explained that her brief 'was to bring in exclusive stories and not to concentrate on the day-to-day stuff which comes in from agencies and comes out through the press bureau at Scotland Yard; my brief was to do investigations and to bring in bigger stories, half a dozen front-page blockbusters every year'. Some, though, like George Hollingberry of the *Sun*, left the features to other journalists on the paper: 'What the *Sun* tends to do, and I am grateful that it does, is to get very good feature writers to do crime features. I point them in the right direction, tell them who to see and probably line the interview up for them. But it is impossible to cover day-to-day crime and break off and do features as well. There is just not the time in the day.'

In many instances, general reporters are drafted in to cover 'run of the mill' stories and to assist on events such as bomb explosions when blanket coverage may be required. This leaves the specialist free to concentrate on his or her areas of expertise. Colin Baker of Independent Television News explained how an internal division of labour had resulted in the development of precisely such a specialism:

It came around about the middle of 1985 when we had a lot of terrorism taking place, not just in Ireland, which we have always covered, but European terrorism, and we saw a rise in the number of terrorist incidents in London from overseas, a lot of it based within foreign embassies, the kind of state-sponsored terrorism that people used to talk about. Also at that time there was the new trend of drugs. Whether it was a new trend or whether it was something the media were just latching on to, I don't know; I suspect that it actually was growing quite fast. So they decided that they wanted someone who would be detached from the general reporters' rota which I was on and concentrate their efforts in those two areas, drugs and terrorism. . . . I did not really have a title but just to look after what was known as 'international crime'—that was a euphemism for drugs and terrorism.

Baker was modest about his credentials for the post, indicating that his background was no different from anyone else's. However, he had lived and worked over a period of ten years in Belfast:

I had developed certain contacts so it was natural to keep my interest going. The difficulty after that was what do you do about international terrorism? You don't just say 'Right, we have got a reporter now.' Or even with drugs—what do you make him do? What do you target? So what we did in the first few months, I looked at the problem on the home front. . . . I looked at the waste of human resources in terms of wealthy and poor who were hooked, I looked at methods of treatment which were controversial, I looked at 'heroin babies'. We did the first pieces on those children who became addicted in the womb, how society copes and looks after them. Then we went back and I tried to do what we called at that time the heroin trail and the cocaine trail.

In many ways, Baker's brief was similar to those specialists on the national Sunday papers and those crime correspondents on the daily nationals who concentrated on features. Terry Kirby of the *Independent*, for example, liked to spend time on longer-term items rather than day-to-day crime stories. Over a 6-month period he had written pieces on drugs in Liverpool, the Police Complaints

Authority, community relations in the London area of Stoke Newington, and the police under stress. He had also covered an international conference on drugs held in Vienna. His conception of his role was rooted in the kind of position taken by his newspaper, which he distinguished from the popular and mid-market locations occupied by others:

> If you are working for the *Sun* or the *Mail*, or a tabloid, you can take a pretty grisly murder or some crime and they will lead the paper with that. They will make page leads out of it. Even though you might not have enough to write more than half a dozen paragraphs they can still go very big on it. Now I know the *Independent*, because of the nature of the paper that it is, would never do that. In however many issues we have been going now the *Independent* has only once, and that was only in the first edition, splashed on a crime story and that was over Christmas when it was a thin period. . . . Now I knew that I was not going to sit around as I had done to a degree perhaps on the *Birmingham Post*, writing, rewriting PA, and making endless phone calls on odd crime stories which I knew were never going to get perhaps more than single-column treatment in the paper. And I did not want to do that. . . . And in fact we agreed that that was really not what I was going to do. . . . I was going to look at it from a much wider angle and in that sense the title crime correspondent is not entirely satisfactory but it is the best one they can come up with and I cannot think of another one.

The *Independent* offers an instructive case when examining the range of briefs in the crime and criminal justice field. Compared to the other national daily newspapers it is a relatively new venture, having started in October 1986. According to the journalists with whom we spoke, the *Independent* originally took a decision not to have a crime correspondent. The initial idea was to have a home affairs desk within which an inner cities correspondent would deal with all the stories that might concern the traditional crime brief, whereas the remainder of the brief would devolve onto another correspondent. This view was later revised when Sarah Helm took over as the sole home affairs correspondent and Terry Kirby as crime correspondent. Some of the quality papers are reluctant to assign the specific post of crime correspondent, preferring instead to rely on a pool of general reporters or the Press Association for covering crime stories. Because of its often sordid nature, some of the qualities (the *Daily Telegraph* being a notable exception) have felt that crime is an area that should be left to the tabloids and mid-market papers. This attitude does not actually prevent them from exploiting some stories themselves by presenting detailed coverage of crimes and court cases. Moreover, the expansion of the general field has enabled the qualities to appoint specialists and to deal with the policy aspects of crime. Terry Kirby, asked why the *Independent* did not wish specifically to designate a crime correspondent, replied: 'They did not think they needed one. It [the *Independent*] was a prestigious upmarket product, etc. We don't want anything as sordid as crime. . . . But they realized that there was a definite need and I suppose I partially elbowed my way into the job.'

Kirby had joined the *Independent* from the *Birmingham Post*, one of the major regional newspapers. According to him there were two specialist posts on that paper which were considered to be of high status: labour correspondent was one and police correspondent the other. The *Birmingham Post* had resisted the title of crime reporter: 'It was curious. They were a bit posher than that. They would not call it crime. They called it police reporter, which I thought was a bit like calling the education correspondent the teachers' reporter. They called it police reporter and then after some time it was changed to home affairs correspondent, which I think is a much more satisfactory title because it covers the whole ambit of the criminal justice system from offence to rehabilitation.'

Co-operation and Competition

The changes in designation of the crime reporter inside news organizations are part of a broader shift in the field as such, in which an older model with specialists closely linked to and identified with the police has evolved into a more ramified set of relations. George Hollingberry once again evoked this, regretting the loss of the 'tremendous *esprit de corps*' that was part of the traditional, quasi-fictional, image of the crime reporter:

. . . suddenly you went charging out in the middle of the night on a murder inquiry in some remote county and by the time you got your story over, phoned from a local pub, you then had to think about where you were going to stay, and very often you'd find yourself—five of you—sleeping in one bed. I've even shared a bath as a bed with another reporter. And this promoted a great camaraderie among the crime reporters and you were forever meeting and helping each other out. Some nights you'd congregate in the bar in some village pub and sometimes one chap might become the worse for wear and a dramatic development may suddenly happen, and I've known reporters to ring rival papers with the story which their own reporter was incapable of putting over. I don't think this sort of situation would happen now, but that's what used to happen in the old days, when you followed the detective with the murder bag.

This tale of collective adventures past conveys a sense of how the culture of crime-reporting has changed in response to structural shifts. This was confirmed by Stewart Tendler of *The Times*, who commented, 'I think the old cigarette and the pint in the pub sort of ethos is disappearing to a certain extent.' He went on to illustrate the point:

Twenty years ago the Yard did almost all the major investigations inside and outside London because very few forces had the expertise. They were all very small city, town, or shire forces. And so the Scotland Yard detective would sail off with the troop of Fleet Street reporters in tow. Now that has gone completely because all the forces are now capable of doing their own investigations and rarely need the Yard. So the matiness that existed in that sort of travelling circus has gone. . . . You could get the situation where the detective, his sergeant, and the press corps all stayed at the same hotel, so they would have a drink during the evening and he might tell them what he had done during the day. And names were made that way, great detectives were born, or not.

The fact that specialists no longer hunt in packs as they once did indicates that the situations that made this part of their working lives have disappeared. However, there is evidence that in other contexts journalists do continue to behave in the same way: the classic instance is that of foreign correspondents who are very often holed up in the same hotel or place together and will therefore support each other up to a certain point.[7] So whilst Hollingberry's *esprit de corps* may have disappeared amongst crime correspondents, it does surface in other areas of journalism.[8]

Indeed, although co-operation may not exist in the same way

[7] See Morrison, D. and Tumber, H., *Journalists at War: The Dynamics of News Reporting during the Falklands Conflict* (London: Sage, 1988). In their study of the Falklands campaign coverage, the authors found that journalists would sometimes support each other, even though they would also remain very competitive.

[8] Another part of the classic image is that all crime correspondents are hard-drinking people who spend all their evenings in the pub. This too has certainly changed.

that Hollingberry outlined, certainly there are moments of collaboration. For instance, at conferences when all cannot cover the same
session, they will swap information. Similarly, at press conferences
or briefings correspondents might also help each other. As Sylvia
Jones of the *Daily Mirror* remarked:

If you've gone to a difficult press conference where people can't hear at
the back, for example, a rape victim or the widow of a murder victim and
she's distraught and in tears, you either all have to crowd around her and
shove microphones under her nose, and that kind of thing, or you have to
sit back and let somebody do it and then the people at the back will get
the quotes from the people at the front. That's just sensible really, otherwise the whole thing would be pretty unworkable. Sometimes if people
have misheard quotes and things, we will actually sit round and agree collectively what the quotes are, so that everybody has roughly the same
thing. One or two people have got tape recorders and it's surprising how
the sound is distorted. Sometimes it comes out as something quite different. So certainly there's a kind of co-operation. One or two people have
arrangements. If they've got a really good exclusive coming out, we all get
woken up at 1 o'clock in the morning to follow it up and you might tell
your best friend that you've got one coming out or you all give it to him
so that he can do it in time for his second edition without having all the
hassle. If you've got a good exclusive, that's fine; nobody will quibble
about that.

Agreement about the use of quotations is a common occurrence
amongst different groups of journalists, who in their own self-
interest want to standardize these. Whereas the analysis of a story
or the opinion columns may be different, agreement on the exact
quote is an important way of signalling that the story has been
adequately covered. Generally, then, on a day-to-day basis, if a
story is not an exclusive there may be substantial co-operation, and
at the time of our research, relations amongst specialists appeared
to be cordial. The crime correspondent of *Today* described these as
follows: 'Invariably it's a very happy ship. I've heard of other specialists moaning and groaning about all sorts of things, but we just
don't have that. And, when something is not totally exclusive, we
do help each other as much as possible.'

Although co-operation exists in certain circumstances, there is
still keen competition between the crime reporters, which many
believe keeps them all on their toes. Those working for the Sunday
papers feel especial pressure to find exclusives, on some papers

more than others. For the Sunday papers there is little point in reproducing what readers have seen earlier in the week. Chester Stern spelled out the kind of difficulty that could occur for Sunday reporting as opposed to that on weekdays:

If you get a shooting, all hell breaks loose; the guys have to get out, get the facts, interview the witnesses, write the piece and get it in the paper within a few hours . . . but then it's all over for them and they're waiting for the next story or working on the next story, and tomorrow it'll be different again. For me, I've just started my week. I have a few ideas or things which may or may not turn into stories which I have got to research and work; things which, if they do look good, I may lose because a daily newspaper may hear about it before next Saturday.

Another area of competition is over exclusivity of contacts. The Press Bureau at Scotland Yard recognizes 'private enquiries'. If a journalist states in advance that a given enquiry is private, the Metropolitan Police know immediately that the journalist at least believes the story to be an 'exclusive'. In that case, if the Met. are prepared to answer the questions posed they will not volunteer the same information to any other journalist unless the same line of enquiry is pursued. A frequent complaint amongst the crime specialists is that this system does not always apply elsewhere, that some sources are likely to issue a general press statement in response to a private enquiry, and that the enterprising individual then loses out. It was emphasized by a number of journalists that many sources do not understand the competition for news and the need for exclusivity.

To the extent that co-operation is institutionalized, this is through the Crime Reporters' Association. This was originally formed in 1945 with 'the dual function of pressure group for better facilities for gathering information, and business-like organization whose members the police could distinguish from less responsible practitioners of Fleet Street journalism'.[9] In common with the organization of relations between official sources and the media throughout the whole of the British state apparatus, this takes the form of a 'lobby'. Most of the specialists are members of the Crime Reporters' Association. In January every year, the journalists hold a reception to which they invite the Home Secretary, the Metropolitan Police Commissioner, and various chief constables.

[9] Chibnall, *Law-and-Order News*, 50.

This is a very informal occasion and the police know that whatever they say is either off the record, or may not even be published. Many of the journalists commented that this was a valuable
encounter during which they could exchange ideas with senior
police officers and get to know them better. The Crime Reporters'
Association is generally held in fairly high regard by senior police
officers, and membership is useful for those who wish to cultivate
their links with the police, providing 'a metaphorical badge of
trustworthiness'.[10] The CRA does operate sanctions against its own
members, but these are extremely rare. As far as we know, no one
has ever been expelled, although some members have evidently
been spoken to 'sharply' over the years.

Although there is a certain measure of cohesion, this should not
be overstressed. The changes that have occurred in the corps of
crime correspondents in recent years have led to a greater
diversification of attitudes towards the police. Steve Chibnall,
researching the field some twenty years ago, found that crime
reporters saw 'their professional responsibilities towards the public
as entailing support for the police in the "crime war"', in particular feeling that they needed to present a positive image of the
police.[11] This view no longer seemed to prevail. One correspondent
remarked, 'I can remember the President of the Crime Reporters'
Association prefacing a meeting with some senior officer from
Scotland Yard with the remark, "We are all pro-police here," and I
said, "Well, hold on a sec. I'm not pro-anybody. I'll do a story as I
see it. I'm not going to have you introducing me as part of a group
with that kind of language."'

In London, CRA members belong to a lobby organized by the
Metropolitan Police, part of the legacy of Sir Robert Mark. This
takes the form of a monthly briefing by the Commissioner. The
specialists feel that this arrangement offers privileged access to
information and that the police trust them not to reveal anything
disclosed under lobby conditions until such time as they are authorized to release the information. These briefings with the
Metropolitan Police Commissioner are the main occasion on which
the group act collectively and were seen as the most valued aspect
of CRA membership, as Sylvia Jones of the *Mirror* put it: 'When
there's a particularly long-running and maybe sensitive story, you

---

[10] Chibnall, *Law-and-Order News*, 151.   [11] Ibid. 145.

get lots of background information on an unattributable basis
which you can't publish legally, or perhaps the police would not be
allowed to give us officially, but it means that you can interpret
things in a more accurate way.'

Competition and co-operation were also part of the working
relationships of the legal affairs correspondents. As noted, this area
of specialization is relatively small and dominated by the quality
press and BBC radio and television. On the whole, legal affairs was
not seen as providing much scope for scoops. Robert Rice of the
Independent observed that lawyers were not tuned in to the
requirements of newspapers, and they also tended to be reticent
about matters that might impinge on their professional relationships with clients. *The Times*'s Frances Gibb felt that the launching
of the *Independent* had created new competitive pressures.
Nevertheless, as with the crime correspondents, the group would
co-operate, for instance, in checking quotations at press conferences and also in agreeing which stories to file, and in what
sequence, when reporting from conferences.

Covering the Courts

Court coverage in London is mainly supplied by the Press
Association, which has three reporters assigned to the Old Bailey.
There are some smaller agencies which also provide stories to the
national papers: Joe Wood, Central News, and National News.
The *Independent* was the only national paper which had assigned a
full-time designated court correspondent to this area of coverage.
Many of the crime correspondents, whilst researching the background to court cases, rely on agency material and full transcripts
for the details. They rarely attend every day, usually turning up for
the opening and returning for the judge's summing-up.[12] Neil
Darbyshire of the *Daily Telegraph* outlined the practice:

In most court cases you get a big show in all the papers for the opening
because they tell you in brief detail what is going to be said throughout
the trial, it lays out the prosecution case. You will then maybe have something from the opening of the defence case and in between it tends to be
detailed evidence. You would not have a particularly big show given to

[12] Contrast this with the court 'beat' described by Ericson, R. V., Baranek,
P. M., and Chan, J. B. L., *Negotiating Control: A Study of News Sources* (Toronto:
University of Toronto Press, 1989), ch. 2.

very detailed forensic evidence because it becomes very samey. . . . The only time you tend to get a lot of copy into the paper in mid-trial is when there is a key witness and you want to hear their version of events or if something unexpected is said. . . . If the defendants are convicted I'll get my previously prepared background into the paper.

Most of the nationals will normally send a general reporter to cover court cases, and the crime correspondents will, as Sylvia Jones of the *Daily Mirror* put it, 'pop in sometimes just to meet people to keep in touch with what is going on'. Heather Mills was appointed to the *Independent* as court correspondent when the paper first started. Previously, she had been the Old Bailey correspondent of the *Daily Telegraph*. The days when the national papers had an Old Bailey correspondent are now past: current practice is to send reporters for each individual trial that is covered, rather than have someone based there permanently. The *Independent*, therefore, was anomalous in having a formally designated courts correspondent. Heather Mills had a certain degree of autonomy in deciding which cases to cover:

I may make a wrong decision and decide to cover something at the Old Bailey when there was a much better story at the High Court. They are all well covered by agencies and if we have not got enough staff to actually send more people out into the courts then we will pick up from the Press Association or one of the stringers [non-staff reporters]. We pay people at the Old Bailey, we pay people at the High Court to keep an eye on things really and they are supposed to let me know if anything good is about to happen.

Correspondents' Contacts

As a consequence of the growth in the scope of crime-reporting, there are now many more potential sources that specialist journalists have to cultivate. Chibnall has argued that crime-reporting has been characterized historically by 'an increasing reliance on one major institutional source—the police'.[13] This remains significantly so, although currently, apart from the police, there are numerous Home Office, Customs and Excise, and City contacts with whom relationships have to be maintained. Contacts have to be turned into sources. And sources are becoming far more proactive in their

---

[13] Chibnall, *Law-and-Order News*, 49.

relationships with the media, as we have seen, with specialists receiving many more telephone calls, press releases, reports, and booklets.

The confinement of the national correspondents to London inevitably means that they concentrate upon London-based news stories. This feature of their work has been long established. In his study of journalists at work, published over twenty years ago, Jeremy Tunstall commented that crime involved little foreign travel, but also that crime specialists travelled out of London much less than, say, their football counterparts. He found that crime correspondents tended to concentrate on London crime and on London police sources, leaving all but the exceptional cases outside of London to local agencies and stringers, who knew their local police better.[14]

This trend has continued, with the national crime correspondents rarely moving out of London except perhaps for special cases or for conferences both in and outside the UK. As a result of the growth in crime specialisms the number of relevant conferences has increased. For example, some correspondents who deal with drugs or terrorism will attend international meetings specifically set up to concentrate on those particular areas. Many local police forces have developed their own murder squads, and at the same time most national newspapers have also built up their own crime-reporting teams in, for example, Manchester and Birmingham.[15] These crime teams are usually staff reporters, and they, in turn, have cultivated local police contacts. These staffers will not simply report crime but will also engage in general reporting. George Hollingbery of the *Sun* underlined this point when he remarked: 'It's very rarely these days that a crime reporter would leave London. It's got to be an exceptional case.' He cited the example of the re-investigation of the Moors Murder case, where some of the London journalists might have gone north, but they would have had to compete with colleagues based in Manchester. Hollingbery, one of the older crime reporters, doubtless in the style of romantic mythicization, as the reference to a celebrated

[14] Tunstall, J., *Journalists at Work: Specialist Correspondents, their News Organizations, News Sources, and Competitor-Colleagues* (London: Constable, 1971), 154–5.
[15] There is also a quite distinctive tradition of crime-reporting in Scotland. For a brief journalistic portrait see Close, A., 'The Criminal Type', *Scotland on Sunday*, 28 Feb. 1993, pp. 29–30.

Hollywood representation of journalism suggests, encapsulated the changes that had taken place and also his own regrets at these:

I can go back to when Scotland Yard was in that lovely old building on the Embankment and we had this little green hut by the side of the building with its nicotine-stained walls, and in the corner there were lots of empty bottles of Scotch and where there was always a poker pool on the go and it reminded me very much of that lovely American film *The Front Page*. It was very much like that with all these old crime reporters playing poker and knocking back the odd nip and suddenly the phone would go and it was wonderful to see their professionalism. Suddenly the game was abandoned and there they were on the phone making all sorts of calls and in those days the Press Office was full of reporters. What's happened since then is that you rarely see anyone in there. The odd reporter calls in and those wonderful old days have long since gone. It's hardly ever used now, except for the odd press conference or somebody passing by. It's rarely used now and I think, in the main, it's due to news editors and editors who want their staff around them and rarely let you out of their sight.

For the crime correspondent, like all journalists, sources and contacts are of crucial importance. As one said to us, 'It's the vital part of any crime reporter's make-up: they've got to have contacts; they've got to have a book, like I've got, full of telephone numbers of people who trust me and you can equally say that you've got to be able to trust the police side too.' Crime specialists' most important single point of contact is still with the police, from whom they obtain most of their information. According to the journalists interviewed, the police made up somewhere between 70 and 90 per cent of all their contacts.

We have noted the growing professionalization of the police as source. Geoff Edwards of the *Daily Star* instanced a younger, high-ranking officer who was very interested in the media and a great believer in the value of good PR and the importance of presenting the police in the right light all the time:

He said to me recently, 'I believe that there is never a circumstance where the police can't say anything about what's happening. Even if you're standing on the pavement with a smoking gun in your hand and there's somebody that you have just shot dead, they could simply say: "This is a very regrettable incident. It's always a tragedy when the police have to use firearms. We are sorry we have had to do this, but obviously the circumstances of it will be properly looked into." That's sufficient.'

Edwards contrasted this singular attitude to the common police practice of trying to say as little as possible for the first twelve hours or so, until they had decided how to play things. He believed that this led to suspicion and had opened up space for critics to accuse the police of cover-ups. Some correspondents compared the police unfavourably to the Home Office. John Weekes of the *Telegraph* dealt frequently with the Home Office Press Office, particularly on drugs, prisons, and police matters, and believed that they were very competent, particularly by comparison with Scotland Yard: 'They seem to me to have press officers who specialize in the various sections, so they know the system. I find that at Scotland Yard they don't. They're too general to be experts.' For journalists, of course, speed is of the essence, and very often they require information at night, particularly when a story breaks, and they have to write a quick half a column on it. As Weekes said: 'Sometimes you can do it off the top of your head and other times you need expert guidance', and where he needed advice, the Home Office had proved to be very useful.[16]

For all journalists, building up contacts is one of the most important parts of the trade, and they have to be cultivated over a number of years. Neil Darbyshire of the *Daily Telegraph* described how this process evolves:

Until the time I started in crime full-time [my contacts] tended to be mostly of junior ranks. So what was happening was I would get a story from the ground, if you like, and there was often a disparity between what the soldiers on the ground think and what is thought at the Yard. The ideal story is where you can take the best of both tales and bounce both things off each party and modify them to an extent where you've squeezed them out hopefully into an amalgamation. I was lucky when I started doing crime full time. Both John Stevens of the *Standard* and John Weekes of the *Telegraph*, who I get on very well with personally, and although they wouldn't necessarily vouch for me on every occasion, we trust each other and they are very helpful in steering me into the right track.

Darbyshire underlined the importance of at least some genuine rapport with a contact and the need to meet regularly in order to keep

---

[16] This view was not shared by Stephen Shaw, looking at the Home Office from the standpoint of the penal reform lobby. He believed that it was 'an article of journalistic faith that nothing the Home Office says is to be trusted'—to the advantage of the penal reformers. Shaw, S., 'Massaging the Media', *CJM: Criminal Justice Matters*, 11 (1993), 19.

this alive. As he said, 'I think you've just got to keep in touch. You've got to identify people who you think you can work with and they feel they can work with you, because there is a certain amount of reciprocal benefit sometimes.'[17]

Some of the national crime correspondents built their first contacts whilst working on local papers and they have been assiduous in maintaining these relationships throughout their careers. Kim Sengupta joined *Today* from the *Daily Mail* about three months before the paper was actually launched and had that period to cultivate contacts and not really demand anything in return. Sengupta made new contacts through established connections, very often networking through a third party. Like many of his fellow correspondents, he believed that police contacts were more receptive to a request for a meeting through a fellow officer than if they had just been approached cold. This was especially so for those working in more sensitive fields such as the Anti-Terrorist Branch, the Special Branch, or the Flying Squad. As Sengupta told us:

I think if you phone them up out of the blue and say 'Hey, I'm so-and-so. I'd like to meet you for lunch', I think they would be a bit apprehensive. But if a fellow detective phones up and says 'Look, I know so-and-so and he's a fairly reliable guy,' then they're that much more relaxed. In the majority of cases that's how I did it. I went to the detective I knew already and said 'Could you be kind enough to introduce me to so-and-so?' and they did.

Peter Archer of the Press Association was fortunate in that his predecessor had very good contacts and introduced him to some of them. As Archer worked alongside him for a few months, he met some of his sources in this way. However, this is quite unusual, as journalists tend to guard their contacts jealously, seeing them as an essential part of their work and, ultimately, as a key to their professional success. However, sometimes they will do favours for a colleague and introduce him or her to a potential source.

Since most of the crime correspondents working for the national papers are based in London, their contacts are almost exclusively with the Metropolitan Police. There are times, of course, when they travel outside London to other parts of the country, but their

---

[17] There are substantial parallels between these remarks and the picture painted by Chibnall's informants, who also spoke of their probationary periods with sources and their long-term investment in building relationships involving a recognition of mutual obligations. *Law-and-Order News*, 150–2.

intimate knowledge is of the Metropolitan Police area, and significant connections outside are quite exceptional.[18] As Geoff Edwards of the *Daily Star* explained:

These are personal relationships that take a long time to build up. It's easy to keep that going, if you've only got to ring up somebody who's a couple of miles up the road or at Scotland Yard or in Finchley or Southwark and say 'I'll pop in and see you for a drink tonight', whereas you might meet some very helpful and nice people in Bristol or Northampton, but it's physically impossible to keep the contact going.

All the journalists—especially those newer to the job—stressed how difficult it was, at times, to build up contacts. Those like John Weekes, who had some thirty years' experience behind him, were in quite a different position. As he had acquired seniority so had his sources risen through the ranks as well. Some younger correspondents believed that the relationship with the police used to be too close, with journalists far too apt to see things from the police's point of view, and thought that the situation was now somewhat different. This view relates to some journalists' perception of a crisis in the police's authority. As one observed:

I'd like to think that people were a bit more cynical and a bit more reserved and I think by and large they are because that circus has disappeared. . . . I remember years ago covering a terrorist committal, I think it was, at a magistrate's court in London where what was then the Bomb Squad had turned up en masse and the prisoners were sent back to prison and everybody retired to the pub opposite to continue to serve drinks after hours to this huge group of men in large trilbies and defunct raincoats. There were a few reporters there and the guy who was then the crime reporter was there and I was there as well. And all these large heavy-weight gentlemen turned round and said 'Who's he?' And the guy I was with said, 'It's quite all right, Superintendent.' 'Oh, sure about that?' 'Yeah.' That doesn't happen now. People will ring you up and say 'Listen, Joe Soap's coming to see me, is he a trustworthy guy? Is he going to drop me in it? Is he reasonable?' But that's probably about as far as it goes.

There is, therefore, both continuity and change in the pivotal relationship with the police: they remain the most crucial source, and yet younger correspondents tend to view them with somewhat

[18] David Murphy underlines the advantages of local knowledge in making the running during news coverage of the Stalker affair. The Manchester specialists had significant advantages over outsiders. *The Stalker Affair and the Press* (London: Unwin Hyman, 1991), 117–19.

greater detachment than was earlier the case. Nevertheless, as of old, it is plainly recognized that covering corruption or misbehaviour was not likely to prove endearing to the main source of information. In turn, the police have accepted that with changed rules of the game the need for greater professionalism in public relations and news management is at a premium.

Handling Sources

Journalists' relations with sources are quite varied. Whatever their difficulties with the media, on occasion the police can obtain privileged treatment. An index of this special position is the kind of co-operation achieved in kidnap cases, where they may request the suppression of particular details or even a news blackout of the case itself in order to protect the victims. In the majority of cases, particularly kidnapping, the rules that have been set out and agreed between the Crime Reporters' Association and the police usually work.[19] However, there are times when this co-operative relationship breaks down. One such example was the kidnapping of the estate agent Stephanie Slater in January 1992, where relations between the police and the press became particularly acrimonious at the end of the kidnap.[20] This had been one of the longest news blackouts in peacetime, and the press had been briefed daily by the Chief Constable of the West Midlands. Problems had arisen when the captive was released. As the West Midlands Police's PR manager put it: 'Up until then we had the press well-hooked and salivating for more information based on what we told them during the embargo. But the snag was she hadn't been fully debriefed and there were sensitive questions which we didn't want her to answer until we knew the full score ourselves.'[21] There is, on such occasions, a classic dilemma between the police's desire to restrict

[19] This kind of agreement dates back to the period of Sir Robert Mark. See Chibnall, *Law-and-Order News*, 186–7. This set the scene for subsequent agreements over siege management in terrorist cases, on which see Schlesinger, P., *Media, State and Nation: Political Violence and Collective Identities* (London: Sage, 1991), ch. 3.

[20] Morgan, J., 'Police and Press Fall out over Kidnap Coverage', *UK Press Gazette*, 24 Feb. 1992, p. 2. See the letter of reply by Cook, T. M., Assistant Chief Constable (Crime), West Yorkshire Police, 'Kidnap Cooperation: Police Put their Case', *UK Press Gazette*, 9 Mar. 1992, p. 19.

[21] Quoted in Humphrey, M., 'Police PR: A Force for Change', *PR Week*, 20 Feb. 1992, p. 11.

operational details and the media's desire for more information to feed the coverage.

At times, the Crime Reporters' Association can act as a quasi-professional body to protest about some practice with which they are unhappy. One such instance occurred over the remand of an international arms dealer which was concealed from the media for four days. The Crime Reporters' Association was particularly worried that their members, who had continued their investigations, were in danger of committing contempt of court.[22] There was also concern amongst journalists that a general practice might develop where people were charged and appeared in court without information reaching the public.

Relations with sources also change over time. Malcolm Dean, the *Guardian*'s Home Affairs Correspondent, observed that a number of professional associations had only latterly taken to promoting their interests publicly. For instance, the Association of Chief Police Officers and the Association of Prison Governors, he thought, had lost some of their insider influence with the Home Office, and had therefore 'gone public'. The advent of professionalized corporate communications, he believed, had interacted with this loss of influence to make previously reticent organizations such as the Bar Council more proactive in their media relations.

From the journalists' point of view, some sources are found to be more reliable, accurate, and aware of the media's needs. One described the desired qualities in the following terms: 'You must always make yourself available. You must always talk when asked. You must always answer journalists' questions. I'm not saying that you have to give all the information that you need to keep confidential until you're ready to release it, but you do have to realize that if you don't answer, then the journalist will write the story anyway.'

Another journalist offered a snapshot of his current judgement of some of his sources:

The Prison Reform Trust has had a high profile lately. It's slightly taken over from things like the Howard League. NACRO has got involved into other kinds of areas more than just prison, but NACRO is still a very, very good body. They are particularly good at getting information and facts over, whereas it's easier to go to the Prison Reform Trust and get a

[22] Morgan, J., '"Secret Courts": Fury over Murder Remand', *UK Press Gazette*, 23 Mar. 1992, p. 1.

quick quote. That's just individual profiles of organizations. I would say that the prison reform and the penal reform lobby is actually very good overall. They are very good in general and there's not much to choose between them.

In general, the police monitoring groups tended to be seen as much more politically motivated than the penal reform groups. One journalist, referring to the monitoring groups, observed: 'There isn't a body which has got the credibility and the authority that, say, NACRO has when it comes to purely dealing with the police. What has emerged is the Police Foundation, who have gained some credibility. We have quoted it, so it gets some credibility as a body which can speak authoritatively and independently about the police, and I think they're going to become quite important.'

Malcolm Dean of the *Guardian* also singled out NACRO as having certain exemplary features in persuading government and public of its liberal approach to prisons. He noted various techniques used. For instance, NACRO provided the Parliamentary All-Party Penal Affairs Group with free secretarial services and managed to gain access to discussions for its own preferred experts. NACRO was also adept at releasing short reports to be picked up for comment at crucial moments, as, for instance, when politically controversial prison statistics were about to be released. He also said it was 'so much better than the Home Office press office has been to provide reporters with immediate answers to statistical queries by just having an extremely good library'.

Such successes by non-official sources, however, do have to be weighed against the fundamental and routine importance of the flow of information from officialdom. The BBC's Joshua Rozenberg offered an example. If the Lord Chancellor's office were to put out a press release about developments in the Criminal Justice Act, he observed, 'that will be a story because it is actually a fact that affects people's lives. The press release may be very boring or badly written. What NACRO says is not often taken notice of directly by the government. So you would attach more weight to something said by the Law Commission than you would to something said by NACRO.'

Terry Kirby of the *Independent* indicated that editorial policy may at times reflect the inputs of pressure groups. Andreas Whittam Smith, the newspaper's editor, was particularly concerned about the prisons. As a result, the *Independent*'s reporters had extensive contact with the prison pressure groups and reform groups. Kirby said, 'I think they're getting a higher profile because we have given them a higher profile.' Peter Archer of the Press Association elaborated further on perceptions of sources, particularly in the prisons field. He gave the example of the Prison Officers' Association, which had become more and more vocal with the increasing problem of overcrowding in prisons. According to Archer, because of this the Association was sending more material to journalists and had become more amenable to enquiries:

They can help us on many things, not just a story on overcrowding, for instance, or something that they've got an axe to grind on, but—without giving away any secrets—say there's a notorious murderer and you need an inside story from the gaol, they'll find, unofficially perhaps, a prison officer who has worked with a notorious murderer and [will] give you a quote. But again, it does very often depend on the individuals involved.

If a pressure group is going to have any lasting impact, it needs well-regarded spokespersons able to deal with media. Neil Darbyshire of the *Daily Telegraph* offered insights into how an organization may begin to establish itself as a credible source. Speaking of the Prison Reform Trust, he remarked that he had never heard of it until twelve months previously but had then found it quite authoritative: 'The Director particularly, he seems to know what he's doing and he backs up more or less everything he says with either statistics or information of another kind.' Derbyshire had made use of the Prison Reform Trust when the famous jockey Lester Piggott was imprisoned for tax fraud. 'This isn't their main function,' he accepted:

They would see their main function, I guess, as improving the state of the lot of Britain's prisoners, or something similar to that. But when Lester Piggott was gaoled, we rang them up and said 'What's going to happen to him now?' As it turned out later, he [the Director of the Prison Reform Trust] knew exactly what was going to happen. He had said first he'll go here to this assessment centre, then he'll go there, and finally he'll be put in a particular place. And that, as a single column piece, was quite interesting for people, exactly what was going to happen to this man. And he knew off the top of his head. Now that sort of knowledge is very valuable in any pressure group if they want to get stuff in the paper. He'll be remembered now by the *Daily Telegraph* as being someone who knows his stuff and one will assume that he knows his stuff about other things as well.

But why had they been contacted in the first place? Darbyshire had come across the Prison Reform Trust when sent a copy of their Annual Report, which apparently included detailed advice on prisoners' rights. The correspondent initially thought that it must have been written by an aggrieved ex-prisoner, which suggested a lead worth following up. By means of this kind of selection process, a portfolio of established sources develops. This is of considerable help for the journalistic routine of checking out stories and 'standing them up' by way of using a range of quotations from interested or informed parties. One consequence is that a predictable 'stage army' tends to appear, as one correspondent commented:

The trouble is when you go to organizations, their responses are so predictable and the people who read newspapers and watch television are so familiar with what their responses are going to be, they make it almost not worthwhile approaching them. You tend to find that because they seem to be so dogmatic, that they lose value in what they can contribute to the story. The same with police monitoring groups. You know really that if you are looking for people to criticize the police, you need to find people who haven't made a career out of criticizing the police. It's well known in journalistic circles that if you want a particular reaction to a story, on whatever it is, there are certain MPs who are practised in that. If we want a story about police harassment of blacks, then you go to Michael Meacher or Linda Bellos because you know you can guarantee virtually what they are going to say. Well, if you want an opposite reaction you can go to Eldon Griffiths, or the Police Federation, or one of the other right-wing people who are just very keen to be seen talking about anything, whether they know anything about it or not. So to me, if you're doing any kind of anti-police story, the best story tends to be those where it's a member of the public who has had a rough deal, or where it's a doctor or a clergyman who has come forward and said 'I witnessed this,' or 'I saw this happen. I think this is terrible.'

Despite these reservations about the use of sources, journalists still go ahead and use standard quotes much of the time. It is convenient and easy when a story has to be rapidly produced or some reaction is needed. Nevertheless, the credibility of the source is very important. In the example cited above, disputes concerning policing, doctors or clergymen are often seen as unbiased figures and therefore as having an independent line. At other times, however, it may be precisely a clash of interests that is sought and therefore the usual rounds are done.

Rewarding Sources

On occasion, crime correspondents attempt to make contact with criminals or people connected with the so-called criminal fraternity, whether ex-convicts or informers. The question of payment to sources is often raised as a matter of public debate about journalistic ethics. The transactions that do come to light generally involve payment for life stories or kiss-and-tell revelations concerning the private lives of politicians or members of the Royal Family. In the field studied here, as far as we could ascertain, money does not normally change hands: contacts' favours are usually rewarded in the form of a drink or a meal. As one correspondent said:

If a police officer volunteered me some information, I'd probably buy him a drink or a meal, but I wouldn't hand him cash.[23] If I approach someone who maybe earns their living by writing or that sort of thing, then I might send them a tip-off fee. For instance there's a guy who's an academic and probation officer, who was very helpful over some stuff I did on hanging and he actually earns part of his living through writing articles, so I thought it was quite OK to send him a tip-off fee. We do that—you're only talking about twenty quid or something. I did that because he was in another part of the country. I'm still here and I didn't have the opportunity to go and buy the meal which I would have done under normal circumstances, and so I did it that way.

Many unsolicited tip-offs, in the form of letters and telephone calls, come into the newsrooms. Those that are paid for are normally stories from stringers or freelancers. The size of payment depends upon the value of a particular story as decided by the news editor. Some information becomes available via the slightly shady area of police radio. There are a number of what are known as 'police watchers', who listen to radio transmissions as a 24-hour way of life, tipsters who ring into news organizations with various bits of information. Although the police do talk about this practice, they do not like to comment on it officially. One of the police's complaints has been that much of the time they find journalists know about things before they have even got their own publicity operation into full gear. As Neil Darbyshire of the *Daily Telegraph* told us, 'One tends to hear of stories in other ways than

[23] Chibnall comments that sociability by sharing a meal and a drink with police sources is preferred to commerce. This would still appear to be the case. See *Law-and-Order News*, 153.

Scotland Yard tapes. There are people that make a life out of listening to police radio, for example in the Met. area, and they'll
often ring us to say this or that is happening long before it appears
on the tape. But the tape is useful for things which have been held
back for various operational reasons and then they suddenly decide
to release it.'

Some of the papers do pay the people who listen to the police
radio by results. Neil Darbyshire told us that 'On the [*Evening*]
Standard particularly there were three or four that used to ring in.
Because the *Standard*'s got such early deadlines, they must have been
up all night.' The callers would be paid what is called a 'tip fee' of a
few pounds if the story was used and slightly less if it was not.

Although most routine contact is with the police, other sources
typically include solicitors, barristers, solicitors' clerks, the military
police, and the SAS. Ex-criminals also figure. Geoff Edwards of the
Daily Star gave an example of contact with a former armed robber
of 'a very high calibre':

He was captured and was looking then at a very long prison sentence. He
became a supergrass, did his time. He was introduced to me by some
members of the police squad who had looked after him when he was acting as a resident informer, who were very impressed with him on a personal basis. He is actually a man of much stronger intellect and
personality than the average Bermondsey type and he became interested in
journalism and so forth. I actually did a couple of stories about him, a big
feature about him. The friendship has endured. He is now totally unconnected with crime. I am happy that is the case. If I thought he was still
involved I would pull the relationship.

This source was paid on the same terms as freelance journalists
and had offered special insights into, for instance, drug smuggling
in prison. However, there was an exception to the routine picture
of token payments, largely in kind, for services rendered.
Correspondents who often work abroad, such as Colin Baker of
ITN, have had to adapt to the customs and norms of the countries
which they visit. As Baker explained: 'Soldiers have to live; policemen have to live. If you pay, as in India, policemen on a border
post, or in Pakistan, £60 a month, but for each trip you go past
him you'll give him £100, what's he going to do? Because if he
doesn't take it, his government will take it. His government's probably taking some anyway, and the state is corrupt as well. . . . So
where's the incentive? Everybody's at it.'

So sometimes journalists or news organizations do have to pay for information, perhaps more often when they go abroad than at home, and sometimes not for information as such, but rather to go on a trip somewhere, or in order to be led to the person who has the required information. Colin Baker explained how this had worked in relation to one of his stories:

In Pakistan to get up the Khyber I needed transport. I needed at least four guys. I wasn't going to go by myself. I wanted a bit of protection going up there and there's no guarantee that they're not going to just take you and take your money off you. So you don't carry very much, enough to maybe get yourself out of trouble, but not very much more. I can't remember what it cost me, fifteen hundred dollars maybe.

At times, the journalist or TV crew may have to pay cash simply in order to illustrate the story being reported. Baker recounted how this had occurred when he was on the 'heroin trail':

On one occasion I sat down on the ground cross-legged and did a deal with this chap who opened up little packets to show me the various qualities that he could provide. I settled for the pure A1 grade, which was nice, brown, good heroin and I paid £850 for that. I wanted to end up taking it off him and holding it, looking into camera and doing a piece to camera and then emptying it and let it fly off in the wind, which I thought would have been a great thing to do. I was told in no uncertain terms that if I did that, I wouldn't come back alive. Part of the deal, which was explained to me while I was doing it, was that the £850 was for taking that kilo, using it and letting the man have it back. So, if you like, a kind of facility fee for him giving up his time and humping it up the hillside. You can't argue with them—there are people with guns around. Then you come back to Heathrow and the customs man says, 'Oh, ITN again. What have you been doing? Oh, buying heroin, ha ha ha.'

Such stories are quite unusual. Crime correspondents typically deal mainly with Scotland Yard and crimes occurring in Britain.

The Police as Source

Crime correspondents routinely listen to the Scotland Yard audio-tape which runs continuously throughout each day and is updated approximately every hour. This tape is used by all the journalists to ensure that they do not miss any major story. Commonly, they follow up given items by using their own contacts and channels. The journalists will usually telephone the tape first thing in the morning and then at intervals during the day.[24] The routine back-up to this police news service is the Press Association, which reports on crime stories regularly. Broadly speaking, the correspondents found the taped news system unsatisfactory as, apart from the police deciding which incidents to prioritize for media attention, their reporting was often delayed, as Terry Kirby somewhat disenchantedly observed:

Occasionally you'll hear about things that happened three or four days ago and they've only just got to the Yard Press Bureau because their local mechanism has failed to notify the Bureau. On the other hand you'll hear about things independently yourself. Maybe one of the news agencies that cover the various parts of London will ring you about it, or maybe one of your own contacts will ring you about it. You then have to go to the Yard and they'll say, 'Oh, yes, it'll be on the tape in an hour or so', or 'Yes, we've got that, but we haven't put it on the tape because it's a bit local.'

Peter Archer of the Press Association would usually call the tape twice in the morning and twice in the afternoon, with the crucial newspaper deadline times in mind. The early morning tape normally runs from about 6.30 a.m. until about 11.30 a.m., when a new tape becomes available. Since the Press Association supplies all the news organizations, it needs to ensure that it does not miss any stories.

The taped news service is part of the Press Bureau at Scotland Yard, and journalists have varying views as to the effectiveness of this facility.[25] Specialist correspondents—whatever their specialisms—are reluctant to rely purely on a press office for information. They prefer to speak to the person in charge, particularly for those stories considered important. John Weekes of the *Daily Telegraph*, a senior crime correspondent, held the view, echoed by others, that the information given out by the Press Bureau was only as good as that given in the first place to their own press office by senior police officers:

In the old days senior officers wouldn't bother to tell them anything. I think the problem is today that senior officers use the system badly because they really don't know what a newspaper wants. It's then up to

[24] There is no single physical 'beat' covered by crime correspondents. This contrasts with the situation described in Toronto by Ericson *et al.*, *Negotiating Control*, ch. 3, which would seem to be typically North American.

[25] In his respect, once again there would appear to be continuity with the picture drawn by Chibnall. See *Law-and-Order News*, 146–8.

the press bureau to advise them, and I think the advice that is coming
from the press bureau and the PR set-ups is not good at all. So I think it's
best for most reporters to get their own contacts.'

Weekes's rather cynical belief was that the press officers and
public relations personnel were mainly there to stop professional
journalists reaching the people who mattered. He also considered
that most policemen were willing to speak to recognized correspondents, but that they were often stopped from doing so by their
press office. In the light of this perception, and offering an external
view on the 'civilianization' debate discussed above, Weekes considered the best directors of information to be policemen rather
than civilians: 'They had the rank to put a bit of clout into what
they want from junior officers. If you've got, for example, as you
have had, a deputy assistant commissioner in charge, then he outranks any commander or detective chief superintendent on a major
case and he also outranks most of the policy-makers. So in that
sense he can put pressure on them to give what he likes.'

This accords with the views of most of the police officers cited
in Chapter 4 above. But not all correspondents were of like mind.
Chester Stern, crime correspondent of the *Mail on Sunday*, had formerly been head of the Press Bureau at Scotland Yard for six
years, and prior to that an area press officer in the Met. He had
been the first journalist recruited by the Yard in 1966 when they
wanted to develop their public relations. Not surprisingly, given his
insider's experience, he came down on the side of the civilians:

The benefit of a civilian is that certainly if you've been a journalist, he
understands at least the basic rudiments of what news value is and deadlines. He's also, if he's a person of any kind of quality and this is the
problem, he will not be bound by rank. He will not be inhibited by rank
from going straight to the chief constable and arguing with him. And the
best people do that and are excellent as a result. The converse, the problem with a police officer is that he's inhibited by virtue of rank. He cannot
go to the chief constable and say 'Sorry, you're wrong, we're going to do
it this way.' And that's where that falls down.

George Hollingberry, another of the senior crime correspondents,
thought that there was insufficient journalistic experience in the
Press Bureau, coupled with problems of overwork that limited
efficient contact. He also underlined the specialist's need to speak
to the investigating officer: 'Every good crime reporter wants his

own story, wants his own interview. He doesn't want it third-hand from a press officer. He wants to ask certain questions on his own. So in that respect there is a failing very often. You really want to get through to the man in charge of the inquiry yourself and put your own questions to him rather than leaving it to a press officer to find out for you.'

Other journalists said that they were well served by the Press Bureau, but they too would follow up stories by talking to the various investigating officers. Once they had time to dig up more about the story, they would add to it for later editions. Stuart Tendler of *The Times*, for instance, used the Press Bureau for checking facts and for keeping updated on certain areas and, as he said, 'If a story is moving very quickly, it's the simplest way of keeping up with it, but what I quite often do is to find out who is doing the job and then ring them up and do it that way, because I always work on the basis that whatever a Press Bureau has got, it's not going to be as much as I would want.'

The crime correspondents do not rely solely on using the Press Bureau, for quite practical reasons. Many found difficulty in getting through because of a lack of telephone lines. Even when they did make contact, some complained that they were kept hanging on. One or two of the correspondents did manage to establish relationships with individual press officers at Scotland Yard. As a result, they were often saved the trouble of calling the tape or the bureau itself as the officers concerned would contact them with the necessary information.

Open Media Relations?

As noted earlier, the more 'open' policy at the Metropolitan Police was initiated when Robert Mark took over as Commissioner. Those correspondents who had direct experience of this certainly believed that matters had improved, but were cautious in their assessments of the overall impact of this policy change. Chester Stern of the *Mail on Sunday*, with his insider background, was particularly well-placed to take a view on the workings of the Yard's media relations. He believed that the police lacked insight into how the media operate: 'They get very cross about stories which they perceive to be anti-police. They get very cross about inaccuracies. They want to use the media for their own ends at certain times for appeals, for publicity to the public. They want photofits published and that sort of thing, but apart from that we're a necessary evil, and hardly any of them understand why we're necessary.'

Stern stressed that the police did not seem to understand the element of competition in the newspaper world nor the need for exclusivity. They would hold press conferences or give general briefings on some stories, he pointed out, when 'Were they to give it to me exclusively, I would get a big show in the paper which inevitably gets followed by the rest of the press. Hold a press conference and the effect is dissipated.' This lack of understanding of journalistic culture is also widespread amongst information officers in government.[26]

Scotland Yard has been brought into line with the general drift of government information service policy. According to Stern, Scotland Yard's emphasis had shifted towards 'straight' public relations, including advertising campaigns, exhibitions, films, and posters: 'As far as background publicity is necessary for the force to get the message across to sections of the community like schoolchildren about crime prevention, that's fine. But it has become the be-all and end-all and become the driving force, and the day-to-day relationship with the news media I feel is what it's all about and this has become more and more neglected.' Other correspondents also thought that the emphasis on publicity was too centred on policy with a relative neglect of operational matters. John Weekes of the *Telegraph* did not believe that Mark's policy had been as open as people had been led to believe: 'What he meant by "open policy" is "I'll be open but nobody else should."' Moreover, he considered that Sir Kenneth Newman's policy whilst Commissioner was open only on policy questions but very tight-lipped on operational matters. Most correspondents were fairly complimentary about Commissioner Peter Imbert's approach, which they thought was based on his background as a detective. According to the crime correspondents, this meant that he had a better understanding of what they wanted.[27]

Stuart Tendler of *The Times*, although considering that the police in London, and to a certain extent outside London as well,

---

[26] Previous studies have noted a lack of understanding of the competitive element amongst journalists. For instance, see Morrison and Tumber, *Journalists at War*.

[27] For a corroborative view see Reiner, R., *The Politics of the Police* 2nd edn. (Hemel Hempstead: Harvester Wheatsheaf, 1992), 264.

had become much more receptive to the press, also had a nuanced view of Scotland Yard's 'openness' policy. He had begun his career as a crime correspondent when Sir David McNee was Commissioner:

I thought as a PR man he was pretty disastrous. Newman was not a very good communicator to most people. I thought actually he was an extremely interesting commissioner, but for a paper like mine, I would, wouldn't I? But what Newman did do was to make it evident to his force that there's a lot to be gained from talking to the press and they've become a lot more open about what they are doing. When I started, a lot of things were not talked about. You didn't talk about Special Branch, but that's changed. . . . When I first started on Fleet Street, the Branch didn't seem to exist. If you rang up, they denied who they were. Now there's no argument about it. So that's changed. The availability of their technical equipment has become more widely known. Things like video-cameras, cameras, micro-films, lasers, all the other bits and pieces that they've now got. They've spent a lot of money on that sort of thing. Well, they're now prepared to talk about it to a certain extent and show it off, whereas a few years ago when I was trying to find out whether they had bought any camera night-sights, you'd have thought I was asking about the Crown Jewels. So they've changed in those ways. In general working they're a lot more realistic, a lot more apparently truthful, whereas I think in the provinces it's not so true.

This opinion suggests a perceptible change over time in police attitudes towards the release of information. Tendler had found that investigating officers were more ready to speak than before, although it must be recalled that he himself had become a familiar figure and familiarity of this kind with sources breeds trust. His views are broadly supported by the *Guardian*'s crime correspondent Duncan Campbell, who thinks that police–media relations have improved in recent years: 'In terms of access, there have been significant improvements and it would be wrong not to acknowledge that.' He also remarked that whilst some regional forces were less responsive on the whole, the police 'have decided that there is nothing to gain by stonewalling the press'.[28]

Others have expressed more disenchanted views. The journalists Andrew Jennings and Paul Lashmar have denounced Scotland Yard's openness as a sham and have detailed obstruction faced under successive commissioners to their long-running investigation

---

[28] Humphrey, 'Police PR', 11.

into corrupt links between a senior detective and a cocaine smuggler. Counter-tactics by the Yard used against them, they report, involved refusing briefings, intimidation of a witness, surveillance of one of the reporters, telephone-tapping, and covert pressures on the media. From this outsider's perspective London's crime reporters are seen as having entered a 'cosy, unsworn compact' via the lobby system.[29]

But there are signs of criticism even from insiders. BBC Radio's Home Affairs correspondent, Jon Silverman, has expressed unease at the Met.'s manipulation of the news media's presence during major drugs raids targeted against dealers in predominantly black areas. He has described bringing the media in to witness such events from the police's point of view as akin to watching a military or paramilitary operation, and also as obscuring the more complex realities of drug-dealing in the interests of apparent police success. Silverman has quite explicitly accused the Met. of image-making on such occasions, saying that they wanted the media ' "on board" as an insurance against rumours that they had used excessive force in a potentially volatile atmosphere'.[30] Writing of one police operation, where twenty-one journalists tagged along, he commented that a meagre haul of crack had been promoted in a 'slickly made video, called *In the Public Interest*, put out by the Directorate of Public Affairs at Scotland Yard'. He went on to ask: 'Is it an unworthy thought that this operation, involving 130 officers and weeks of secret surveillance, finds its justification, not as a punitive strike against the merchants of crack, but as a PR promotion for the Met.?'[31] In the light of such doubts, there is a case for a more in-depth investigation of what 'openness' in the era of corporate identity politics might really mean.

Media Relations as a Resource-Building Strategy

The majority of crime specialists thought that HM Customs and Excise had notably improved their media and public relations in recent years. This perception was soundly based as there had

[29] Jennings, A. and Lashmar, P., 'The Wall of Silence that Refuses to Fall', *Guardian*, 13 Aug. 1990, p. 25.
[30] Silverman, J., 'Media Management by the Met', *British Journalism Review*, 3 (1992), 44.
[31] Silverman, J., 'Crack Magic Puts Us under its Spell', *New Statesman & Society*, 25 Oct. 1991, 24.

indeed been a consciously developed media strategy inside Customs and Excise. By attempting to increase support from the public through more favourable media coverage, the Customs aimed to influence government. If ministerial paymasters see good results receiving public attention, then the battle for an increase in resources may be partly won.

Graham Hammond, head of information at HM Customs and Excise, confessed to much concern about a negative public image. Due to past actions over Value Added Tax (VAT), they felt they were perceived as jackbooted men who visited during the night and kicked down the door. Secondly, even though the Customs were scoring major drug-busting successes as a result of their investigations, their efforts were going largely unnoticed by both government and public because they did not have a very active public relations and press policy. As Graham Hammond put it:

When we were in the arena bidding for money in competition with the National Health Service, the police, and so forth, because our case wasn't in the forefront of ministers' minds, we became neglected, and in fact the department suffered quite savage cuts in staffing as part of the government's review of Civil Service staffing. Subsequent to our higher publicity profile, I think it is no accident that we are getting more resources and more staff devoted to both tax and drugs enforcement.

This comment emphasizes that it is not always sufficient for different departments to win the battle for extra resources merely by internal bureaucratic politics. At times, it is necessary to go outside. It was necessary to use publicity to stress the efficient ways in which the Customs were collecting VAT, seizing drugs, and so forth. Hammond had joined Customs and Excise from the Ministry of Defence, where he had been involved in handling news on the Falklands campaign. When taking up his new post, he was instructed by the Commissioners of the Board to develop a more open policy towards the media. The Customs and Excise had previously been an archetypical secret service, with the press office considered to have done well if they had kept the press completely at bay. As a result, the department felt that it was not gaining the resources to which it felt entitled, especially by contrast to the police, who at that time were selling their cause fairly well. Adopting a more open stance—including, for instance, giving access to the BBC to make a television series about their activities—had evidently brought in more resources, permitting more staff-time to be devoted both to tax collection and drug enforcement.[32] According to Hammond, the government could see the mileage in being seen to support a law enforcement agency that was succeeding in the fight against crime. This was in any case in line with a broader philosophy of 'selling government', as he pointed out:

I speak both as a journalist having dealt with previous governments and also now as an insider. It is now much more easy to get good information from government sources than it ever was before because information officers like myself are encouraged to present the government's case in a very forceful manner. That does the government a lot of good. I am not suggesting that the government are doing this for any great philanthropic reason—there is a degree of selfishness in the proper sense in this—but, nevertheless, because I think government recognizes that it is essential to use the media to get its case across, to explain to the public about tax policy, the reasons for this policy, then that is one of the reasons why it is now easier to get information.

The Customs' higher profile approach to publicity had not gone unnoticed by crime correspondents. It was noted that the service had begun to initiate contact with journalists before important trials. Customs and Excise had decided to brief their own press officers from the start of a major drugs operation. They had also decided to build up a library of photographs and videos of their activities and make these available for use by the media, thus maximizing the smooth management of coverage. After taking legal advice, the various investigating officers would now brief journalists on the background to a given case as well as the line to be pursued by the prosecution. This is extremely useful for journalists writing in-depth end-of-trial reports. Whilst the jury was considering its verdict, a non-attributable briefing would be given on the understanding that it would not be used in the event of an acquittal.

Despite these developments, some specialists still felt that there was an inadequate flow of information. Generally, however, the Customs service was found to be much more accommodating than before. As one correspondent pointed out: 'There was a time when they refused point-blank to discuss any ongoing operations or to

[32] *The Duty Men*, 8 episodes (BBC TV, 1988, prod. Paul Hamann).

discuss anything when anybody had been arrested. Now that's all been changed with background briefings for different cases and they are generally much more open than they were.'

Conclusion

The field of crime-reporting has ramified considerably in the past two decades to include coverage of legal affairs and aspects of home affairs, both much more recent specialisms. The traditional focus of crime-reporting has itself widened, and investigation of correspondents' conceptions of the field shows some fluidity in how a given brief is defined and also points to variations in practice across different news organizations. Correspondents do compete for exclusive stories, but they also engage in considerable co-operation. Their relations with sources are of central importance to their work and, as has been shown by other studies, these links are carefully cultivated. There are widespread rules of thumb at work for assessing the value and credibility of news sources, and a body of lore about these is carried in the memories of older correspondents. Specific journalist–source relations often last for the duration of a reporter's or source's career, and, given their complexity, are not simply reducible to an economic exchange of information for publicity.

6

Figures and Fear

OFFICIAL statistics on the incidence of crime tend to be taken as a kind of barometric reading of the condition of law and order in society. Consequently, given the potentially negative political consequences of an adverse reading, a recurring preoccupation in official quarters has been the impact on the public of news-reporting of the crime statistics for England and Wales.

This focus of official concern is far from new. However, it was given some prominence recently by the Home Office's *Report of the Working Group on the Fear of Crime*, chaired by Michael Grade, Channel Four Television's Chief Executive. The report suggested that one effect of crime coverage by the media is almost inevitably to increase public fear. The crime statistics were a focus of some comment by the Working Group:

The quarterly crime statistics for England and Wales are currently fed to the media by the Home Office in a form that is hard to digest and therefore easily distorted. The public deserve accurate and comprehensive information about crime. We question whether their interests are best served by the present frequency and format of publication. We recommend that the Home Office should always publish these statistics in a more easily digestible and detailed report. To do this without additional expenditure we recommend that publication should be reduced from four times, down to twice a year. Further, we recommend that all criminal statistics should carry a prominent 'health warning'.[1]

This kind of perspective links in to a well-established theme in academic commentary on crime news and its relationship to the real incidence of crime. It also connects to how reporting is frequently seen as inducing misleading perceptions of crime by the types of story that it tends to privilege.

---

[1] Grade, M., chairman, *Report of the Working Group on the Fear of Crime* (London: Home Office, Standing Conference on Crime Prevention, 1 Dec. 1989), 2–3.

From News Content to Public Fear

The study of crime news content has been a long-standing concern of social scientists and in many respects has tended to be shaped by the kinds of broad public policy consideration noted above. Several closely related issues have been the focus of academic research in this area. For instance, the 'representativeness' of crime news has been judged by using official crime statistics as a point of comparison between news coverage and the situation on the ground. This has connected with concern about the impact of media representations of crime (especially that of violent crime, and violence more generally) on public fear and anxiety. In turn, this has linked crime news and political action, where, for instance, reports of 'crime waves' have produced public pressure on the authorities for policy changes and solutions to perceived rises in crime.[2]

A succession of American studies covering a wide variety of newspaper markets has shown that interpersonal crimes, particularly those involving violence, are consistently over-reported in relation to official statistics, whereas routine property crimes are under-reported.[3] The US media researcher Doris Graber has observed that an 'exaggerated picture is presented of the incidence of the most violent kinds of crime, while the incidence of lesser crimes is minimized'. She compared the coverage of street crimes officially recorded by the Chicago police with coverage of corresponding crimes in the *Chicago Tribune*. Graber found, for instance, that murder, which constituted 0.2 per cent of all crimes recorded in the police index, constituted 26.2 per cent of all crimes mentioned in the *Tribune*. Non-violent crimes, such as theft and car theft, constituted 47 per cent of all crimes on the police index, but only 4 per cent of those mentioned in the *Tribune*.[4]

The British evidence tends towards the same conclusion. For instance, Bob Roshier's analysis of the *Daily Mirror*, *Daily Express*, and *Daily Telegraph* found the expected over-reporting of crimes

---

[2] For a useful review of the literature see Garofalo, J., 'Crime and the Mass Media: A Selective View of Research', *Journal of Research in Crime and Delinquency*, 18 (1981), 319–50.

[3] Davis, F. J., 'Crime News in Colorado Newspapers', *American Journal of Sociology*, 62 (1952), 325–30 is often cited as the post-war initiator of such research.

[4] Graber, D., *Crime News and the Public* (New York: Praeger, 1980), 39.

against the person (particularly murder).[5] It was also found that up to one-third of the stories analysed concerned a variety of trivial offences. This suggests that instead of talking about 'crime news' as though it were a unitary category, it is necessary to distinguish between at least two types of story. On the one hand, there are 'sensational' stories which are given extended treatment, often on the front page and with accompanying pictures. On the other hand, there are the short, terse, 'mundane' items that are tucked away on the inside pages.[6]

In an analysis of Scottish newspapers, the criminologists Jason Ditton and James Duffy showed that violent and sexual crime constituted 45.8 per cent of all crime news, compared to the police statistics for violent and sexual crime which amounted to 2.4 per cent.[7] Our own research revealed similar findings. Violence against the person constituted 3.62 per cent of all notifiable offences reported by the police. However, such criminal acts comprised 24.7 per cent of crime-related items reported in the quality press, 38.8 per cent in the mid-market press, and 45.9 per cent in the popular press.[8]

Doris Graber found that white collar crimes were 'slighted' to a lesser degree than might be expected, even though they were mentioned less frequently than street crime stories. More interestingly, Graber showed that 'contrary to general belief, white collar crimes received basically the same display as street crime stories in prominent page and section placement, headline size, story length and pictorial coverage.'[9] More recently, the publicity given to cases concerning fraud and insider dealing in the late 1980s both in the USA and Britain has given white collar crime a prominent position in the media.[10]

[5] Roshier, B., 'The Selection of Crime News by the Press,' in S. Cohen and J. Young (eds.), *The Manufacture of News: Deviance, Social Problems and the Mass Media* (London: Constable, 1973), 28–39.

[6] A point developed by Dahlgren, P., 'Crime News: The Fascination of the Mundane', *European Journal of Communication*, 3 (1988), 189–206.

[7] Ditton, J. and Duffy, J., 'Bias in Newspaper Reporting of Crime News', *British Journal of Criminology*, 23 (1983), 159–65. Figures cited from p. 164.

[8] The figures are drawn from official statistics for 1987, the year in which data for the media content study was gathered. They are compared with findings in Schlesinger, P., Tumber, H., and Murdock, G., 'The Media Politics of Crime and Criminal Justice', *British Journal of Sociology*, 42 (1991), 412, table 1.

[9] Graber, *Crime News and the Public*, 37–8.

[10] For a discussion of business scandals see Tumber, H., '"Selling Scandal": Business and the Media', *Media, Culture and Society*, 15 (1993), 345–61; on the

Certainly, the disjuncture between the real incidence of crime (as officially measured) and the patterns of reported crime (as represented by the news media) has remained a continued focus of comment, and there are reasonable empirical grounds for considering that news coverage may colour at least some public perceptions of crime, although this should not be exaggerated. For instance, Roshier's study showed that newspaper readers overestimate the proportion of crimes solved. This was probably because all the English newspapers that were analysed consistently over-represented solved crimes in their coverage. Coupled with the over-representation of trials involving serious sentences, such reporting also exaggerated the odds in favour of a criminal's arrest and conviction.[11]

It has also been suggested by the US sociologist Mark Fishman that the police may at times reinforce journalistically produced concern about a 'crime wave' by selecting further incidents for reporters based on what has been covered before. Furthermore, the police are in a position to initiate perceptions of a crime wave themselves by the way in which they select crime incidents for their press releases. In late 1976, for example, a great deal of publicity and anxiety was generated over an apparent 'crime wave against the elderly' in New York, which even led to a police-sponsored community defence programme. However, official statistics revealed that for the categories of crime committed against the elderly (homicide, purse-snatching, and robbery) a comparison with the previous six months showed a decrease in the figures at the same time as the media were reporting a crime 'surge'.[12]

Under some circumstances, official intervention at an early stage in media crime waves could effectively stop them, provided that the relevant authorities judge them to be undesirable, and that other interests do not try to make political capital out of them.

Guinness affair see Levi, M., 'Sentencing White-Collar Crime in the Dark?: Reflections on the Guinness Four', *The Howard Journal of Criminal Justice*, 30 (1991), 257–79; and on the use of PR in some cases in the USA see Roschwalb, S. A., and Stack, R. A., 'Litigation Public Relations', *Communications and the Law*, 14 (1992), 3–24. For a detailed Dutch study of the social construction of fraud which considers the role of the media in defining the problem, see Brants, C. H., and Brants, K. L. K., *De Sociale Constructie van Fraude* (Arnhem: Gouda Quint BV, 1991).

[11] Roshier, 'The Selection of Crime News', 37.

[12] Fishman, J., 'Crime Waves as Ideology', in S. Cohen and J. Young, (eds.), *The Manufacture of News* (London: Constable: rev. edn., Beverly Hills: Sage, 1981), 98–9.

One such instance concerned the sharp increase in coverage of subway crime in New York in 1977. A few days after the onset of this wave the Chief of the Transit Police publicly denied its existence, and a news conference shortly afterwards given by senior transit authority figures stressed that the subways were safer than the city streets. From that point on subway crime coverage apparently steadily decreased to its previous level of reportage.[13] If correct, this kind of finding does suggest a strategy for official news management where damping-down law and order anxieties is desired— provided, of course, that it is rooted in the real incidence of crime.

In related vein, contemporary concern about television repeatedly focuses on whether or not viewing crime and violence might result in delinquency. For instance, questions have been posed about whether or not violent fictional representations and crime-reporting of disorder might 'cultivate' widespread fear, bring about imitative behaviour or a deadening of public sensibilities.[14] Such themes are part of a discourse upon the 'violent society', in which the representation of such diverse phenomena as inner city riots, football hooliganism, political assassinations, terrorism, and war have been the objects of often spirited debate and considerable research.[15]

Alongside the view that media variously produce deviance or desensitize the public, the debate about fear of crime is largely premissed on the assumption that the media are fear-producing, or, putting it differently, that some kind of clearly distinguishable

[13] Ibid. 112.

[14] The 'cultivation' approach has been extensively developed by George Gerbner and his associates. A relevant example is Gerbner, G., and Gross, L., 'Living with Television: The Violence Profile', *Journal of Communication*, 26 (1976), 173–99. Substantial polemics have ensued. For a useful bibliography see Gerbner, G., Gross, L., Morgan, M., and Signorielli, N., 'Cultural Indicators: A Research Project on Trends in Television Content and Viewer Conceptions of Social Reality', Annenberg School of Communications, University of Pennsylvania, 1 Aug. 1986. Recent British critiques include Gunter, G., *Television and the Fear of Crime* (London: John Libbey, 1987); Docherty, D., *Violence in Television Fiction* (London: John Libbey, 1990); Sparks, R., *Television and the Drama of Crime: Moral Tales and the Place of Crime in Public Life* (Buckingham, Philadelphia: Open University Press, 1992).

[15] This theme has been pursued in a number of studies concerned with deviancy. Of these, amongst the best known are Chibnall, S., *Law-and-Order News: An Analysis of Crime Reporting in the British Press* (London: Tavistock Publishing, 1977); Cohen, S., *Folk Devils and Moral Panics* (London: MacGibbon and Kee, 1972); Cohen, S., and Young, J. (eds.), *Images of Deviance* (Harmondsworth: Penguin, 1971); Hall, S., Critcher, C., Jefferson, T., Clarke, J., and Roberts, B., *Policing the Crisis: Mugging, the State, and Law and Order* (London: Macmillan, 1978).

effect occurs in the perceptions and perspectives of the news consumer as a result of the act of consumption.[16]

For instance, it has been held that portrayals of crime and crime-related themes have led to increased public anxiety and fear of going out on the streets. In fact, the evidence on the relationships between media coverage and fear of crime is far from clear-cut. It would be mistaken to take an undifferentiated view either of crime news or of the audience. There are significant differences in how distinct types of newspapers represent crime, and television likewise differs again. There is some evidence, too, that how the audience consumes news is also subject to substantial variation.[17] Moreover, there is the added complication of how television crime fiction relates in multifold ways to public anxiety and the possibly widespread desire to have at least a fictive resolution to problems that remain threatening and open-ended in everyday life.[18]

If patterns of media crime content vary, then how they are variously consumed by different categories of viewer and reader also becomes rather important. Demographic factors such as age, sex, class background, level of education, area of residence, and so forth, are all germane to the perceptions that audience members bring to bear upon their viewing of television or frame how readers read the newspapers. These factors may significantly shape the extent to which given individuals might or might not personally be anxious about crime and violence.[19]

Although the news media may constitute the main source of factual information about crime, they may not be the key variable in promoting fear of crime. Graber found that her respondents used the media as prime sources for data about crime and criminal justice matters, but used them less frequently as sources for making

[16] For a useful overview on effects see Cumberbatch, G., and Howitt, D., *A Measure of Uncertainty: The Effects of the Mass Media* (London: John Libbey, 1989); also see McQuail, D., *Mass Communication Theory: An Introduction*, 2nd edn. (London: Sage, 1987), ch. 9; and for a relevant review of crime studies in this context see Ericson, R. V., 'Mass Media, Crime, Law, and Justice: An Institutional Approach', *The British Journal of Criminology*, 31 (1991), 219–49.

[17] On television see Gunter, B., *Dimensions of Television Violence* (Aldershot: Gower, 1985). On the press see Williams, P., and Dickinson, H., 'Fear of Crime: Read All about It? The Relationship between Newspaper Crime Reporting and Fear of Crime', *British Journal of Criminology*, 33 (1993), 33–56.

[18] For an extensive discussion of these issues see Sparks, *Television and the Drama of Crime*.

[19] See Schlesinger, P., Dobash, R. E., Dobash, R. P., and Weaver, C. K., *Women Viewing Violence* (London: BFI, 1992) and Williams and Dickinson, 'Fear of Crime'.

evaluations.[20] Thus the identification of the key mediating factors influencing fear of crime is a crucial issue for public policy and, in particular, for crime prevention. Shapland and Vagg suggest that 'When taking decisions on crime prevention programmes, a delicate balance has to be struck between on the one hand, persuading people to take crime (and crime prevention) seriously, and on the other, alarming people, thereby increasing the level of fear.'[21] They go on to list eight aspects of public concern, worry, and fear that have been identified in large-scale surveys, particularly in the British Crime Survey. It is this kind of complex set of factors that lies behind the oft-used slogan 'fear of crime'. This umbrella term includes respondents' opinions about the amount of crime in society; their opinions about the amount of crime in their own area; their perceptions of the likelihood that they will be victimized; overall concern about crime as a problem; concern about the problems posed in their areas by specific forms of crime; fears about going out of doors; avoidance behaviour; precautions taken.[22] From the available survey evidence, each of these aspects appears to have a slightly different association with variables such as age, sex, and class.[23]

A related question concerns the level of public support for and compliance with institutions in the criminal justice arena. Popular detachment from official crime-fighting makes the work of these institutions much harder. Writing about police, courts, and prisons in the USA in the 1970s, Doris Graber remarked:

Lack of support makes the work of these institutions far more difficult and success less likely. It may also lead to reduced appropriations, particularly in periods of tight money when public officials become more conscious of linking budgets to demonstrations of satisfactory performance and public approval. The evidence does not indicate that any of these consequences currently flow from media publicity, but the potential exists. It is quite likely that adverse media stories have been used by parties to

[20] Graber, *Crime News and the Public*, 50.
[21] Shapland, J., and Vagg, J., *Policing by the Public* (London: Routledge, 1988), 110.
[22] Ibid. 111.
[23] For discussion of the variables associated with fear of crime see Toseland, R. W., 'Fear of Crime: Who Is Most Vulnerable?' *Journal of Criminal Justice*, 10 (1982), 199–209, and Maxfield, M., *Explaining Fear of Crime: Evidence from the British Crime Survey*, Home Office Research and Planning Unit Paper no. 43 (London: HMSO, 1987).

political discourse to erode support for these institutions, as currently constituted.[24]

Our own study of Britain in the late 1980s and early 1990s has shown how the police and other groups in the criminal justice arena have developed a public relations offensive to counteract negative publicity and, at times, to gain extra resources. This kind of investment in image-building is likely only to be enhanced given the contemporary debate about police effectiveness in tackling crime.[25]

Making Figures Count

It is questionable whether any easily identifiable causal relationship can be drawn between exposure to television or the press and public perceptions of crime.[26] However, the doubts that beset much academic research about variations in media treatments and their impacts do tend to be wholly absent from most official pronouncements, which still assume the existence of an undifferentiated media effect. In September 1992, for instance, in line with previous such comment, Michael Jack, a Home Office Minister, told the annual conference of the Howard League for Penal Reform that crime statistics were exploited by the media for sensational headlines. He also accused the media of creating disproportionate fear amongst the public: 'Individual crimes, such as the murder of a young mother on Wimbledon Common, are not put into context. Newspapers shouldn't obscure the truth about crime.'[27] Naturally, speaking for a party that had identified itself strongly with law and order, and was evidently failing in the 'war against crime', it was only to be expected that a Conservative spokesman would seek to lay the blame for government shortcomings on the media.

As noted, the Working Group's report had urged the government

[24] Graber, *Crime News and the Public*, 126.

[25] As we conclude writing in July 1993, the Sheehy report concerning the restructuring of the police has just been published and we are witnessing the first steps in debating the government's proposed reforms, centred precisely on questions of resources, performance, and cost-cutting.

[26] For a review of the evidence see Cumberbatch and Howitt *A Measure of Uncertainty*. Wolf, M., *Gli effetti sociali dei media* (Milan: Bompiani, 1992) rightly notes that whatever the methodological problems the question of 'effects' seems inescapable, and it will continue to be discussed and reconceptualized.

[27] Bunting, M., 'Media Exploit Crime Fear', *Guardian*, 10 Sept. 1992, p. 2.

to use the British Crime Survey more often to measure crime: 'the Home Office must ensure that in publishing figures for crimes recorded by the police, due emphasis is given to the findings from the British Crime Survey, which provides a better long term indicator of the level of crime, and any changes'. It also added that the 'British Crime Survey should be carried out more often, and on a regular basis'.[28]

The crime survey was developed as an alternative to the well-recognized deficiencies of government statistics of recorded offences, which are based on the crimes recorded by the police. These 'necessarily exclude those crimes of which the police are ignorant', and the rules for classifying and counting incidents change over time, and also have to be interpreted by police officers when recording them.[29] Crime surveys were developed as an alternative mode of establishing the extent of crime by obtaining testimony directly from victims, but are not without their own shortcomings. For instance, they require identifiable individuals as victims and cannot easily count crimes against organizations, or 'victimless crimes'.[30] The main problem of conducting the British Crime Survey more frequently is one of expense. Whereas recorded crime statistics cost probably no more than £100,000 a year, one sweep of the British Crime Survey is considerably more.[31] The Working Party also suggested that the police needed to provide statistics about local crime in a way that was informative and, if appropriate, reassuring, 'so as to help the media and other groups to set the record straight'. Local crime figures, it was argued, could well be more encouraging than national averages, so it was recommended that chief constables should use their annual reports as a means to this end.[32]

As well as making available the notifiable offences recorded by

[28] Grade, *Report of the Working Group*, 3.
[29] Hough, M., and Mayhew, P., *The British Crime Survey: First Report* (London: HMSO, Home Office Research Study no. 76, 1983), 2.
[30] Ibid. 3–4. Appendix A provides some relevant methodological discussion.
[31] Lewis, C., 'Crime Statistics: Their Use and Misuse' in *Central Statistical Office Social Trends*, 22 (London: Government Statistical Service, 1992), 13–29.
[32] Grade, *Report of the Working Group*, 4. We have illustrated above how media coverage may be used in order to try and extract resources from government. Richard Wells, Chief Constable of South Yorkshire, addressing the same Howard League conference, criticized chief constables for 'massaging' the crime figures precisely for this purpose. He also urged the government to replace crime statistics with a range of performance indicators measuring police effectiveness. See Bunting, 'Media Exploit Crime Fear'.

the police on a quarterly basis (the quarterly statistical bulletins were started in the 1970s), the Home Office also publishes criminal statistics, in an annual series dating back to the nineteenth century.[33] The Home Office has expressed concern that the information the media use could be incorrect or variously misinterpreted, which might then lead to misconceptions about crime and criminal justice issues. It is acknowledged that crime statistics, like all official statistics, may be used by different groups for different purposes. Whereas the authorities may use the figures to inform and guide their policies—and, of course, to justify them—their critics may use them in support of their attacks. There is a consequent wish to reduce their potential for contentiousness. In the words of one Home Office researcher, 'the problem is how to formulate crime figures in a way which is not misleading and informs and improves our understanding of crime.'[34]

Since the publication of the Working Group's report in 1989, debate has continued intermittently over the collection, production, and dissemination of crime statistics. However, there is no complete agreement that the frequency of crime statistics should be reduced. In police quarters, questions have been raised about whether journalists are sufficiently well trained to report crime statistics accurately, whereas editors have riposted that the police remain too censorious or simply do not provide information rapidly enough, thereby preventing background investigation.[35]

Doubts have also been raised about whether publishing local crime statistics would indeed have the effect of reducing fear of crime. Paul Condon, the current Metropolitan Police Commissioner, found in his previous post as Chief Constable of Kent that the crime figures had been deliberately under-reported and clear-up rates had been inflated. He decided to produce 'honest' figures, which partially contributed to a 35 per cent increase in reported crime in 1991. Condon's approach was linked to a redefinition of the role of the police in society, in particular the wish to reduce

---

[33] e.g. the Notifiable Offences Recorded by the Police in England and Wales for 1991 were published in the Home Office *Statistical Bulletin*, issue 2/92 on 9 Mar. 1992.

[34] Lewis, 'Crime Statistics', 13.

[35] See the rather contentious debate at the Guild of British Newspaper Editors' Spring Seminar in Birmingham between Mike Granatt, Director of Public Affairs of the Metropolitan Police, and editors of various regional newspapers, reported in the *UK Press Gazette*, 4 May 1992.

public expectations of their ability to act as 'the sole agency stopping crime'. He observed that 'The public have got sick and tired of hearing chief constables react to rising crime simply by demanding more resources.'[36] If ultimately successful, this ploy in the politics of policing could have far-reaching consequences, as crime figures would be demoted as an indicator of police effectiveness.

To illustrate current practice in reporting crime statistics, we analysed the press and television coverage of the Home Office *Statistical Bulletin of Notifiable Offences Recorded by the Police in England and Wales for 1991*, published on 9 March 1992. The bulletin comprised ten pages of written text, five pages of tables, and a set of notes on the back page. The front page consisted of six main points in the style of headlines, based on the more detailed bulletin inside:

- 5.3 million notifiable offences were recorded by the police in 1991, a rise of sixteen per cent over 1990;
- ninety-four per cent were crimes against property, five per cent were violent crimes;
- car crimes accounted for just under a third of the overall increase of 730,000 offences;
- violent crime increased by six per cent, but incorporated a twenty-five per cent increase in robberies;
- recorded crime increased in all police force areas;
- 1.5 million offences were cleared up in 1991, an increase of seven per cent over 1990.

Beneath those six points, a graph covering the period 1981–91 illustrated the rise in notifiable offences recorded by the police. Accompanying the *Bulletin* was a one-page statement, making eight points, by the then Home Office Minister of State, John Patten. The key point was the first, which offered an official line of interpretation for the statistics:

Today's figures show a welcome slow-down in the trend at the end of 1991 with a comparatively smaller increase in the crime rate towards the end of the year. They also confirm the picture revealed by previous quarterly bulletins that 1991 saw property crime, most strikingly car crime, continue to rise, but violent crime not increasing at the rate it was.

[36] Rose, D., 'The Beat Goes on, but to the Public's Tune', *Observer*, 12 Apr. 1992, p. 55.

The rise in reported crime was presented as a 'slow-down' in the overall trend, and property crime was taken to be the major problem as opposed to violent crime, with car crime singled out. The statement went on to mention measures to discourage crime, concluding with the line that it was personal responsibility that counted (thereby implicitly dismissing causal explanations of criminality). To what extent were these priorities successful in shaping coverage?

Several general points offer a guiding thread through the range of reports discussed. First, the figures were released earlier than anticipated in the politically charged context of the run-up to a General Election campaign. Certainly, this was a distinctive context, but a political framework for reporting is not exceptional since the crime figures are inherently a matter of controversy between the parties. Whilst pre-electoral, or electoral, campaigning may give the debate a particular edge, it is naïve to suppose that crime indicators can ever be treated as above the fray. The party battle conditions news-reporting profoundly, and calls for greater 'responsibility' have to take realistic account of this.

Second, some quite standardized patterns of using news sources were evident, with a highly defined structure of access that privileged spokespeople for the major political parties, the police, and then, in a much lower key, a few 'experts'. Broader contextualization and explanation of crime statistics is apparently the exception rather than the rule. This raises questions about the range of interpretation possible amongst the public.

Third, even if we were to regard the Home Office's press release as the 'primary definition' with the capacity to establish an agenda, there was considerable variation in the priority accorded the story, and in the credibility attached to the government's position. Although the statistics and press release certainly formed the point of departure for all reporting, and the story was an 'obligatory' one, beyond that, however, it was not treated uniformly, and the use of news management was a matter of wide comment.

Fourth, an analysis of news content cannot tell us how such reporting might have been interpreted by different sections of the television audience and newspaper-reading public, or whether or not it contributed to fear of crime. In the analysis that follows we look across a range of national press and television reporting in order to bring out both the common features and variations in how the story was handled. The fact of difference in media coverage ought at least to be a feature of debate about the assumed impact of reporting crime statistics on fear of crime. Confronted with variation, we cannot automatically assume uniformity of response. Nor can we generalize from the one case, and it would be valuable to look at the practice of the news management and reporting of crime statistics over time.

Television Coverage

The crime figures were reported by the BBC's *Nine O'clock News* and ITN's *News At Ten* on their day of release, 9 March 1992. The BBC gave the story marginally more prominence than ITN. Both programmes led with the pensions fraud of the late media magnate, Robert Maxwell. The BBC then devoted its second item to the crime statistics story and its third to the libel case between the boxer Barry McGuigan and his former manager. *News At Ten* chose to run the McGuigan story in second place, placing the crime statistics third.

The *Nine O'Clock News* opened the story with the newsreader stating that reported crime had gone up by more than 16 per cent, with virtually all parts of the country up. The story was then presented by the home affairs correspondent, Neil Bennett, speaking over a short film clip shot inside a police car, followed by a pie chart representing the main categories of crime. It was noted that crimes of violence were still only 5 per cent of the total. The correspondent said that since the Tories had come to power reported crime had more than doubled. This was voiced over a graph showing the rise in crime from 1979 to 1992. It was then observed that the figures had come out early, sparing the government embarrassment in the election campaign, this being voiced over a short film clip of police patrolling at night. The report switched to John Patten, the Home Office Minister, sitting at a desk with books behind him, saying that the crime rate had gone down and that the only people to blame were the criminals (points made in the government's press release). Patten was given twenty seconds. The correspondent then stated that spending on policing had been a priority, but that the level of crime had remained stubbornly resistant; this was spoken over another film clip of police in a computer room, followed by another sequence of police on the beat. Twenty seconds of Roy Hattersley, Labour's Shadow Home Secretary criticizing government inaction, the lack of police officers, and inadequate crime prevention came next. Hattersley was standing at the foot of some stairs. Baroness Seear, speaking at a Liberal Democrat press conference, said that there was a lack of appropriate youth training and social security benefits. She too was given 20 seconds. This precise equality of time accorded spokespersons for the major political parties clearly reflected the rules of equal time applied during election periods, although this was actually a pre-electoral phase of campaigning. In a concluding piece to camera, the home affairs correspondent, outside the Home Office, commented that the early release of the figures would not stop opposition parties from seizing on law and order during the election campaign and that the crime statistics were making the Tories vulnerable in an area of traditional strength.

The BBC's main news programme, then, treated the crime statistics as a major story. Handled by a specialist correspondent, it brought out the rise in crime over time, 'balanced' the government's views with those of opposition figures, and placed the issue in the context of electoral politics. Its visual treatment mixed graphics of statistics with the talking heads of politicians and a recurrent background of police work.

News At Ten led the story similarly to the *Nine O'Clock News*, with the newsreader first saying that recorded crime had risen by 16 per cent, and that the increase was lower than expected, and with the Home Office Minister, John Patten, reported as saying that the crime figures showed a welcome slow-down. Opposition parties had said the figures were truly appalling and accused the Government of issuing them early to avoid bad publicity in the run-up to the election. The report then moved to the crime correspondent, Robin White, who, over film of the Home Office exterior, said that the figures released from the Home Office were every bit as bad as predicted. Over film of Parliament, the crime correspondent said that MPs were on the starting-block for the election and that the crime figures could not have come out at a worse time for the government. They had risen by 16 per cent, with 94 per cent being crimes against property, and crimes of violence up by 6 per cent. *News At Ten* showed a graph of the rise in crime from 1981 to 1992 under the Conservatives (in line with the Home Office's data, rather than from 1979 as did the BBC). The crime correspondent voiced over the graph, saying that the last two years had seen the largest jump since the Tories had come to power and that Labour saw this as a source of urgent concern. Roy Hattersley, standing outside Westminster, said he intended to make sure that the issue was prominent in the election because it affected people's lives. He was given 15 seconds. The item then cut straight to John Patten in a shot largely identical to the BBC's, commenting on the Tories' lead in opinion polls over other parties on law and order. He too was given 15 seconds. Following Patten, the crime correspondent voiced over a film of Baroness Seear at the Liberal Democrats' press conference, quoting her as saying that crime was intolerable. Over film of the Home Secretary, Kenneth Baker, leaving Number 10 and a clip of a policewoman investigating a car break-in, the correspondent observed that the Home Office had antagonized some police officers by new initiatives on crime. The correspondent went on to state (over shots of a police officer) that police feared that this was an attempt to divert attention from what they perceived to be the real problem, what one police chief had described as the social and economic malaise caused by the recession. Next came Helen Peggs of Victim Support, with 10 seconds to state that some victims could be burgled four times in a year. Over a further clip of two police catching a criminal on the street, the correspondent reported that many rank and file officers thought the problem was exacerbated by serious undermanning. This was followed by 10 seconds of Richard Critchley of the West Yorkshire Police Federation, who said that the police were losing the battle. The report ended with the correspondent's piece to camera noting that some polls suggested that crime was running close to the economy as the major election issue.

ITN's report offered access to more varied sources than did the BBC's, with more perspectives on policing and on victims. However, as with the BBC, the story was given prominence, handled by a specialist, and placed in an electoral context. In both programmes, John Patten was seated in a ministerial setting, with connotations of authority, whereas Roy Hattersley's appearances suggested that he was between meetings, and the Liberal Democrat context was a press conference. This might conceivably have played some role in how the audience perceived the political arguments. Nevertheless, access was as of right for the main parties, which, as we shall see, was not the case in all of the press. Moreover, the thrust of both programmes was to report the rise in crime (rather than to stress, as did the government's press release, the 'slow-down in the trend'). The relevance of rising crime as an electoral issue and the likelihood of news management by the government were also made apparent.

The Quality Press

The story was covered on 10 March 1992 by *The Times*, the *Independent*, the *Daily Telegraph*, the *Guardian*, and the *Financial Times*. The *Independent*'s front-page story began thus: 'Crime increased by sixteen per cent in England and Wales during 1991 according to figures released yesterday', and went on to say that publication had come nearly three weeks earlier than expected, provoking opposition accusations that the government was getting damaging statistics out of the way before the election proper began. The *Guardian* also mentioned their early release (this time in its long page 2 report), as did the *Financial Times* (in a short story on page 10 headed 'Recorded Crime up 16 per cent a Year'). *The Times* and the *Telegraph*, however, did not mention the question of the early release of the figures.

The *Financial Times*'s story, one column of sixteen centimetres on page 10, covered most of the headline points mentioned in the Home Office bulletin, quoting Patten's view that the figures showed a welcome slow-down in the rate of increase and adding 'figures for October 1990 to September last year showed a record nineteen per cent annual rise.'[37] Roy Hattersley, Labour's Shadow Home Secretary, was next quoted as saying that the figures were truly appalling. The story then largely paraphrased the press release on violent crime, car crimes, and the police's successes, but noted that there had been a fall in the clear-up rate.

The Times covered the published statistics on page 5, in a column of 21 centimetres. The first paragraph noted that recorded crime in England and Wales had risen by 16 per cent in the past year to 5.3 million—a point made in common with all the other qualities. However, the second paragraph (helpfully from the government's point of view) went on to say 'the statistics obscure the fact that the average annual rate of increase between 1982 and 1992 was 6 per cent and that there are numerous reasons why an increase might be recorded. Almost 30 per cent of all crimes

---

[37] Column centimetres are comparable between newspapers of the same type.

involve cars, 94 per cent were against property and 5 per cent violent crimes.' It continued: 'a total of 730,000 more offences were recorded last year, the increase includes 140,000 more thefts from motor vehicles (up 18 per cent); 90,000 more thefts of vehicles (up 18 per cent); 210,000 more burglaries (up 21 per cent); and 88,000 more offences of criminal damage (up 12 per cent).' This ran against the government's up-beat gloss on the figures.

The *Independent*'s front-page report discussed the question of possible news management extensively. It quoted Patten 'as rejecting allegations of manipulation' and as explaining early publication by needing to publish before Parliament dissolved. The article went on to cite senior Home Office civil servants as suggesting 'that there was nothing sinister about the early release of the figures. There was no set date for the issuing of crime statistics, as soon as they were ready they were out.' The next paragraph, testing this claim, noted that 'the 1990 figures were released on 26 March last year, the previous year's on 29 March 1990. On both occasions the Home Office issued graphs of other statistics which some observers suggested was designed to divert attention from high increases.' Hattersley's 'truly appalling' remark was quoted, together with his view that the figures had been rushed out to keep law and order off the election agenda. The *Independent* was the only quality paper to quote the Liberal Democrat spokesman, Robert MacLennan, who said that the rate was 'intumescent because the government had failed to tackle the social roots of lawlessness'.

In a further article, on page 3, headlined 'Total Number of Crimes Could Top Six Million this Year', Terry Kirby, the crime correspondent, examined the trends shown by the crime figures. The report spread over four columns to a total of 84 centimetres; half reproduced two tables from the Home Office *Statistical Bulletin*. Apart from John Patten, Professor Jock Young of the Centre for Criminology at Middlesex Polytechnic was quoted as saying 'it's completely wrong to keep looking at the figures in terms of a percentage increase over the previous year because the base rate keeps going up.' In addition, the Association of Chief Police Officers was cited as cautioning 'against using reported crime as a measure of police performance'.

The *Guardian* devoted its main page 2 story—five columns totalling 90 centimetres—to the crime figures, under the headline 'Tories Try to Play down Sixteen per Cent Rise in Crime'. A report by John Carvel, home affairs editor, included a map of Britain showing the increase in notifiable offences recorded by the police according to force areas. The other graphic was of the percentage increase in all types of recorded crime, along the same lines as one reproduced in the *Independent*. The *Guardian*, apart from quoting the Home Secretary and Roy Hattersley, also cited a Liberal Democrat spokesperson as saying that the rise in crime was intolerable. The Chairman of ACPO also figured as a quoted source.

A further story by John Carvel, headlined 'Researchers Link the Recession with Number of Offences', took up two columns totalling 36 centimetres. The article noted that Britain was suffering the worst reported crime wave on record and that it had been forecast by government researchers, who had established a statistical relationship between rising crime and economic recession.

The story in the *Daily Telegraph*, though similar to that of the *Financial Times* and *The Times*, was deemed important enough to be put on the front page. The first five paragraphs covered the main points in the Home Office bulletin, and like the *Financial Times*, in the final two paragraphs first John Patten's views were reported, followed by Roy Hattersley's comments. The piece occupied one column of 21 centimetres.

The quality press, then, reported the story in distinctive ways. Whereas *The Times*, *Financial Times*, and *Daily Telegraph* largely concentrated on retailing and briefly interpreting the crime figures, both the *Independent* and the *Guardian* took a more broadly contextual approach that offered scope for a wider range of sources to express their views, with the three main political parties represented, as well as an 'expert' view and that of the police. They also gave the story major treatment. The *Independent* raised questions about Home Office news management, whereas the *Guardian* squarely presented the figures in the context of electoral politics, and also sought a socio-economic explanation for the growth of crime.

The Mid-Market Press

None of the mid-market papers carried the story on their front pages. The *Daily Express* ran it on page 4 under its 'Election Countdown' logo and did not signal it clearly, mixing it up with a gay sex arrest 'MP Quits' headline. The crime statistics story, by

Will Stuart, political editor, was sub-headlined 'Worrying Rise in Rape and Murder' and ran for two columns totalling 42 column centimetres. Over half of the space was taken up with a pie chart showing different types of crime committed in 1991. The written text reported that 'Each day two people were murdered and eleven women raped,' and suggested 'government figures also reveal that the police are failing to keep pace with the rising tide, in that fewer than 3 in 10 of all crimes in 1991 were solved.' The sole quotation came from John Patten, welcoming the 'slow-down', and the below average rise in violent crime and sex offences. The report noted the 19 per cent rise in rape, the record figures for gross indecency with children, and the rise in car crime.

By contrast with this relatively low-key treatment, the *Daily Mail* gave the story major treatment across four columns on page 9, with a pro-government headline, 'The Tide Is Turning against Crime Wave'. Bylined Peter Burden, chief crime correspondent, the story ran for 68 column centimetres. It contained a graph of changes in quarterly crime from 1987 to 1991, and a table showing the rise in offences during 1991. In line with the Home Office's press release, the report began by stating that crime had grown by 16 per cent, with recorded offences reaching 5.3 million, but stated that the surge had begun to slow down. John Patten was quoted as welcoming this and police chiefs as explaining that increases were partly due to greater public readiness to report crime. The last paragraph noted that the government's record on law and order had faced criticism in the build-up to the election: 'Last month senior police officers in London linked the crime figures to the recession and social deprivation. The one-year figures to the end of December that are normally released at the end of March were published early because they were ready, said the Home Office.' Thus professional and political criticism were, in effect, buried at the end of the report.

For its part, *Today* reported the crime figures as the main story on page 4, headlined 'Ten Crimes a Minute', subheadlined 'Offences Top a Record 5.3 Million, Kidnapping Cases up by 40% and Burglary is the Number One Offence'. The story spread over four columns totalling 48 column centimetres. Written by Evelyn Black, political correspondent, the report highlighted offences showing a marked increase, singling out burglary, car thefts, and kidnapping. It then noted that all police forces had reported more crime, the biggest rises coming in rural areas. The early release of the figures was mentioned, as was the Home Office's denial that this was a political ploy. John Patten and Roy Hattersley's stock quotations were used, with a concluding prediction from Jock Young that the crime rate would hit 6 million by 1993.

The mid-market press, then, handled the crime figures in a variety of ways, and these clearly related to political priorities. The *Express* departed from the agenda of the press release to articulate popular concern about violent and sexual crime, identified problems of policing, and named only John Patten as a source. The *Mail* took an overtly pro-government line in its interpretation of the statistics, although it noted the controversy over their early release in passing. Finally, *Today* went against the grain of the Home Office line by underlining specific increases in various crimes, and also quoted an opposition spokesman and an expert.

The Popular Press

The *Sun*'s coverage emphasized sexual murder and violent crime, initially concentrating on rape. The crime figures were covered on page 7 in two small columns, totalling 12 centimetres, headlined 'Tory Vow on Crime':

Home Office Minister John Patten yesterday pledged more action to combat Britain's rising crime wave. He spoke as new figures reveal a record 4,046 women were raped last year compared with 3,391 in 1990. The average of 11 rapes a day in England and Wales in 1991 is an increase of 19.3 per cent over the past five years. The figures showed a record of 5.3 million offences of all kinds, most, 94%, were against property.

Tory vows to boost police numbers and a reference to tougher laws concluded the piece.

By contrast with this short report, the *Daily Mirror* carried the crime statistics as the main page 2 story on its Home News page. Headlined 'Crime is Twice as High Under Tories', the report by Sylvia Jones, crime correspondent, took a quite explicit oppositional stance, and ran across five columns, amounting to 77 column centimetres. It carried a graphic of two men attacking an elderly person captioned 'Robberies up 25%, Rape up 19%, Car Offences up 18% and Violence up 6%,' and opened saying 'crime figures soared to a record 5,300,000 last year, more than double the total when the Tories rode to power on promises of better law and order.' It continued:

The latest devastating statistics, released early to avoid embarrassing the government in the middle of an election campaign, will finally crush the myth that the country is safer under the Conservatives. The Home Office figures released yesterday show that every 6 seconds a crime is committed somewhere in England and Wales, every 20 seconds a car is broken into, every 30 seconds a burglar strikes and every minute someone's property is damaged.

Reversing the usual order, Hattersley was quoted first as saying the figures were appalling, with Baroness Seear, the Liberal Democrat, cited as further commenting that the rise was intolerable. The story then quoted Patten, but prefixed this with: 'In an extraordinary attempt to whitewash the figures Home Office Minister John Patten claimed "they show a welcome slow-down from the even bigger jump the previous year". In fact the difference was just one per cent.' Criticism from Jock Young (described as a top crime analyst) followed, as did a Scotland Yard commander's view that a direct link between crime levels and social and economic malaise existed. Albert Pacey, Chief Constable of Gloucestershire, was reported to dispute government claims to have greatly strengthened police manpower. More than in any of the other papers, the story was overtly geared to attacking the Conservatives, using named sources as well as its own interpretation of the figures to effect this.

The popular press therefore offered two sharply contrasting approaches. Whereas the *Sun* gave the story very little space, the *Mirror* gave it considerable play. The *Sun* stressed the rise in rape, but otherwise privileged the government's line. The *Mirror* emphasized the rise in various forms of crime, blamed the Conservatives for this, noted the news management attempt, quoted opposition parties and an expert view together with police concern, and where it quoted Patten, did so to discredit him.

News Source and Reporting Rituals

Our study of news source strategies and their battle for the news agenda has been detailed above. As we have shown, the complex processes involved in this are by no means readily discernible from a reading of the news text. However, the 'battle for public interpretations', as the Australian media researcher, Rodney Tiffen terms it, is more directly manifest in news content.[38] Explanations

[38] Tiffen, R., *News and Power* (Sydney: Allen & Unwin, 1989), 91.

of crime in the news are undoubtedly linked to current political struggles and are deployed predictably.[39] Our case study of the reporting of crime statistics is an instance of the attempt by politicians of different political parties to win the battle for legitimacy by apportioning blame, whether on the criminal, the police, or the opposition. In other instances—notoriously terrorism and riots— the media themselves often become a prime object of blame.

Gaye Tuchman has argued that this way of representing explanation is characteristic of journalistic production routines. By presenting 'conflicting possibilities', or by opposing alternative explanations of events, the journalist solves the problem of seeking out the truth. In her terms, objectivity is attained by quoting from, or referring to, credible sources. This practice functions as a 'strategic ritual' to deflect criticisms of partiality.[40] Apart from such journalistic rituals, in the conflicts over crime statistics we also regularly witness the enactment of political rituals, where politicians take established stands and utter expected comments.[41] There is, therefore, a fit between the ritualized reporting adopted by the media and the ritualized position-taking of political news sources. Moreover, as news sources gain credibility with journalists they enter into more routinized relations. As we have shown in Part I, pressure groups such as NACRO may achieve increased legitimacy the more journalists rely upon them to provide alternative comments or positions to those of the government or other state bodies. As such news sources become more sophisticated in recognizing the routine formats of news production, and learn to provide well-tailored information subsidies, their comments or explanations may become part of the 'strategic rituals' of journalists.

Many studies of news production and content have indicated the lack of causal explanation in news discourse. More specifically, as Ericson et al. point out, 'crime stories rarely address the causes of

---

[39] Tumber, H., *Television and the Riots* (London: BFI, 1982), 50; Ericson, R. V., Baranek, P. M., and Chan, J. B. L., *Representing Order: Crime, Law, and Justice in the News Media* (Milton Keynes: Open University Press, 1991), 269.

[40] Tuchman, G., 'Objectivity as Strategic Ritual: An Examination of Newsmen's Notions of Objectivity', *American Journal of Sociology*, 77 (1971/2), 660–79.

[41] These may take various forms, are especially obvious and elaborate in moments of profound threat to the social order, and often articulate with major media coverage. See Elliott, P., 'Press Performance as Political Ritual', in H. Christian (ed.), *The Sociology of Journalism and the Press* (Keele: Sociological Review Monograph 29, 1980), 141–77.

crime.'[42] The crime statistics story would appear to bear out this contention. In addition, the comments by Patten and Hattersley accompanying the media publication of the crime figures conform to a pattern discerned by other researchers. Suggesting a number of reasons why explanations are not a routine feature of news discourse, Ericson *et al.* state: 'Beyond the format constraints of the medium and the organizational constraints of journalists, news sources often wish to eschew causal explanation, especially in terms of the structure and process of their own organizations. When sources do offer explanations, it is typically in pursuit of their own legitimacy and often through a process of blaming others.'[43] Both Chibnall and Ericson *et al.* have argued that when explanations can be discerned, they tend to be signalled by terms such as 'violent' and 'criminal' which 'carry unambiguous connotations and meld together disparate phenomena and their meanings'.[44]

The above case study has shown how important was the argument over the early release of the crime figures. The timing was contentious because of an impending General Election. The Labour party argued that the statistics were being released early in order to get some bad news out of the way before the election. In fact, law and order did not, in the end, figure very prominently in the election campaign.[45]

The argument over the early release of the crime figures was also part of a wider and continuing row about the compilation and publication of government statistics. In particular, the number of changes made by the Conservative government in how unemployment figures are calculated has led to accusations of abuse, manipulation, and bureaucratic propaganda each time the figures are published and reported by the news media.[46] Drawing attention to

[42] Ericson *et al.*, *Representing Order*, 268.

[43] Ibid.; also see Tumber, *Television and the Riots*.

[44] Chibnall, *Law-and-Order News*, pp. xi–xii; also see Ericson *et al.*, *Representing Order*, 269.

[45] See Butler, D. and Kavanagh, D., *The British General Election of 1992* (Basingstoke: Macmillan, 1992), chs. 8 and 9.

[46] See Altheide, D. L. and Johnson, J. M., *Bureaucratic Propaganda* (Boston: Allyn & Bacon, Inc., 1980), esp. ch. 1. For a discussion of government management of statistics and information policy under President Reagan see Demac, D., *Keeping America Uninformed* (New York: Pilgrim Press, 1984) and *Liberty Denied* (New Brunswick: Rutgers University Press, 1989). On the UK see Tumber, 'Taming the Truth', *British Journalism Review*, 4 (1993), 37–41 and 'Marketing Politics: The

news management in the reporting of official statistics, therefore, has become a regular element of news discourse. In our case study, the impending General Election was the main reason why news management became a matter of journalistic reporting and analysis.

Conclusion

Evidence as to which aspects of media coverage cause or constitute fear of crime is inconclusive. The sensational reporting of sexual crime and violent crime, the representation of victims, dramatic reconstructions, fictional representations, stories of police failure or corruption, and various combinations of the above, have all been cited as possible or potential inducers of fear.

The reporting of crime statistics has also been targeted as a culprit because news coverage invariably distorts the official account. However, the publication and reporting of crime statistics is one of the few ways that the public can obtain a wider picture of crime, however unsatisfactory this may be judged to be. Most reporting is highly selective, as might be expected, and does not offer any significant background explanation. There is a case for discussing how this might change. So far as the public is concerned, to the best of our knowledge no detailed study of how specific social groups react to crime statistics has been undertaken. Thus, it is largely on the basis of mere presumption about questionable effects that a reduction in the frequency of publication of crime statistics is advocated. However unsatisfactory present journalistic practice may be judged to be, a diminution in the published evidence available is likely to deny necessary information to the public. It is only on an informed basis that the public may exercise its democratic right to make judgements about the conduct of policy. The routine reporting of crime statistics enables debate to occur about both the government's and the police's effectiveness in tackling crime. Moreover, the specific case for showing how they contribute to fear of crime has yet to be convincingly made.

Americanization of Government Information Policy in Britain', in P. H. Melling and J. R. Roper (eds.), *Encountering America: The Impact of American Culture on Europe, 1945 Onwards* (Lampeter: Edward Mellen, in press).

7

A Tale of Acquittal

CRIMES disrupt the social order by infringing the law. The criminal justice process is an institutionalized way of restoring legally guaranteed order, and within the implementation of legal sanctions against criminals, the trial is a particularly important symbolic moment. Inasmuch as law is taken to be the embodiment of the social will to enforce certain kinds of rule, the media representation of what goes on in the courtroom communicates judicial judgments to the public about specific kinds of rule-breaking action. In the present chapter, and the next, it is not our intention to analyse the process of court reporting as such.[1] Rather, we have taken the conclusions of two important trials during our fieldwork period as the objects of analysis and examine the media reaction to the judgment in each case. We have provided our own interpretation of the texts. How these stories were variously interpreted by different categories of reader and viewer must remain a matter of speculation, although other studies suggest that, at one level, the daily consumption of crime news is a routine way for the public to work out its views on human behaviour and morality and use this knowledge in everyday life.[2]

The story presented in this chapter concerns the shooting of an innocent citizen by a law-enforcer, by no means an isolated event, although in Britain certainly a rarity. This is particularly interesting, because violence properly used by the police is normally seen

[1] This still remains to be done. The nearest to such an account is to be found in Ericson, R. V., Baranek, P. M., and Chan, J. B. L., *Negotiating Control: A Study of News Sources* (Toronto: University of Toronto Press, 1989), ch. 2.

[2] We know virtually nothing about what crime news means to readers, viewers, and listeners. Two insightful speculations based on qualitative content analysis are to be found in Katz, J., 'What Makes Crime "News"?', *Media, Culture and Society*, 9 (1987), 47–75, and Dahlgren, P., 'Crime News: The Fascination of the Mundane', *European Journal of Communication*, 3 (1988), 189–206. Both believe that crime news is integrated into everyday problem solving about often quite unconnected practical issues in people's lives.

as the legitimate exercise of force.[3] When the rules governing such uses of force are broken, the edifice of official legitimacy is shaken, and how news-reporting handles fear of the arbitrary or wrongful use of authority becomes an issue. It is this theme—fear of official violence, rather than the more conventional focus on fear of crime—that we wish to highlight.

The trial of a law-enforcer runs counter to the conventional public expectations about who constitutes a criminal. For most citizens, on an everyday basis, the police are the symbolic and physical embodiments of the law. When a police officer is tried for a misdemeanour, therefore, in a sense the very process of law-enforcement is itself put on trial, and the outcome may be taken as a particularly significant comment on the effectiveness of criminal justice.

The Lovelock Acquittal

The case in question was one of police deviance with profound racial implications. The police officer was white and the victim black; moreover, the action was taken by a man against a woman, thereby adding a further, complicating, gender dimension, although this did not attract any significant attention.

An experienced police officer, Inspector Douglas Lovelock, in the course of searching for a young black male, Michael Groce, wanted for questioning about an armed robbery, had shot and disabled that suspect's mother, Mrs Cherry Groce. The incident had occurred in the London district of Brixton, where many black people live, and had sparked off serious public disorder. A comprehensive analysis of news coverage of the officer's acquittal on a charge of unlawful and malicious wounding discloses a repertoire of available themes which are combined in various ways by different news media to produce distinctive treatments.

First, there is a policy question, namely the danger of armed policing where weapons training might be inadequate; second, the matter of how race is linked to public order, otherwise framed as the police *v.* the black community, which links into an established history of race-reporting in Britain; and third, a human interest

---

[3] A discussion of related issues concerning political violence, media, and legitimacy is in Schlesinger, P., *Media, State and Nation: Political Violence and Collective Identities* (London: Sage, 1991), chs. 1–4.

angle—the trauma experienced by two families, black and white. In what follows, we analyse the coverage by media sector, bringing out variations in news treatment whilst at the same time demonstrating some striking commonalities, particularly in the use of sources.

The Quality Press

The story received front-page coverage on 16 January 1987 by the *Guardian*, the *Independent*, *The Times*, and the *Daily Telegraph* and, in each case, apart from reporting of the outcome of the trial, a variety of related news reports and features was carried. The *Guardian*, *Independent*, and *Telegraph* also carried editorials.

The *Guardian* and *Telegraph* had front-page photographs of a serious-looking Inspector Lovelock leaving court with his daughter, and *The Times* ran one in its extensive page 3 spreads, sharply contrasting it with a close-up of Mrs Groce lying in a hospital bed, her face framed by a pillow. The *Telegraph* had a full-face passport photo of Mrs Groce. All the front-page headlines focused on the police officer's acquittal: 'Inspector cleared by jury of malicious wounding' (the *Guardian*); 'Inspector cleared of Groce shooting' (the *Independent*); 'Inspector who shot woman is acquitted' (the *Daily Telegraph*); 'Police gunman in Brixton raid cleared by jury' (*The Times*).

It was the *Telegraph*'s headline that stressed the 'transitivity' of the crucial action: namely, who had done what to whom.[4] *The Times* used the ambiguous term 'gunman', which carries connotations of outlawry. The front-page news reports, carried over on to the back page by both the *Guardian* and *Telegraph*, and on to page 3 by *The Times*, all covered largely the same points.

All noted that the jury (which included two black men) accepted the Inspector's account that the shooting had been 'accidental'; that Mr Lovelock and other officers involved in the raid would be facing internal disciplinary hearings, although the Inspector would be reinstated; that Mrs Groce would be pursuing a claim for damages for negligence against the police (*The Times* reported 'police sources' as saying this could be as much as £300,000). All the reports noted in passing that the acquittal brought gasps of relief

---

[4] See Fowler, R., *Language in the News: Discourse and Ideology in the Press* (London and New York: Routledge, 1991), 70–80.

and sobs from friends and relatives of the accused. The Inspector's whispered 'Thank you' to the jury was also briefly mentioned. These latter characterizations of the end-of-trial moment connected with the human interest factor displayed in the photographs, but in low-key form; as we shall see, by contrast this approach received considerable play both in the mid-market and popular press. Finally, the reports all provided some minimal details of the police's search for Mrs Groce's son, Michael, believed by them to be armed, and the circumstances under which a tense and exhausted Inspector Lovelock shot Mrs Groce in her bedroom.

Extensive use was made of quoted, or of otherwise identified, sources.[5] Indeed, these constituted a set of building blocks from which the reports were largely assembled. For instance, the *Guardian* quoted a statement from the Metropolitan Police saying that the officer would be reinstated that went on to say: 'Inspector Lovelock has suffered considerably on a personal basis from his experience and it is therefore unlikely that he would ever wish to carry a firearm again.' This was followed by a quotation from Mrs Groce's solicitor, the left-wing lawyer Paul Boateng (now a Labour MP), saying that both she and the policeman would have to live with the consequences. His statement concluded: 'Nothing can ever really compensate her for what has happened. She meanwhile continues to pick up the pieces of her life without bitterness or hatred and wishes only to be left alone to do so.' These words were also carried by the *Independent*. *The Times*, *Telegraph*, and *Independent* all quoted from a statement issued by Lovelock's solicitor (glossed by the *Guardian*): 'Inspector Lovelock wishes to express sincere personal regret for the injury caused to Mrs Groce in this tragic accident. He also wishes to thank his family and friends for all their support and assistance.' Such statements, all issued on behalf of parties to the dispute, stressed either personal suffering or regret for causing injury, thereby underlining the human or tragic dimension. They also embodied attempts to define the nature of the event and the main actors' attitudes.

Other kinds of statement by named sources centred on the policy and procedural features of the case and the wider consequences for criminal justice and law-enforcement. Right at the end of the *Guardian*'s main report, Julian Lewis, chairman of Lambeth

---

[5] For a discussion of the use of quotations and sources in race reporting see van Dijk, T. A., *Racism and the Press* (London: Routledge, 1991), ch. 6.

Council's police committee, described the acquittal as 'a gross mis-
carriage of justice', whereas in the *Independent*, also near the end,
he was quoted saying, 'This verdict seems to suggest that police can
gun down black people with impunity.' Other observations critical
of police conduct also appeared in the body of the front-page
reports. *The Times* cited Michael Groce, the victim's son originally
sought by the police, as saying: 'Justice was not done. . . . It was
not a court out there today. It was a show,' and that such shootings could be repeated 'whether you are black or white'. The
Independent was alone in presenting the view of Linda Bellos,
leader of Lambeth Council, who predicted 'If the police use the
word "exonerated" there will be a violent reaction.'

The critical statements cited above—in general coming late in
the story—first raised major questions about the efficacy of the
criminal justice system in providing remedies for violence committed by the police, and second, drew attention to the racial dimension, which was otherwise not touched upon as a structuring
theme, but rather left implicit. The National Council for Civil
Liberties, cited only once in all the news coverage, and then at the
end of the *Guardian*'s report, called for Home Office guidelines on
the use of police guns to be given the force of law. This theme will
be considered below.

With the exception of the *Independent*, the quality press coverage did not take up such critical themes in its follow-up reports,
largely restricting the perspectives available to those that derived
from police sources. A range of alternative reactions to the acquittal were therefore made available in the page 1 reporting but, given
the 'inverted pyramid' style of news-reporting, did not frame the
overall construction of the event. Background articles and features
were mainly concerned with how the police's procedures had
allowed such an incident to occur. Indeed, the acquittal became the
occasion for a police procedural story.

The *Telegraph*'s page 3 spread consisted of four articles, topped
by a cartoon strip containing four frames which showed, first, the
door of the Groce house being knocked down by armed police;
second, the police entering; third, Lovelock kicking open a door;
and finally, 'A "shape" moves on his left. He "tenses" and the gun
goes off. Mrs Groce is hit in the chest.' The caption under the last
image derived directly from Inspector Lovelock's testimony in
court. The entire sequence of images was described as 'The split

second of "tension" that paralysed Cherry Groce.' The quotation-marks signified the newspaper's formal distance from the point of view expressed. However, at the same time, the cartoon precisely reproduced the standpoint of the police officer and not that of Mrs Groce, the agent's angle of vision rather than that of the acted upon. Moreover, of the *Telegraph*'s four stories, the police were evidently the sole source for three.

The longest story, a two-column report headlined 'Mistakes that led Lovelock into tragedy', began thus: 'A combination of misinformation, inter-force friction, failure to make routine checks and the volatile nature of Brixton led Insp. Douglas Lovelock into a position where senior officers believe the tragic outcome was almost inevitable.'

This formulation—stressing 'inevitability'—constructed the violent action as the result of forces virtually beyond the control of the individual. The report listed a series of police errors detailed in a '15-inch thick report by Mr John Domaille, Assistant Chief Constable of West Yorkshire for the Police Complaints Authority'. Central to these was inaccurate information about whether or not Michael Groce had been armed and a failure to establish who was in Mrs Groce's house in advance of making the raid. Inspector Lovelock's belief—retailed to the court—that 'I would be confronted with an armed and dangerous criminal' was cited. The report quoted extensively from named and unnamed senior police officers, of whom one said, 'Considering that the entry party knew nothing about the layout of the house, and had no idea of whom they might find inside, what happened next could have been anticipated. But what do you do in a place like Brixton? Those involved believe that what they did was right. It would be very hard to convince them otherwise.'

This comment both 'explained' the shooting and justified it from the police point of view, setting the action taken in hostile territory—a theme developed more extensively elsewhere, as we shall see. However, the alternative option of following standard procedure—waiting until an armed gunman surrenders—was embodied in a quotation from Chief Superintendent Bob Wells, head of Metropolitan firearms training. Another senior officer was quoted as questioning the action but also as pointing out the problems of policing Brixton. Directly underneath the long report, the *Telegraph* carried a brief profile of Inspector Lovelock titled 'A reliable leader', described by 'one of his senior officers' as a man '"others were happy to follow, as he always knew what he was doing"'. This offered a mere glimpse from a human interest point of view, telling of the policeman's place of birth, his police career, and his family circumstances, including a second marriage.

The remaining two reports concentrated on other distinct aspects of the story. The first, headlined 'Innocents could still get shot, say police' quoted 'senior police officers' as saying 'they have accepted that people will be shot in a society that requires the use of firearms by police, and have decided that there will be no further changes in firearms training as a result of the Brixton incident'. Once again, this stressed the 'inevitable' outcomes of a system and thereby diminished the individual responsibility for the use of violence. The article noted the reduction in authorized armed police in the Metropolitan force from 4,600 to 3,000 since the 1983 shooting in error in London of Stephen Waldorf, a film editor mistaken for a wanted criminal. It also recounted the 'stringent selection process' for those being trained. Police professionalism in training, it implied, could not prevent the occasional accident from happening. This view was summed up in a graphic quotation from Chief Superintendent Wells: 'There is nothing in what we have done that would change the position once two people are three feet apart, in the three-eighths of a second they have to decide, one may fire.' Echoes of this comment abounded in the press-reporting.

The final article—'Shot that shattered harmony in Brixton'— detailed the impact of the Groce shooting on Brixton (impliedly 'harmonious' rather than a site of long-standing tension between police and black community) and told of 'two nights of rioting, leaving Brixton a "no-go" area', of the death of a *Sunday Telegraph* photographer, the rape of two girls, damage to business, and Brixton police station under siege. It was concerned with public disorder as effect, but not with its causes. Three of the four *Telegraph* stories, then, privileged the police as source, with space to put their tactics in context. General reassurance about firearms policy was also offered, based on police testimony.

Apart from carrying over its page 1 story onto page 3, *The Times* ran two other substantial reports. The main story was topped by 'Guidelines ignored as officers stormed house in search of armed man: Repeated police bungling led to rioting.' By referring to procedural error and inefficiency, this offered a much more forthright condemnation of police practice than did the *Telegraph*'s headline. The lead paragraph also took this line: 'A disastrous police operation plagued by rule-bending, inter-force rivalry, hastiness and negligent intelligence was exposed during the trial of Inspector Douglas Lovelock, who was cleared yesterday of maliciously wounding Mrs Dorothy "Cherry" Groce.' The report continued by referring to Inspector Lovelock's belief that he might confront a 'violent young criminal who had already fired at police with a sawn-off shotgun and was likely to fire again to resist arrest'. Instead the house contained Mrs Groce and other members of her family. The effect of the shooting was to cause public disorder, described in terms broadly similar to the *Telegraph*. The report then detailed the poor communication between Hertfordshire detectives seeking Michael Groce and the Metropolitan Police. In particular, the Met. were under the erroneous impression that Groce had fired a shotgun at the Hertfordshire policemen seeking to arrest him, and Met. officers misidentified Mrs Groce's house as a likely location for the fugitive.

Again, the problem of policing in Brixton was noted: 'A surveillance operation was ruled out because it was certain to be discovered. An approach to Lambeth Council, which owned the house was ruled out because it was feared that the left-wing local authority might leak details of the plan.' This tended to shift responsibility from the police to the unpropitious circumstances in which they had to operate in a hostile community run by an impliedly politically suspect council. The police, however, the report continued, had failed to follow the official policy of containment when armed suspects were believed to be in a house. Investigating officers were reported as saying 'that once the inspector was inside the house with his revolver drawn, given his training and the circumstances that prevailed, there was a very great chance that he would fire'. Again, the police-derived view of 'inevitability' came to the fore.

The linked report was headlined 'Scotland Yard disarms 238 detectives' and connected the proposed reduction in authorized armed officers in the Metropolitan Police with the Groce shooting and an impending Home Office report on armed policing. It went on to note extra training requirements and the reduction in numbers of those authorized to handle guns. Police rethinking had come in the wake of the Waldorf case in London in 1983 and that of John Shorthouse, a young boy shot by police in Birmingham in 1985. The officers involved in both these shootings were cleared of, respectively, attempted murder and manslaughter. The report, as in the *Telegraph*, quoted the head of the Met.'s firearms unit and underlined the safeguards now built into training. Clearly, the leak from the Home Office about its forthcoming report was well timed, since its coincidence with the end of the trial meant that the promise of procedural reforms would tend to be coupled with procedural errors, possibly reducing their impact.

By comparison with the *Telegraph*, then, *The Times* laid greater emphasis upon the failings of police procedures and its reporting tended to underline the dangers of armed policing rather than play them down, or excuse the blunders by focusing on the difficulties of policing Brixton.

The *Guardian*'s treatment of the story paralleled that of the other quality papers. A major 8-column article occupied half of the main feature page built around a photograph of an officer undergoing arms training. The main headline was 'Armed police and the luck of the draw', connoting the role of chance in armed action. Alongside, a brief item headlined 'Tragic shots' resumed several incidents of unarmed people 'accidentally' shot by the police, labelling these 'a hallmark of the eighties'. More detailed than the reports carried in any other paper, this began with the case of Gail Kinchin, a 16-year-old girl shot in Birmingham. 'Several incidents followed when officers pursuing armed men mistakenly burst into the homes of innocent people.' Those involved included pensioners and children. The report went on to list the Waldorf case and some others before concluding with the Groce incident. The cumulative impact of this account was to give the impression of a pattern of shootings, counterbalanced, however, by the concluding paragraph which, reflecting the official view, observed that 'For every bullet fired by a police officer, 100 are fired by the criminal.'

The main feature took the form of a detailed investigation that concluded that whether or not the police shot in stressful circumstances was as much a matter of luck as one of judgement based upon careful training. Alongside the 'inevitability' theme, then, the role of chance was also invoked. The story was pegged to the imminent Home Office report on police use of firearms and likely pressures on the Home Secretary to create élite squads of marksmen attached to each force. Again, this indicated how the procedural reform agenda had been effectively imposed by good news management.

The *Guardian*'s report offered a revealing account of a visit to the Metropolitan police's weapons training establishment. Unlike any other report, this quite explicitly brought out the Met.'s broader media strategy:

It was particularly ironic that five days before the shooting of Mrs Groce, the Metropolitan Police had held an 'open day' for the media at D11's home in Lippitt's Hill, in Essex. Its purpose in part was PR image-building, but it was also to explain, and as much as possible demystify, the Blue Berets' work. In this it succeeded in a very cogent manner. The D11 officers—formerly mysterious figures only glimpsed at sieges and the like, walking calmly into action with their long, blue riflebags slung over their shoulders—turned out, almost to a man, to be extremely fit, alert and competent but relaxed and amusing men who would 'every time prefer to send in a "furry Exocet" (German Shepherd Dog) to meet a maniac cornered with a sawn-off shotgun' rather than risk life.

The police's need for a public relations success in this contentious area was made clear, as was the mystique surrounding élite armed squads in Britain—highly familiar from the SAS and their high-profile use in sieges.[6] However, the mystery is rapidly dispelled by the reference to D11's essential humanity and accessibility. A close reading of the *Guardian*, then, begins to suggest the successful steering of the controversy about the Groce shooting into a recognition of the police's fallibility, despite all their best efforts, essential decency, and good will. Even the most expert and best trained of police marksmen—a category into which Inspector Lovelock did not himself fit—said 'unequivocally, that such shootings "could happen tomorrow, or next week"'. Once again, we are invited to see such tragedies as inevitable.

In the end, according to the *Guardian*, observation and assessment of character by experienced superiors were found to be the only sound basis for selection, and even then officers might go wrong in the 'three-eights of a second' available to them (Superintendent Wells's phrase, as noted above, echoing throughout the reporting). Observations about the occupational psychology of the police gunman set the context for explaining the pressures and uncertainties facing Inspector Lovelock in the same terms as those rehearsed in *The Times* and the *Telegraph*. The *Guardian*'s

[6] See Paterson, R., and Schlesinger, P., 'State Heroes for the Eighties', *Screen*, 24 (1983), 55–72; Bruce, B., *Images of Power: How the Image Makers Shape our Leaders* (London: Kogan Page, 1992), 96.

investigation rationalized the logic of armed response without condoning its undesirable consequences.

Of the quality papers, only the *Independent* developed a different perspective. It converged with the others in a short, 2-column piece, carried below its main follow-up report on page 4. The article catalogues the '"Host of errors" that led to shooting', noting points already discussed, and indicating its distance from that explanation by its use of quotation-marks.

What distinguished the *Independent*, however, was a lengthy report stretching across all eight columns at the top of page 4 which examined some of the background tensions, headlined 'Brixton has uphill struggle to build spirit of trust.' In the centre of the article, a photograph, four columns across, depicted, in the words of its caption, a 'flashback' to the 'disturbances' following the shooting. Unique amongst the quality papers' visual representations, this picture was taken from behind a group of five police officers in riot gear, standing in a street looking at a burning car, with a black man and woman passing by.

'Crime levels in Brixton', the piece began, 'are still high many months after the riots that followed the shooting of Cherry Groce. . . . It remains an area where the potential for a breakdown of law and order is ever present.' The report continued by quoting the views of a youth worker, a campaign worker for unemployed workers, and the leader of Lambeth council, all of whom pointed either to pressures on the black community deriving from poverty, unemployment, and bad housing, or problems with the police. A social diagnosis therefore counterpointed the public order framework that predominated elsewhere. Only this report mentioned the recommendations for improving policing made by Lord Justice Scarman in his report on the riots of 1981, and some developments in building trust since then, notably in gaining public support for combating drugs dealing. Superintendent John Murray of Brixton Police was cited as offering an optimistic view of the future of police–community relations.

Of the quality papers, then, the *Independent* alone addressed the wider social background of Brixton, departing from the predominant Home Office agenda of the reform of arms handling to wider questions of racism and police–community relations. In doing so, it offered contextual information virtually absent from the rest of the qualities.

The Mid-Market Press

These papers all gave the acquittal front-page and inside-page treatment. Most prominent coverage came in the *Daily Mail*, which made the story its front-page lead, splashed across two-thirds of the front page. The *Daily Express* ran the story down its right-hand column, whereas *Today* blocked it in at the bottom of the page. The distinctive news angles—which varied more than those of the quality press—were encapsulated in the following headlines: 'Shooting case inspector cleared—but Yard is to change the rules: CID WILL LOSE ITS GUNS' (*Daily Mail*); 'Wife shot by police to win giant payout' (*Daily Express*); 'NEVER AGAIN: Lovelock walks free but he gives up guns' (*Today*).

The *Mail*'s headline took up the police procedural angle of acquittal-but-reform, closely approximating to the predominant line in the quality press. Framing the headline at the top of the page were two photographs: on the left, a half-profile of Inspector Lovelock, taken when leaving court, and on the right a full-face passport photo of Mrs Groce. The *Express* first highlighted the compensation sought by Mrs Groce, but in terms that suggested that she had won the pools rather than been the victim of a crippling shooting. Half-way down the column was a photograph of a smiling Cherry Groce, a choice of image that tended to signify a prize-winner rather than a gunshot victim. Finally, *Today*'s headline profoundly personalized the story as that of a lawman hanging up his gun: the headline and sub-head were built around a colour photo of Inspector Lovelock's face on the left, captioned 'cleared', to which, on the right, was counterposed one of Mrs Groce in a wheelchair on the street, captioned 'crippled'.

The *Mail*'s front-page story ran over onto page 2, where there were a further three reports. The front-page report was dominated by the 'radical shake-up of Metropolitan police firearms policy' theme, placed in the context of the Waldorf and Groce shootings, followed by the implications for improved training, selection, and routine practice in order to 'reduce the chances of police accidentally shooting members of the public, or mistakenly shooting each other because some officers are in plain clothes'.

The human interest slant received much more play than in the quality press: 'There was huge relief in police circles last night that Inspector Lovelock had been cleared at the Old Bailey.' The angle of the main page 2 report was summed up by the lead-in and head-line 'Verdict delights police . . . but angers victim's family: Lovelock sobs as court ordeal ends.' It focused first upon the consequences for Inspector Lovelock, treating him as though he were the principal victim:

Inspector Douglas Lovelock, whose accidental shot paralysed Mrs Cherry Groce and sparked the Brixton riot, left the Old Bailey a free man amid emotional scenes. He collapsed sobbing into the arms of his 27-year-old wife Julie after being cleared of unlawful and malicious wounding. But although the harrowing court ordeal is over, Mr Lovelock could decide to resign from the force. His work broke up his first marriage and put his life under pressure.

In other respects the report provided details already familiar, though it stressed the support of friends and family emotions far more than did the quality papers.

Besides carrying the statement of regret, the *Mail* also quoted the statement from Mrs Groce's solicitor, Paul Boateng, described as 'the Left Wing head of the former GLC's police committee'. Given the *Mail*'s right-wing political orientation, this label was hardly intended to endear, since the Greater London Council (GLC) police committees generally were *bêtes noires* for Conservative politicians and newspapers.[7] Quotations carried elsewhere by the Lambeth police committee chairman and Michael Groce also featured, but not prominently.

Alongside the main report, two further articles deployed the *Mail*'s anti-leftism more overtly. In 'How the Left halts fight against crime', the theft of vehicle batteries from council premises, and a refusal to allow the police to enter for the purposes of investigation, were instanced. These were linked to police evidence during the Lovelock case suggesting that an approach to Lambeth council for plans of the Groce house would have been leaked. The second, shorter report, 'Murder probe block', cited police allegations (denied by the council) of obstruction in two murder inquiries and a sexual abuse investigation. Together with the generally sympathetic treatment afforded Lovelock, this counterposition of obstructive leftism in Brixton inserted an overtly ideological perspective absent elsewhere.

[7] See Curran, J., 'Culturalist Perspectives of News Organizations: A Reappraisal and a Case Study', in M. Ferguson (ed.), *Public Communication: The New Imperatives* (London: Sage, 1990), 212–33.

The *Express*'s front-page story principally took up the compensation likely to be paid Mrs Groce, in an evident leak from the police: 'The Brixton housewife paralysed for life by a police bullet could get a record-setting £300,000 compensation, sources said last night. The Metropolitan Police have accepted all along that mother of six Mrs Cherry Groce, 39, was an innocent victim when she was accidentally shot in a police raid on her home.'

The terminology used—'Brixton housewife', 'record-setting'—fits in with the pool-winners frame. The report is also reticent about the 'sources' of this tale of largesse.

A much longer report featured on page 7, headlined 'Tears as gun case policeman is cleared', with a picture of Lovelock and his daughter. The *Express*, like the *Mail*, played up the human interest aspects of the case, with Lovelock as principal focus:

The policeman who shot and crippled a housewife wept yesterday as an Old Bailey jury cleared him of unlawfully and maliciously wounding her. As the verdict was announced Inspector Douglas Lovelock shook slightly and closed his eyes. He then turned to the jury and whispered a simple 'thank you.' The strain of months of tension was etched on his face. Mr Lovelock's wife Julie burst into tears as colleagues rushed forward to congratulate him.

The language used stressed emotional strain, the courtroom drama, and the end to the suffering of the police officer. Only at this point did the report turn to the 'mother-of-six Cherry Groce, 39, who will be in a wheelchair for the rest of her life', to say that she was not in court. The remainder concentrated on the jury's decision and some of the background to the raid, citing Lovelock's apology. In a brief boxed news item, 'Verdict slammed by Council chief', the critical views of Lambeth council's Julian Lewis were cited, including his fears of further confrontations, reservations about the jury system, and call for a public inquiry. The report concluded with reassurances from Scotland Yard.

Today took this last theme as its lead paragraph: 'Inspector Douglas Lovelock, whose shooting of a mother of six sparked off the Brixton riots, will never be armed again.' Playing on the human interest theme, the report counterposed one family's joys with another's sorrows—unique amongst the mid-market (and quality) press in doing so: 'But as Inspector Lovelock and his family celebrated, Mrs Groce's family claimed the verdict meant they would forever be legitimate targets for the police.' Mrs Groce's mother was quoted as fearing for the rest of her family and as expressing doubts in British justice. At this point, the report covered Lovelock's apology, his reaction to the verdict, and Mrs Groce's likely compensation, ending with the police's errors and reassurances from Scotland Yard of lessons learned.

The mid-market press, then, tended much more towards personalization, with Inspector Lovelock, often described in emotional terms, as the main focus of attention, presented more as victim of adverse circumstances than as the agent of someone else's misfortune. The policy dimension received some play in this sector of the market, most considerably so in the *Mail*.

The Popular Press

Much of the coverage here was in line with the mid-market papers, although no popular paper made the case into a front-page story. The *Sun* and the *Daily Mirror* each carried the story on page 7, whereas the *Daily Star* slotted it into page 11. All three papers made similar decisions on the use of news photographs, each carrying a father/daughter picture. (The absence of the Groce family from the trial meant that the photo opportunity for this kind of strongly resonant image did not exist.) The main pictorial variation came in the images of Mrs Groce. The *Sun* showed her in a wheelchair, the *Star* had a close-up of her face in a hospital bed, whereas the *Mirror* showed a full-face photo of a young Mrs Groce wearing a wedding dress.

In line with much of the mid-market approach, the popular papers concentrated on personalization, although the *Mirror* distinguished its headline from the other two by focusing on police giving up guns: 'THANK THE LORD! Joy of the gun cop's wife as he is cleared' (the *Sun*); 'Jury clears Lovelock over raid that ended in tragedy: THANK YOU, SOBS GUN COP' (the *Star*); '120 POLICE HANG UP THEIR GUNS IN FEAR: But cop is cleared over bungled raid' (the *Mirror*). Respectively, these concentrate on Mrs Lovelock's elation, Lovelock's gratitude, and emotional police reaction coupled with the acquittal.

In its leading paragraphs, the *Sun* highlighted the emotional impact of Lovelock's acquittal:

The policeman who sparked a riot by shooting and paralysing a black mum-of-six burst into tears yesterday as he left court a free man. Inspector Douglas Lovelock, 42, had to be supported by colleagues after an Old

Bailey jury found him not guilty of unlawfully wounding 39-year-old Mrs Cherry Groce. His weeping wife Julie, 27, rushed to cuddle him and sobbed: 'Thank the Lord he has been cleared—the last 15 months have been torture.'

The report went on to tell of how Lovelock's colleagues took leave to support him, mentioning the continuing police internal inquiry and his regrets. In terms not carried in any other newspaper, the *Sun* said that the trial had been 'deliberately boycotted' by the Groce family 'because they felt the policeman would be acquitted'. Two shorter articles took up the policy themes: 'Top police face probe' looked at the possibility of disciplinary action against those who devised the raid, whereas the three-paragraph 'He'll never go armed again' quoted Scotland Yard as saying Lovelock was unlikely to wish to carry a gun.

The *Star*'s opening paragraphs also stressed the emotion felt by Lovelock on acquittal, briefly rehearsed his account of how the shooting happened, and then cited his statement of regret. His reinstatement and Mrs Groce's quest for compensation were also mentioned, as was Paul Boateng's statement on Mrs Groce's behalf. A short piece at the end of the main report, detailed 'Four vital mistakes' made in carrying out the raid.

For its part, the *Mirror* first highlighted the handing-in of weapons by 'at least 120' armed police 'for fear of landing in court if they kill or maim', a storyline pursued nowhere else. Moving onto the Old Bailey acquittal, it recounted the emotional reactions this had aroused. Scotland Yard's statement was quoted, together with the policy change concerning armed CID officers. Lovelock's statement of regret was followed by comments from the Police Federation and a police firearms expert on the difficulties and stresses of gun-handling. In a separate short piece, 'Cherry is not bitter', run somewhat bizarrely under Mrs Groce's wedding photo, she was quoted via Paul Boateng's statement as feeling no hatred.

In the popular press, then, the human interest angle largely predominated in the *Sun* and *Star*, and received considerable play too in the *Mirror*, where the underlying policy issues received most attention, again in terms largely set by the police.

Editorial Commentary

Editorial treatment was concentrated in the quality press, with second leaders in each of the *Guardian*, the *Independent*, and the

Daily Telegraph. In line with its extensive news coverage, The *Daily Mail* gave over the whole of its comment slot and, less predictably, so did the *Daily Mirror*. In essence, all of these spoke in terms that had implications for policy, although most editorials drew quite different lessons from the incident.

The *Guardian*, decrying the developing pattern of police trials and acquittals for killing innocent citizens, stressed the inadequacies of the criminal law. Given that such incidents were likely to continue, it was essential to make the police corporately responsible for compensation. This, therefore, accepted the 'inevitability' argument, and looked for compensation for those who fell victim to armed policing. In contrast, the *Independent*'s focus was on the problems of police overwork and stress, which suggested the need to reform management structures to prevent the recurrence of such incidents: unlike the *Guardian*, its rhetoric was one of prevention rather than cure. The *Telegraph*, noting there could be no accusations of a cover-up, and that the situation in Brixton had made it difficult for the ground rules to be applied, argued, without specifying how, that the lives of the innocent needed to be safeguarded. This tended to be exculpatory by invoking the 'hostile territory' argument. It was the *Mail*'s editorial that bore the closest relation to parts of its news coverage. Arguing that the police had now tightened up on their procedures, it urged more black people to join the police and attacked left-wing Labour councils for obstructing the police in their duties. Thus, the procedural reform message was uncritically taken on board, the left trounced, and ethnic minorities simplistically urged to enter the mainstream. Finally, the *Mirror* took the view that there were serious shortcomings in police weapons training and that this needed to be addressed to forestall any future tragedy, sharing with the *Independent* a prevention before cure argument.

Television Coverage

Television news gave extensive coverage to the Lovelock acquittal on all channels. Most reporting took place on 15 January, the day the trial ended, although there was some follow-up on the morning of 16 January. On the night of 15 January, the case was covered by BBC's *Six O'Clock News* and *Nine O'Clock News*, and also received substantial attention from the BBC2 daily current affairs programme, *Newsnight*. ITV carried the story on its 5.45 p.m. *ITN*

News and then subsequently on *News at Ten*; it also featured on the 7 p.m. *Channel Four News*. The following day, BBC1's *Breakfast Television* reported the acquittal and, to a lesser extent, so did ITV's TV-am. In the present analysis, we concentrate on the main night-time news reports.

On BBC1's *Nine O'Clock News*, the Lovelock acquittal ran as the second item, at just over 3 minutes, following almost 9.5 minutes on the 'Big Freeze' that had paralysed transport throughout Britain. The story was introduced by the newsreader as follows:

Police Inspector Douglas Lovelock, who shot and paralysed Mrs Cherry Groce at her home in Brixton, South London, has been cleared of unlawfully and maliciously wounding her. Police raided the house looking for her son Michael in connection with an armed robbery. After the shooting there were riots in Brixton which left one man dead, fifty injured and led to over 200 arrests. Inspector Lovelock told the court it had been a terrible accident.

Over footage of Lovelock pushing through a crowd to reach his car, the narrative continued:

Inspector Lovelock left the Old Bailey with his wife and daughter, free to return to his job, but unlikely to ever carry a gun again. He wept when the jury's verdict was announced. Now a claim for damages by Mrs Groce, the mother of six he shot and paralysed, is being vigorously pursued.

The story was initially framed in terms of the shooting, its public order impact, and the human interest consequences for policeman and victim. This last theme was reinforced by footage of Lovelock's solicitor expressing regret. Over footage of police marksmen with weapons, the focus then shifted to the question of the police's use of arms and the Home Office's imminent report on training methods. The report then moved to library film of the Groce's home in Brixton in 1985, noting that the police had ruled out 'official firearms policy' because they 'claimed the area was too hostile':

Inside, Inspector Lovelock, under stress and believing he was confronting a dangerous criminal, shot Mrs Groce. The bullet which wounded her at close range was a new softnosed type, not dum-dum bullets but with a similar effect. Instead of passing cleanly through her body, the bullet splintered leaving a fragment lodging in her spine. She's now confined to a wheelchair, but today bears no malice towards the policeman who shot her, despite such a terrible injury.

This was narrated over, first, a close-up of Mrs Groce in a hospital bed with a relative by her side, and then footage of her being brought home in a wheelchair by ambulance men. It reprised Lovelock's court testimony, played down the emotive implications of the police using 'dum-dum'-like bullets, and then focused on the victim's present condition and her forgiveness. The report concluded with footage of riots in Brixton and burning buildings, tracing this 'violent aftermath of another police shooting' to the belief that Mrs Groce had been shot in the back.

News at Ten made the acquittal its lead item, devoting over 8 minutes to the story, almost three times as much as the *Nine O'Clock News*. With a background photo of Lovelock, the newscaster opened the narrative:

The police inspector who shot and crippled Mrs Cherry Groce is free tonight to take up his duties once more after being cleared of unlawfully and maliciously wounding her, but it's unlikely he'll ever carry a gun again. Inspector Douglas Lovelock had told the Old Bailey he'd been tense during the police raid on Mrs Groce's home in Brixton last year. The shooting started riots in the area.

Over a photo of Cherry Groce, and then of Douglas Lovelock, the newscaster continued:

Mrs Groce will spend the rest of her life in a wheelchair. She said she'd pick up the pieces of her life without bitterness or hatred. The police are expected to pay compensation which may run into six figures.

The story was framed at first in the same terms as the BBC's but then, distinctively, strongly addressed the impact on the victim. After showing film of Lovelock's solicitor expressing his regrets, the report turned to the theme of police arms training. Over footage of the Lippitt's Hill training centre, the narrative noted that Lovelock had been authorized to carry firearms: 'There has never been any question about his expertise or his psychological approach. He even passed the most rigorous of tests which included having to look, identify and react to a target in less than a second.'

Showing film of four policemen in training with an instructor, the report noted that they were being trained in the same way as Lovelock. However he had been wrongly briefed and had told the court that 'just before the door was broken down the blood was "pumping around my body" and when he went in he said, "I felt a mixture of excitement, fear and tension and apprehension."' Thus, the report privileged Lovelock's court testimony and attempted to position the viewer inside an analogous situation by showing training. Switching to film of Mrs Groce in a hospital bed, the story went on to say that she had been the victim, detailing the physical damage done. An independent inquiry by the Assistant Chief Constable of West Yorkshire had led to the malicious wounding charge being preferred by the Director of Public Prosecutions. Over footage of Michael Groce walking in the street, it was reported that he had given himself up after the shooting. The narrative continued over library film of riot police in action in Brixton in September 1985: 'The shooting was seen in Brixton as another example of heavy-handed policing. That night, there was rioting, looting and burning. It went on for two days with police coming under constant attack from stone-throwers and petrol bombers.'

Over film of policemen aiming guns, the report concluded by saying that police regulations covering the use of firearms were 'more stringent' than those laid down in Parliament.

Both BBC2's *Newsnight* and ITN's *Channel Four News* offered other perspectives on the acquittal story. *Newsnight* ran the story as its first item for a duration of 11 minutes. It took the policy question as its central theme: 'The policeman who shot Cherry Groce is cleared. What safeguards are needed to stop further tragedies?'

In the main body of the story, the narrative noted that Inspector Lovelock had been acquitted, that Mrs Groce had been injured, and that riots had occurred, and that the incident had also raised a number of important questions about arming police officers. The events surrounding the shooting were rapidly resumed over film of the Groce home in Brixton, Michael Groce, and Mrs Groce in hospital, the segment concluding with the statement by Lovelock's solicitor. Unlike the *Nine O'Clock News* and *News at Ten*, *Newsnight* also carried Paul Boateng's statement and detailed previous shootings, in a sequence that began: 'But in addition to the element of personal tragedy, one of the most alarming things about this case is that Mrs Groce is not the first innocent person to have been shot by the police by mistake.'

After brief details of various incidents, over a full-face photograph of the pregnant teenager Gail Kinchin, shot in 1980, film of Stephen Waldorf's yellow mini after his shooting in 1983, further film of the aftermath of a post office shooting in 1984, a photograph of 5-year-old John Shorthouse shot in 1985, the commentary continued:

After the Shorthouse and Groce shootings, the Home Secretary, Douglas Hurd, set up a working party to look into the use of guns by Britain's police. The result of the report, which will be submitted to Mr Hurd soon, is expected to lay down new guidelines for police tactics during raids in pursuit of armed suspects.

The narrative continued by noting that the report would recommend more careful monitoring of firearms officers and closer supervision by senior police, that in the light of Lovelock's errors a greater emphasis would be laid on intelligence-gathering before armed raids, and that more specialist squads should be used. The presenter then turned to Leslie Curtis of the Police Federation to discuss these proposals. Curtis immediately responded as follows: 'Can I say two things very briefly? First, I am very glad to see the outcome of this very sad case in relation to Mr Lovelock. And secondly, and equally importantly, we share the sympathies Mr Lovelock's expressed over Mrs Groce. It's very, very sad.'

This comment presented the widely reported relief-but-regret response adopted by the police. He then went on to express doubts about whether specialist squads were an adequate answer, saying that 'everyone, whether they be expert or not, that goes into these situations is a human being just like you or I, and they will suffer the same traumas and the same problems that everyone else does.' However, he did accept, under questioning, that better intelligence and supervision could help, but returned once again to the human factor. Mr Curtis was the only expert source interviewed before the programme moved on to its next item. In effect, by taking the public policy line on the issue, and by not examining any alternative perspective to that of the professional police officer, *Newsnight* largely fell in line with the Home Office's and the Met.'s news management identified earlier in the discussion of the press.

Channel Four News also took a line distinct from the mainstream news programmes, running the story second for almost 4.5 minutes. After resuming brief details about the verdict, the programme departed from the run of coverage by offering a report on 'the aftermath of the police raid and the present relationship between the police and the community in Brixton'.

The report began with riot footage from 1985, and a clip of Mrs Groce being wheeled out of hospital, followed by one of Michael Groce. Unlike any other news outlet analysed it made the following point: 'After the violence in Brixton had died down, the Cherry Groce Defence Campaign was established. For several months they campaigned for the policeman who fired the gun to be prosecuted. Five months after the shooting Inspector Lovelock was charged.'

To the background of film of Campaign members in discussion, the reporter noted anger about the handling of the case. Interviewed, Devon Thomas, a Campaign member, said: 'There appeared to very little attempt to go in harder when there was obviously softness in the defence case. The prosecution, the way they were putting their case was in a very gentlemanly approach; there wasn't a cut and thrust of a court that I expected in such a crucial case as this.'

This was followed by a comment from Julian Lewis of Lambeth Council Police Committee: 'We have a situation where the police burst into this family's home and shot down the mother in front of her family. That is going to do nothing to help heal the rift in confidence between the black community and the police.'

To background film of Brixton streets, it was reported that there was an attitude of cynicism abroad, with no further trouble expected. The reporter went on to raise the police's claim that they had not sought plans of the interior of the Groce house for fear of a leak that might endanger the operation. This was described by Devon Thomas as an unsubstantiated allegation.

Shifting tack, the report then noted that this was 'one of several recent incidents where innocent people have been hurt by police guns', showing film of Stephen Waldorf in hospital and of John Shorthouse's funeral. Over footage of police training at Lippitt's Hill in a simulation similar to the Groce incident, it was noted that the police had no plans to change their training, although reference was made to the new Home Office guidelines now awaited. The report concluded with film of Inspector Lovelock leaving court, noting his regrets and the Metropolitan Police's acknowledgement of lack of trust between it and 'ethnic members of the community'.

Channel Four News, then, departed significantly from the common television news agenda, in ways comparable to the *Independent*'s investigation of the Brixton background. It gave access to views that had no airing elsewhere either in the television or press coverage, and rather than take armed policing as the key news angle it focused on police–community relations.

Conclusion

The story analysed draws our attention to public fear of official violence rather than the more customary focus on fear of crime. On this occasion, given the story's central racial dimension, the police's relationship to the black community was of special importance as a contextual factor but was largely ignored. Where a policy discourse prevailed, mainly in the quality press and in television coverage, the procedural reform agenda was privileged. Where human interest prevailed, the impact on the police officer came to the fore.

Although the contemporary focus on fear of crime has all but obscured discussion of fear of official force, our reading of media coverage of the Lovelock acquittal strongly suggests that this is widely recognized to exist, not least in official circles themselves. What was so striking about the case was the overwhelming effort undertaken to reassure the public as a whole—through adept news management—that the official and legitimate use of force could be contained, and that where it could not, this was because of inevitability, accident, or human error. We can only conjecture whether or not the repair work was successful on this occasion amongst the public as a whole. We may reasonably doubt that it allayed the fears of the black community.

8

A Tale of Conviction

OUR final case study of news reporting concerns a sexual murder that received a great deal of attention. It was subsequently to be revisited several years later in the BBC's victim-oriented television series, *Crime Limited*, in July 1993. The coverage analysed here came at the conclusion of a trial for the murder of a young woman, Tessa Howden, aged 19, who had been attacked and then killed whilst sleeping in her own bedroom at her parents' home in Selsdon, Surrey, by a local man, Gary Taken. This was a gruesome murder that so violated the sanctity and security of the home as to unavoidably raise questions about public fear of violent crime encroaching into the domestic space. Its handling in some sections of the media also puts voyeurism on the agenda.

Men's violence against women—whether sexual or domestic—is a staple of media output, both in news-reporting and in broadcast fiction and the cinema. The ways in which such violent relations are represented crystallize conceptions of masculinity and femininity in the media. The extent to which we identify with such representations, or do not, is, arguably, related to the kinds of social experience that we have as consumers of media products, and may be shaped by factors such as gender, class, and ethnicity.[1]

The 'Sleeping Beauty' murder story was given major attention.[2] In this analysis, we first focus on how television news reported the story on the day of the sentencing itself, 13 January 1987, and then consider how the press dealt with the story on the following day.

[1] For a discussion of varying responses by women to the televised representation of men's violence against women see Schlesinger, P., Dobash, R. E., Dobash, R. P., and Weaver, C. K., *Women Viewing Violence* (London: BFI, 1992).

[2] The attention attracted by this story reflects a shift in reporting patterns. Compared to previous post-war periods 'it is the sudden impact of three or four rape cases each year given massive front-page coverage over a range of national dailies which make the 1980s somewhat distinctive in rape reporting.' The case had the added news value of being a gruesome murder as well as a sexual assault. See Soothill, K., 'The Changing Face of Rape?', *British Journal of Criminology*, 31 (1991), 385.

The end of a trial for sex crimes is a conventional point for news media to conclude a narrative that has involved the search for the criminal and then committal, trial, and sentencing, often with comments on the severity or leniency of the sentence passed—although that was not at issue in the present case.[3] A trial is also an important moment in the ritual process of restoring social order when a criminal act has been committed. It closes off one phase in the process of bringing retribution to those who have broken society's rules as expressed in the law. The next phase, where guilt is proven, is imprisonment, which, in effect, constitutes the vanishing of the offender from society. Thus the public moment at which the judge pronounces the sentence is of considerable importance in offering an opportunity for news media to elaborate the implications of a particular crime. In the present case, one angle on the story was that despite the imprisonment of the offender the story had not ended because his actions had claimed victims other than the dead girl: namely, those close to her, who had survived her death and continued to suffer its consequences.

Television Coverage

The Tessa Howden murder trial was covered by both the main channels, BBC1 and ITV, on 13 January 1987, the day the trial ended. BBC1's *Six O'Clock News* ran the item fourth for just over half a minute. It was introduced as follows by the newsreader: 'At the Old Bailey a 20-year-old man has been sentenced to life custody for strangling a teenage girl in her bed as her family slept.'

Over a photograph of Tessa, followed by one of Gary Taken, the narrative continued:

Tessa Howden, who was nineteen, was found the next morning by her father at their home in Croydon, South London. The verdict was unanimous. The evidence against him was said to be 'overwhelming'.

The remainder of the report was spoken over footage of police searching through woods near the Howden home, a view of the home and street, and a close-up of a bedroom window:

The discovery of Tessa's body on January 10th last year sparked off a huge search in the Croydon area. Taken was arrested after his fingerprints

[3] See Soothill, K. and Walby, S., *Sex Crime in the News* (London: Routledge, 1991), 17.

were found in her bedroom. The prosecution said he'd probably picked out Tessa from a photograph which appeared in the local newspaper where she worked.

The report only offered the bare bones of an account and left out any reference to the sexual dimension of the crime, although it did suggest the menace for young women of being picked out from a photograph by a dangerous male. By contrast, there was greater explicitness in the 6.30 p.m. BBC local news programme *London Plus*, which ran the story third at almost a minute's length. After the newsreader's introduction, over a photograph of Tessa, a reporter voiced over a sequence of shots focused on various windows of the Howden home and described more graphically what had happened:

Taken climbed in through a small window at the back of the Howden's home and then to the bedroom of 19-year-old Tessa. While her parents slept, the unemployed scaffolder threatened her with a knife before sexually assaulting her. Taken then strangled Tessa with her own tights. Her body was discovered by her father, speaking here a year ago.

This was followed by a clip of David Howden speaking of his distress at a press conference. The report closed over further film of a policeman holding Taken's 'distinctive red sunglasses'. However, even this greater explicitness operated within the kind of reticence about details of the crime adopted by the quality press, as we shall see. It contrasted strongly with the handling of the story on ITV, which much more closely resembled the mid-market and popular press treatment discussed below.

The 5.45 p.m. *ITN News* ran the story third for one and a half minutes, three times the length of the equivalent BBC report, and the tone and content were significantly different. Over photographs of Tessa and her murderer, the story was introduced as follows:

An unemployed scaffolder, Gary Taken, has been sentenced to youth custody for life for the sex murder of blonde teenager Tessa Howden. Taken, aged 20, crept into Tessa's home in Selsdon, Surrey, through a kitchen window, while she and her parents were asleep. He was also sentenced for 15 months for stealing women's underwear from washing lines.

This unambiguously underlines the sexual nature of the crime—it is labelled a 'sex murder'—and indeed the theme of the perpetrator's sexual perversity was the key to how the entire report was constructed. The reporter, speaking from outside the Old Bailey, continued:

Gary Taken deteriorated from a man who stole women's underwear to a sex beast and a murderer. 'His crime', said the judge, 'was a foul outrage'.[4]

Cutting to scenes of the Howden home and street, the report went on:

One night in January last year he broke into the house and entered Tessa's bedroom. There he slashed her across the throat, sexually assaulted her and finally strangled her with her own tights. Her body was discovered the next morning by her father, David, who'd been sleeping across the landing.

Over a sequence of press conference footage Mr Howden was quoted: ' "I can only describe it as if your stomach's been wrenched out," he says now. "It's totally devastating." ' The report went on to describe the clues left behind—fingerprints, some in blood, and the murderer's red sunglasses (once again over footage of a policeman holding them). The report referred to Taken's attempt to bribe another man to confess to the crime and the devastating impact of the crime on the Howden family. ITN's treatment, then, emphasized the sexual content of the crime—in sharp contrast to the BBC's—and stressed the human interest angle of profound disruption to an ordinary family.

The story was given even greater play—3 minutes—on the local *Thames News* that followed ITN's broadcast, where it ran as the fourth item. Here, the human interest theme of family tragedy predominated, with the sexual interest in a slightly lower key. The story opened in much the same vein as ITN's over photographs of Tessa and her murderer:

Gary Taken has been put behind bars for life for the sex murder of newspaper promotions girl Tessa Howden. Tessa was slashed, sexually assaulted, and then strangled with her own tights at her home in Surrey while her parents slept in the room next door.

After noting the judge's condemnation, Taken's entry points to the house were shown, and then the human interest theme was taken up more fully. Following film of the Howdens looking at a photograph album, an interview clip with Mrs Howden was shown, who said: 'Tessa was a quiet, shy, easy-going, pleasant girl. She never

---

[4] Ibid., ch. 3. 'Sex fiend' imagery has been a staple of popular press reporting of sexual crime.

had an enemy as far as I know in the world. Everybody who came into contact with her loved her.'

Following an interview with a female colleague who described all her workmates as 'dumbfounded', the reporter went on to detail the various clues that had led to Gary Taken. Film of his parents at home followed, saying they were 'convinced he's innocent', and then an interview clip with the convicted man's father, who broke down after several incoherent sentences. The sequence closed by cutting back to the Howdens, at home, detailing the impact on their family. The similarities between this treatment of the story and that of ITN are obvious.

Television news, then, went in for minimal detail in the case of the BBC and more elaborate treatment in the case of ITV, where sexual detail and human interest were more fully explored. As we shall see, these variations came into play in the press reporting as well. For the popular papers, especially the *Daily Star* and the *Daily Mirror*, the story offered a chance to go in for some complex and detailed treatment, covering a variety of angles, typographies, and photographs, making it the key story of the day. In the mid-market press, the *Daily Mail*'s coverage strongly resembled that of the popular tabloids in extent though not in style, whereas the *Daily Express*, although giving the story substantial play, gave it more contained treatment (as had the *Sun* at the popular end of the market). ITV's coverage places it with the popular and mid-market papers. The *Guardian*, the *Independent*, *The Times*, and the *Daily Telegraph* all gave full accounts of the murder, with reasonable prominence. But the style and scope of this reporting was at sharp variance with both the popular and mid-market papers, being centred upon the conventions of court reporting, rather like the BBC's.

The Popular Press

The *Daily Mirror* made the impact of the murder on Tessa's family the central theme in its reporting, with a double-page feature on this in the centre pages, although other angles were also explored in detail. Almost the entire front page was given over to the story, the page dominated by a large white headline on a black background: 'OUR NIGHTMARE'. This 'our' by implication included the reader as well as the dead girl's family whose phrase this was.

Alongside a photograph of Tessa in the right-hand corner of the front page ran the legend 'AS SLEEPING BEAUTY KILLER GETS LIFE Tessa's parents tell of the terror that shattered their lives.' The headlines were followed by another in lower case, this time a quotation from the dead girl's father, David Howden: 'I thought I might have gone mad and killed her.' In line with this was a photograph of Mr Howden, face pressed against that of his wife, Heather, captioned: 'BRAVE: Tragic parents David and Heather'. The text of the story followed, with a small photograph of the bearded killer set in the outside column, captioned 'MURDERER: Taken'.

The newspaper's lead paragraphs highlighted the horrifying impact of the murder on the family:

Sleeping Beauty Tessa's Howden's parents told of their never-ending nightmare yesterday as her killer was locked up for life. After seeing evil sex pervert Gary Taken sentenced, Tessa's father David said the murderer had shattered his once-happy family. The trauma was so horrific that at one point 47-year-old David even thought he might have killed Tessa himself. And his wife Heather, 44, was so upset that she took to wearing her daughter's clothes to feel closer to her.

The 'Sleeping Beauty' image conjures up a fairytale princess, innocently waiting to be awakened by a kiss from a handsome prince. Instead, the victim was subjected to a horrifying sexual ordeal and death by strangulation. The nocturnal visitor, then, was a figure of darkness—evil and perverted. The attack had violated one of society's central institutions—the family—and in this case a harmonious one. It also breached the Englishman's private space, his home, and brought the parents to the edge of madness: the father to imagine his own culpability, the mother to seek contact with her daughter by wearing her clothes.

The front-page story continued onto page 2, telling how the father's business had collapsed and how both parents were being treated for depression. The murderer was described as showing no emotion in court, and as believed to be innocent by his father.

The *Mirror* then developed the story further, with page 7 dominated by 'MY GENTLE TESSA: Anguish of Boyfriend', with a large photograph of the couple wearing party hats. The story quoted Tessa's boyfriend, Geoffrey Collyer, who described her as 'lovely', 'perfect in every way', and 'gentle'. Details were given of Tessa's academic achievements, her sales promotions work for a local newspaper, and of the couple's holiday and marriage plans. Alongside this detailed picture of shattered normality was juxtaposed another story headlined 'What a weirdo says ex-lover', where the 'sex fiend's former girlfriend revealed that he was 'obsessed with girlie magazines and slinky underwear. But when it came to lovemaking, he was a flop. "I'd only give him five out of ten," she said.' The girl-friend, Lisa Histed, went on to tell of pornographic magazines in Taken's bedroom and how he had harassed her at night-time after the relationship broke up. Page 7, then, contrasted the 'normal' boyfriend and boy–girl relationship with the perverse. It compared the loving behaviour of the employed boyfriend with the sexual fantasy life of the unemployed murderer and evoked a fetishistic collector of women's underwear who acted out pornographic fantasies. The article also mentioned in passing Taken's claim to have been Tessa's secret lover.

Finally, the *Mirror* devoted a centre-page spread to revisiting the scene of the crime; it featured a large photo of Tessa's room, restored to the normality it had enjoyed before the violation, and now a virtual shrine for the family: 'The pretty painted china sign on the door says "Tessa's Room". Inside, her favourite soft toys are scattered on the bed.'

Into this scene of cosy protectedness, now rendered pathetic by the death of its occupant,

Gary Taken broke in, crept upstairs and opened the 19-year-old girl's door as she lay sleeping. While the winter wind howled and the rain poured down outside to mask her cries, he abused her, slashed her hands and throat and finally strangled her with a pair of her own white fishnet tights.

This evokes horror, in terms redolent of the cinematic genre, in which a predatory, voyeuristic force of evil erupts into a scene of innocence and vulnerability. Could we be more vulnerable than when asleep?

The story then went on to describe Mr Howden's horror on discovering his dead daughter, and the details of how he raised the alarm, having to go through the ordeal of being the police's initial prime suspect. Much of this feature was an exploration of the loss to the parents and the suffering that they had endured. In the middle of the centre-page story (captioned 'Sleeping Beauty Murder Trial') was a quote from Mr Howden: 'I found her by the bed. I just grabbed her and hugged her. I knew she was dead.'

The *Mirror*'s treatment was the most extensive and its themes were paralleled by other popular and mid-market papers, but with interesting variations. The *Star*'s front page was also given over to the story. But this time, Taken's bearded photograph dominated, at almost twice the size of Tessa's smiling portrait. A huge white headline against a black background proclaimed: 'HE SHOULD NEVER HAVE EXISTED: Tessa's killer jailed for life.' The front-page story emphasized Taken's sexual perversity, the theme that dominated the *Star*'s coverage. It began:

Pervert Gary Taken was jailed for life yesterday for the sex killing of Sleeping Beauty Tessa Howden. Afterwards, Tessa's grieving father said: 'As far as I'm concerned, he should never have existed. People like that shouldn't.' Taken, 20, who began as a Peeping Tom when he was only 7 and stole women's undies for kicks, submitted 19-year-old Tessa to a horrific ordeal. He got drunk, broke into her bedroom as her parents slept, and slashed her 11 times with a knife when she struggled.

The sexual element in the story was heavily underlined: the label 'pervert' opened the story, the murder was described as a 'sex killing', and Taken's history constructed as sexual: a childhood Peeping Tom obsessed with 'undies'. The story also immediately linked drunkenness and violence, the police officer who had led the investigation quoted as describing Taken as evil and out of control because of drink. Running on to page 2, the report continued: 'Although pretty Tessa was sexually assaulted, detectives are not convinced that Taken raped her. "We don't think he was capable of that", said one. The killer, who got turned on by women's scanties, had systematically spread Tessa's knickers over all the bedroom.'

As illustrated above, the *Star*'s portrayal of an impotent killer with fetishistic behaviour had a salacious tone. The report went on to speak of the discovery of more women's underwear at his home. This theme was picked up again in a 2-page spread, labelled a '*Star* News Special', on pages 4 and 5, which gave a detailed sexual portrait. It was dominated by the headline 'WEIRDO'S SICK LUST FOR TESSA', whose portrait occupied the centre of the right-hand page.

The main report catalogued an obsession dating back eight years and detailed how Taken stalked Tessa, took secret snapshots of her with a concealed camera, and stole her underwear from the washing-line. He had also stolen the back door key, one of her swimsuits, and two years previously had almost been caught peering through her bedroom window. The story continued with details of women's underwear recovered from his home, secret photographs of women, and his voyeurism, which included watching his parents make love and women going to the toilet.

This seems an obvious invitation to the (masculine) reader's own voyeurism and fantasies, further played upon in the story headlined 'I SAW KNICKERS UNDER THE BED Shock for lover'. Alongside a photo of 'pretty Lisa Jane Histed', the report disclosed more about Taken's sex life:

She said: 'I thought he was generous—but he was nothing special in bed. I knew he had a reputation as a weirdo who collected girls' knickers and he was always buying me black underwear so I would look nice. On one occasion his mother told me I had left my knickers under his bed. When I told her they weren't mine she looked very embarrassed. Gary had a big collection of girlie magazines and the walls of his bedroom were covered with pictures of topless models.'

Taken's sexual inadequacies were underlined and the sexual attractions of his own perversity suggested. The pornographic cliché of black underwear was invoked, and the complicity of the two women in the tragic outcome, faced with so much evidence of Taken's dangerous obsessions, hinted at. The ex-girlfriend knew of Taken's voyeuristic photography and she also (as reported in the *Mirror* and, as we shall see, in the *Mail*) claimed to have been threatened when the relationship ended.

Two other articles dealt with the impact of the case on the parents. Topped by a photograph of David and Heather Howden, and headlined 'Lifetime of agony for family', the accompanying story covered the psychological impact on her parents of Tessa's murder. Mr Howden was reported as jobless and in debt and both parents as receiving psychiatric help and finding it terribly hard to cope. The story also ran through the details of Mr Howden's shock discovery of his daughter's body. Finally, in a brief item, tucked away at the bottom of the page, 'Parents claim: He's innocent', Gary Taken's mother and father were quoted denying his culpability, talking of his distress in prison, and accusing the police of making a mistake.

The *Sun* also combined the two major themes—impact on the family and sexual deviance—but with a different balance from either the *Star* or the *Mirror*.

The story was carried on the bottom half of the front page,

topped by the usual bearded photograph of Taken, and headlined 'KILLER'S £4,000 BRIBE'. This highlighted an angle mentioned only in passing by the other papers:

Weirdo killer Gary Taken—jailed for life for murder yesterday—tried to bribe a fellow prisoner to take the rap for his crime. Bearded knicker thief Taken offered the man £4,000 to confess that HE had throttled sleeping beauty Tessa Howden.

But the police dismissed the second man's 'confession' as a 'pack of lies'. Running on to page 7, the report noted the jury's unanimous verdict of guilty and the judge's life sentence and gave brief details of the crime itself.

The *Sun* ran the story in much more contained form than either of the other two popular papers, but with such economy as to cover most of the same ground. Page 7 was topped by a photograph of 'Victim . . . pretty Tessa' and the headline 'MY NIGHT-MARE, BY MURDER GIRL'S DAD: "I shut my eyes and see her body . . . the horror will not go."'

The story described how Mr Howden was haunted by the memory of discovering his daughter and emphasized the following poignant quotation in bold typography:

I was hysterical, I screamed. I kissed her, trying to breathe life into her. But inside I knew it was hopeless. As a parent you worry about your daughters every second they are out of your sight. You can't rest until they are home at night and safely tucked up in bed. For this to happen in your own house almost defies belief. It is the ultimate nightmare.

This evoked an image of protective fatherhood totally undermined, bringing out the emotion and despair. It crystallized parental fear for children's safety—underlining an implicit perception of a disorderly and dangerous society 'out there' and, at the same time, coupling this with the eruption of that disorder into the sanctuary of the home, where it is supposed to be kept at bay. The article was run alongside a photograph of the parents comforting one another, captioned: 'Parents . . . weeping David and Heather Howden yesterday'.

Beneath this was a further story headlined, quite simply: 'THE WEIRDO', followed by two bullet-points: 'He stole panties off lines; He bored spyholes in loft.' Here the second theme—that of sexual perversion—was given play, quite literally, as the sober tone of identification with parental grief gave way to a synoptic catalogue of deviant obsessions and activities. After describing 'Kinky killer Gary Taken' as 'a weirdo who loved cavorting around in his darkened bedroom wearing knickers stolen from washing lines', the *Sun* went on to note, in a series of bullet-points, how detectives had discovered some sixty pairs in his bedroom.

Taken also:

- Bored holes in the loft ceiling to watch his parents making love—and in the toilet wall so he could see women using the lavatory.
- Spent hours prowling the streets as a peeping tom.
- Thought any girl who posed in a swimsuit was a slut.
- Took hundreds of snapshots of girls showing a leg getting into cars.
- Hung a huge vanity mirror in his bedroom so he could study himself wearing the stolen undies.

Much of this style of reporting, once again, invites the reader to watch the voyeur at work. It is a catalogue of titillation that constructs the reader as voyeur. The story continued by offering some salacious detail about Taken's sex life with Lisa Histed, referring once again to the discovery of 'knickers' by his mother. The ex-girlfriend was quoted as saying 'He was only interested once a week and then I had to take the initiative—I'd have to crank him up so to speak. But he was a good lover—and well-endowed.' And then the tale of discovery followed: 'Taken's knicker fetish was almost discovered one day when his mum found a pair under the bed and handed them to Lisa. She said: "They weren't mine—mine were in my handbag. I'd no idea why he had them and was too scared to ask."'

The reference to Taken's low sex-drive, the size of his penis, the misplaced knickers, all bring a kind of comic relief to this dreadful story. The tragic theme was resumed in the final, very brief, boxed article headlined 'Grief of fiend's mother', which reported 'Taken's weeping mum' as refusing to believe her son guilty and speaking of him as 'good and kind'.

The Mid-Market Press

The *Daily Express* staked out different ground by looking at the impact of the crime on both victim and perpetrator's families. The story was contained on page 7 and dominated by the following theme: 'Anguish as the Sleeping Beauty's murderer is sentenced to life—Tessa: Tragedy that destroyed two families'.

The main story ran beneath this headline in the centre of the page, with a large picture of Tessa to the left. Unusually, by comparison with the other papers, here she was posed in a very short, low-cut dress, reclining on one arm—a photograph that strongly hinted at, rather then denied, her sexuality. The caption ran: 'Victim Tessa: A shy intelligent girl who planned to marry.' Opposite was the full-face photograph of a bearded Gary Taken. The storyline stressed the petit bourgeois virtues of the Howden family: 'Hard-working garage boss David Howden and his vivacious wife, Heather, had everything going their way. They had a comfortable life-style, a successful business and two lovely daughters.' All this was lost when Tessa was killed. The story discussed the impact on the Howdens, especially their business loss and psychological distress.

Below the photograph of Tessa were pictures of both sets of parents (the only occasion on which Taken's parents also become the visible representatives of this tragedy), and the second main story, 'I can't believe my Gary did it.' In this story, despite the headline, the convicted man's mother indicated her growing doubts about his innocence.

The remaining two stories focused on one theme well-developed in the other papers and one less explored. At the bottom of the page, headlined 'Killer's deadly obsession', Taken's long-standing passion for Tessa was described, as was his illicit photography, thefts of underwear (the *Express* talked of 'panties'), and peeping tommery, culminating in the fateful visit. The final story, 'Why did they have to blacken her name?', reported an attack by the 'grief-stricken father' on 'pervert Gary Taken for besmirching the memory of his murdered daughter, Sleeping Beauty, Tessa Howden' by claiming that he had had an affair with her.

The *Daily Mail* gave the story very substantial play, once again using many of the same basic elements, but also with some quite distinctive inflections. In a major article starting on the front page, the 'ex-fiancée's' story, accompanied by a large photograph (captioned: 'Lisa Histed: "I was frozen with fear"') was headlined 'My terror with Tessa's murderer'. The story revealed when she 'realised he was a psychopath'—namely when she had broken off their relationship and he had refused to accept it. The story ran on to page 3, the whole of which, together with almost half of page 2, was given over to 'The Sleeping Beauty Murder'. She now believed that it had really been her who was the intended victim. The story reported that Taken was illiterate, that they had had a normal sexual relationship although she now thought him to be 'rather undersexed and inadequate', and that the engagement had been broken off because she discovered his 'fetish for women's underwear'. After several weeks of threatening phone calls, Taken next waited near the house at night, and three months after stopping this had killed Tessa. The ex-girlfriend was quoted as saying 'As soon as I heard that poor girl had been murdered I knew it was Gary.'

The main angle in the *Mail*'s treatment was conveyed by the headline that ran across pages 2 and 3: 'The killer's face at the window: Peeping Tom who stalked his pretty victim for two years.' A prowler, spotted by Tessa two years before her death, the article reported, was believed by the police to be Taken. It went on to talk about the 'trappings of a pervert' that had been uncovered in his bedroom, detailing the pornographic magazines, 90 pairs of women's knickers, and the dozens of photographs of local girls. The report and its accompanying imagery were strongly inflected by a consciousness of class difference which emerged in the attribution of motive (the most coherent and explicit version to emerge anywhere). The account came entirely from police sources: 'Yesterday detectives said they believed Taken was a Peeping Tom whose perverted desires drew him into murder.' A senior officer was next quoted as saying: 'He was an illiterate, unemployed yobbo and she was a well brought-up career girl living in a nice house with a good job and a boyfriend.'

This contrast between two worlds was underlined by the accompanying photographs: a picture of a gaping-mouthed Taken, lying back smoking a cigarette, juxtaposed to one of a smiling Tessa outdoors with her clean-cut boyfriend. The two families' homes and their social environments (orderly *v.* disorderly) were also contrasted in photographs with the accompanying caption: 'Only half a mile apart: Left, the once-happy Howden home in a quiet cul-de-sac, and the bedroom where Tessa was brutally killed. Above, Taken's home on a sprawling council estate.'

The main article gave a detailed account of how Taken had entered the house, forensic detail about the victim and the nature of her injuries, and how Taken's fingerprints (on record for another offence) had given him away and led to his arrest within a few days.

The last piece ('I will never forget says father') focused on the family's trauma, stressing the change in the family's fortunes—

from a successful garage-owner to a social security case with debts of £17,000. The couple's insecurity in their home—alarm systems in each room, lights on at night—the recurrent visions of their dead daughter, and sense of loss were all featured here, as was her fiancé's loss of a 'wonderful wife' to be. The *Mail*, then, stressed class difference, the impact on the institution of the family, and police procedural success, and handled the killer's perversion in a detached manner.

The Quality Press

Most space was given to the story by the *Daily Telegraph*, which in any case generally has more crime coverage than the other papers in this category. The *Telegraph*, *Times*, *Guardian*, and *Independent* all carried the item on page 3. The *Telegraph* had three photographs, a small portrait each of Tessa and of her boyfriend, and a much larger shot of Mr and Mrs Howden together after the trial. The story was divided into two: the main one, headlined 'Tessa's killer sentenced to life term', occupied two columns, whereas 'Family's life of anguish' occupied one.

The main story concentrated upon the court proceedings and had a factual style: 'Gary Taken, 20, an unemployed scaffolder, was sentenced to youth custody for life at the Old Bailey yesterday for the sex murder of teenager Tessa Howden. Passing sentence, Sir James Miskin, the Recorder of London, said Parliament did not permit any recommendation on such a sentence.'

The report went on to summarize the main elements of the prosecution's case against Taken, the arrest on fingerprint evidence, and the incriminating material in his bedroom. His mother's testimony (she was described as a London bus conductress) that she had been told that he was having an affair and had been given access to the house was reported. This account was ridiculed by the prosecution, and the jury was described as taking four and a half hours to reach a unanimous verdict of guilty.

In the second, shorter story, 'Family's life of anguish', the *Telegraph* covered the main points dealt with elsewhere about the business losses, financial problems, and lasting psychological damage to the parents. What was not reported elsewhere was that 'Tessa's long-term boyfriend, Mr Geoffrey Collyer, 20, was himself briefly a suspect. The jury heard the couple had sexual intercourse only hours before her death.'

This was an important detail, as it disclosed Tessa's sexuality, entirely denied in the other reporting by her construction as 'Sleeping Beauty'. But we shall return to this point. The *Telegraph*, then, combined court reporting with a human interest approach in two separate stories.

The Times's headline over a 3-column story—'Sex-obsessed killer of Tessa is given life term in custody'—also took the form of a court report, but with notably more attention given to the sexual dimension than in the *Telegraph*. Alone of all the newspapers apart from the *Independent*, *The Times* carried no accompanying photographs. The report began, like the *Telegraph*'s, by noting the conviction and then moved to the horrific impact on the parents. It then resumed the main evidence against Taken, giving details of the thefts of 'women's underwear' (the phrase also used by the *Telegraph*) and the girl's swimsuit that were found in his room. Accounts of Taken's voyeurism both at home and outside were given in the report, as was his attempt to persuade his mother that he had been Tessa's lover and that she had been left fit and well. The report concluded with a legal point:

Sir James Miskin, the Recorder of London, passed sentence in accordance with policy for offenders aged between 17 and 20, who can receive the same maximum penalty as adults. Taken received 'custody for life'. The judge said he was unable to make a recommendation on the length of the time he should serve as he would in the case of an adult.

The style of reporting here, then, was similar to the *Telegraph*, but with much more detail about the sexual dimension of the crime and the *modus operandi*.

The *Guardian*'s 2-column story, 'Life for sleeping girl's killer', once again showed stylistic similarities with the other quality papers, its opening paragraphs noting the sentence and the legal limitations on any further recommendation. Alongside the report was a large photograph of a smiling, smartly dressed Tessa, with two smaller pictures of her boyfriend and father below this.

The report resumed the prosecution's case in terms very similar to the other quality dailies, but like the *Telegraph*, and unlike *The Times*, the sexual content was kept to a minimum. Where the *Guardian* differed significantly from both, however, was in its reference to a social dimension:

The court heard that Taken was referred to a psychological unit when he was 11, and afterwards received home tuition. He was transferred to another unit and then went to a boarding school in Sussex. In 1980 his parents removed him from that school and he again received home tuition. He had done a variety of manual jobs and was unemployed when he was arrested. The court had heard that he suffers from dyslexia.

With the exception of the sentence about dyslexia, exactly the same words were to be found in the *Independent*'s 1-column story 'Strangler gets life for sex murder.' This report also began by resuming the judge's sentence, going on to describe how Taken entered the house, the sexual assault, slashing, strangulation, and the fingerprint evidence. The *Independent*'s report also mentioned the discovery of the swimsuit and a suitcase full of 'women's underwear'.

The *Guardian* and the *Independent* were the only newspapers to evoke a casework approach to the offender, however fleetingly. For the *Guardian* he was 'dyslexic', whereas elsewhere he was described as 'illiterate'. Immediately after the social dimension was evoked, in both papers the police officer in charge of the hunt was quoted as saying Taken was an 'evil man', as was the father's relief that he had been found guilty. The *Guardian*'s report concluded with Mr Howden's comment: 'I don't know who decides when he is to be let out of prison but it has got to be a very brave person who lets him loose on society again.'

The construction of the story in the press drew upon a number of common themes and images, but with significant variations between different sectors of the market and within them. One obvious point concerns the mode of address adopted. For the popular papers, and ITN, Taken was a 'weirdo' or 'sex beast'. The popular papers drew a firm line between the world of abnormality, therefore, and that of wholesome normality. However, the extent to which graphic detail of the killer's sexual obsessions was employed also made some newspapers part of the voyeuristic world that they described. What was placed in the realm of the sexual horror story by the popular press was handled differently by both the mid-market and quality papers, which tended to talk more neutrally of Taken as a 'killer' or 'murderer', and to some extent, to use clinical designations such as 'psychopath'.

The different modes of address were also apparent in the discussion of his central fetish. For the popular papers this was about 'knickers' or 'scanties' (terms much associated with blue comedy and the world of tabloid journalism), the mid-market term was 'panties' (not quite common parlance), whereas the qualities and television news talked of 'women's underwear' (the kind of designation found in a large chain store). Clearly, such terminological shifts are far from trivial, as they are indices of the imagined audiences of specific forms of journalism.

All the popular and mid-market papers constructed the victim, Tessa Howden, as 'Sleeping Beauty' and as possessed of many virtues. In the underlying morality tale, these positive attributes functioned to throw into relief the sleazy and inadequate profile of her killer. The quality press did not use the 'Sleeping Beauty' label, nor, in the same way, construct an image of a victim who so strongly aroused a sense of pathos.

Taken emerges as a figure of uncontrollable sexual desire who destroys that which he desires. Tessa, as Sleeping Beauty, was denied her sexuality. Arguably, for it to have been acknowledged would—quite wrongly—have damaged her standing as an innocent victim of male aggression by constructing her as a woman with a sexual history. In our sexist culture, as has been repeatedly shown in rape cases, for a woman not to be a virgin is to be regarded as damaged goods, and as 'asking for it'.[5]

A close reading of the press brings out the work of suppression that went on. There was the photograph in the *Express*—quite exceptional in treating Tessa as a woman to be desired, rather than as a dutiful daughter or employee, or perfect would-be wife. There was the evidence in court that the *Telegraph* reported about her active sexual relations with her boyfriend. There were references in several papers to her being photographed by her brother-in-law, posing in her favourite black and white swimsuit—the one stolen by Taken, along with the photograph itself. Such observations cut across the image of utter purity that dominated the construction of the story. It is as though Tessa could not be regarded as a genuinely undeserving victim if she were not imagined to be virginal.

Another theme that warrants discussion—and this could hardly

[5] See Soothill, K. and Walby, S., *Sex Crime in the News*, 45 and 147. For an account that also demonstrates the US press's tendency to label the female victims of rape and sex crimes in terms of guilt or innocence see Benedict, H., *Virgin or Vamp: How the Press Covers Sex Crimes* (Oxford: Oxford University Press, 1992), esp. chs. 1 and 2.

be surprising when writing about the British press—is that of class. Constant reference was made to a reasonably well-off family economically destroyed by this tragedy. The businessman who had built his own success was reduced to a social security case because of his impaired capacity to work. A virtuous family was brought down in a fall from grace occasioned by an evil force. This line was most evident in the *Mail*'s treatment of the story, which made the class differences extremely explicit, where they were implicit elsewhere. Consistent with this, the *Mail* provided an explanation of the murder partly couched in terms of class resentment. This stands out most clearly when contrasted with the sex fiend/weirdo level of explanation provided by most of the press and the muted, rather implicit reference to social deprivation made by the *Guardian* and the *Independent*.

Conclusion

This analysis suggests the potential of major sensationalist crime-reporting for reinforcing fear of crime. By comparison with the abstractions of crime statistics, and the policy discourse that surrounds them, the scope for engaging viewers' and readers' fear—through various forms of identification—seems much greater in human interest stories that receive major treatment. We might ask how such a story of sexual murder is interpreted by young women—and young men. There is also the question of how such tales work on parental anxiety for the safety of daughters, as well as the more generalized fears that might be aroused of having one's home violated by an intruder. Finally, and quite distinctly, there are questions to be posed about voyeuristic forms of reporting that might pander to male fantasies of destruction visited upon the bodies of women.[6] We merely note these as questions that arise from this analysis and which point to the need for relevant forms of audience research.

[6] For pertinent reflections see Theweleit, K., *Male Fantasies*, 1. *Women, Floods, Bodies, History* (Minneapolis: University of Minnesota Press, 1990); Dworkin, A., *Pornography: Men Possessing Women* (London: The Women's Press Ltd., 1981); Kappeler, S., *The Pornography of Representation* (Cambridge: Polity, 1986); Kuhn, A., *The Power of the Image: Essays on Representation and Sexuality* (London: Routledge & Kegan Paul, 1985), ch. 2.

9
'Don't have Nightmares . . .'

THIS chapter analyses the origins of the popular BBC crime programme, *Crimewatch UK*, and the initial constraints that have
shaped its subsequent evolution. The programme has broken new
ground in British television's co-operation with the police as the
production team are given an unusual measure of access to the
details of cases under investigation. In that respect, it exemplifies a
limiting case of source–media relations: the police are the sole,
authoritative, source of information and can determine the conditions under which their knowledge is used. Drawing upon the
vogue for audience participation, *Crimewatch* has sought to bring
about a new relationship between the police and the viewing public
by its attempt to mobilize a public response to the crimes that are
covered.

Apart from a two-month Summer break, *Crimewatch UK* is
broadcast monthly on the BBC's main channel, BBC1. Since 1984,
when the programme was first launched, it has regularly attracted
an audience of between 9 and 13 million viewers—with no signs of
falling popularity—and has enjoyed a very high audience appreciation rating. It has been the precursor of what is rapidly becoming
an expanding form of popular television programming.

Each month a selection of crimes is portrayed using a variety of
televisual techniques including reconstructions, photofits, and security videos of robberies in progress, and the audience is invited to
assist the police with their inquiries by providing relevant information. The idea of using television to make such public appeals is
not new. For some thirty years a programme called *Police Five*,
fronted by Shaw Taylor, ran in the London area. But this was a 5-
minute slot, more like a short news bulletin than a fully fledged
programme, with little scope for televisual inventiveness and none
at all for audience participation.

A more recent and even shorter version of this has been
Crimestoppers, which makes 30-second and 1-minute appeals con-

cerning a given crime. This format has been imported from the USA. In North America such programmes have been sustained by collaboration between the police, the news media, and private corporations.[1] Started in Albuquerque, New Mexico in 1976, *Crime Stoppers* has used the old technique of rewards for information coupled with anonymity. Its innovative twist was to bring in the media to promote stories of crime.[2] In Britain, *Crimestoppers* has been promoted by the Community Action Trust, a registered charity whose stated objects are 'the advancement, promotion and preservation of public law and order'. The first initiative was launched in the London Metropolitan Police area in January 1988 and subsequently extended to the rest of England, Scotland, and Wales.[3]

Crimes covered by *Crimestoppers* are specific to the ITV regions, each of which has a board that brings together the police, the media, major companies, and other interests.[4] The public are encouraged to provide information about the 'target crimes' to the police, who will take information without asking for the identities of those giving it. This is the same model as that used in the USA. Since October 1989, London Weekend Television has featured *Crime Monthly*, a programme mix of reconstructions and 'casebooks' of solved crimes which has a clear mission to entertain and which is now being networked in the wake of *Crimewatch*'s

---

[1] See Carriere, K. D. and Ericson, R. V., *Crime Stoppers: A Study in the Organization of Community Policing* (Toronto: Centre of Criminology, 1989). In the UK, the activities of the Community Action Trust, which co-ordinates *Crimestoppers*, are also supported by private companies and the news media, working in co-operation with the police.

[2] For an officially sponsored assessment see Rosenbaum, D. P., Lurigio, A. J., and Lavrakas, P. J., 'Crime Stoppers: A National Evaluation', *National Institute of Justice: Research in Brief* (Washington, DC: US Department of Justice, Sept. 1986).

[3] See *CAT: Fighting Crime for a Safer Community* (Community Action Trust pamphlet, n.d.); *Community Action Trust Annual Review 1992*.

[4] We were granted access to the Scottish *Crimestoppers* board-meeting in Glasgow on 26 Nov. 1991, the centrepiece of which was a report from the police co-ordinator. The board meets quarterly. At that time Scottish Television was considering whether or not to continue giving *Crimestoppers* airtime. In Scotland the press (especially the popular Sunday papers) is particularly important in stimulating the flow of information, according to Detective Inspector Bryan McLaughlin, Scottish Regional Co-ordinator. The IBA's research also suggests the particular importance of the local press in Central Scotland. See Wober, J. M. and Gunter, B., *Crime Reconstruction Programmes: Viewing Experience in Three Regions, Linked with Perceptions of and Reactions to Crime* (London: IBA Research Department Paper, Aug. 1990), 9–10.

success. In 1992, individual broadcasts had attracted over 9 million viewers.[5]

Crimewatch has become national popular television in its own right, justified by a public service remit and addressed to the entire UK audience. Unusually for a factual programme, Crimewatch has proven popular enough for its presenters, Nick Ross and Sue Cook, to write a book about it. This proudly proclaims that 'As a direct result of viewers' phone calls, over eighty people were arrested and charged in the first three years, mostly with very serious offences such as murder, rape and armed robbery.'[6] Subsequently, in June 1988, after forty programmes had been screened, its producer claimed that of 410 cases, '81 had been cleared up as a result of the programme. Those 81 cases involve 142 arrests, with 71 convictions so far (31 cases are still awaiting trial). Murder cases have produced 15 arrests, with six convictions so far, the rest awaiting trial; attempted murder, five arrests, two convicted; robbery and armed robbery, 46 arrests, 10 convictions.'[7] In September 1990, *Crimewatch* was claiming 251 arrests as attributable to the programme, with 171 convictions out of 686 cases covered in the first six series. For its part, *Crimestoppers* maintained that it had produced some 600 arrests by the Metropolitan Police.[8] By September 1992, *Crimewatch* claimed to have solved 922 cases after 80 programmes, leading to 321 arrests and 184 convictions.[9] These repeated claims underline just how important this kind of success is to legitimize this type of programming.

Crimewatch has occasioned bouts of critical attention. These usually amount to accusations of sensationalism and worries about its alleged contribution to the creation of fear of crime.[10]

---

[5] According to its executive producer, Simon Shaps, speaking at the 'Making Crime Pay' Training Day, The Manchester Symposium, Channel Four Television, London, 7 Nov. 1992. On the same occasion, Detective Inspector Adrian Holder, London Regional Co-ordinator of *Crimestoppers*, offered an example of the programme's impact. *Crime Monthly* had produced 300 calls on one occasion, claiming to identify a particular car security key. In his words: 'Anyone can phone up and shop their friends if they want to.'

[6] Ross, N. and Cook, S., *Crimewatch UK* (London: Hodder & Stoughton, 1987), 11.

[7] Herbert, H., 'The Nightmare of Nark's Corner', *Guardian*, 2 June 1988.

[8] Minogue, T., 'Putting Real Crime on Prime Time', *Guardian*, 3 Sept. 1990.

[9] Campbell, D., '£4m on Offer for Amateur Detectives', *Guardian*, 9 Sept. 1992, p. 2.

[10] Dunkley, C., 'Today's Television', *Financial Times*, 17 Mar. 1988 and

Questions have also been asked about the propriety of using crime for entertainment purposes.[11] The Home Office's *Report of the Working Group on the Fear of Crime* expressed considerable concern about 'crime scarer' style media coverage, pointing a recriminatory finger at *Crimestoppers*. The Report noted that *Crimewatch* did at least issue a 'Health Warning' to its viewers, telling them that the crimes it features are uncommon.[12]

The *Crimewatch* format was imported into the UK from the Federal Republic of Germany. Since October 1967, the German second channel, ZDF, has broadcast a programme every four or five weeks. Called *Aktenzeichen XY . . . Ungelöst* (*Case XY . . . Unsolved*) this has drawn audiences of some 20 million in the Federal Republic, Austria, and Switzerland. Between 1989 and 1991 it was still attracting up to a quarter of the television audience when transmitted.[13] The German media researcher Claus Rath has suggested that this format is 'a perverse realisation of Brecht's theory of radio, which called for the distribution system of radio to be turned into a communications apparatus in which everyone is involved . . .'. The perversity, he suggests, lies in the way in which 'the TV-citizen becomes a member of the police, the restorer of "law and order", the eye of the law'. Hence, he continues, 'the social arena functions as a hunting ground, the living room as a hunter's hide. Mixing documentary, fiction and live action, the show also mixes the enjoyment of television with the denunciatory activity of a viewer who passes on advice to central office.'[14]

These remarks assume a very tight relationship to exist between broadcasting and the coercive arm of the state. Television is perceived as an uncomplicated transmission-belt for the state's policing demands. Furthermore, the 'active spectatorship' of the

'Fantasy, Hypocrisy and Verité Viewed', *Financial Times*, 20 Apr. 1988; Sweeney, 'Where Fear and Loathing Stalk the Set', *Observer*, 10 May 1992, p. 48.

[11] Woolley, B., '"Crimewatch": An Arresting Programme', *Listener*, 23 Aug. 1984, pp. 10–11.

[12] Grade, M., chairman, *Report of the Working Group on the Fear of Crime* (London: Home Office, Standing Conference on Crime Prevention, 11 Dec. 1989), 32–4.

[13] See 'Télévision vérité: La Nouvelle Frontière de la télévision?', Le Dossier du Mois, *Eurodience*, 44 (1991), June, p. 13. A Dutch version of this programme type is *Opsporing Verzocht*, which on average attracts 14% of the audience on transmission.

[14] Rath, C-D., 'The Invisible Network: Television as an Institution in Everyday Life', in P. Drummond and R. Paterson (eds.), *Television in Transition* (London: BFI Publishing, 1985), 200.

audience is also assumed to be uniformly co-operative, resulting in an 'invisible network' of surveillance. But it is precisely at this point that sociological analysis is needed in order to assess whether those lines of determination from state to public via the medium do indeed obtain in the way suggested. The evidence suggests that they do not.

The German programme was prominently used in the hunt for the Baader-Meinhof group, and political crime was part of its normal menu.[15] Those 'years of lead' had a major impact on West German political culture and have clearly affected Rath's analysis of the relationship between broadcasting and the state in the area of crime. Political violence (particularly that emanating from Northern Ireland) has significantly affected the relations between broadcasting and the state in Britain. This has had an undoubted impact on *Crimewatch* because it has affected the programme's remit.[16]

To analyse the British case, we need to look carefully at the objectives, professional practices, and institutional needs both of the police and of the broadcasters and consider where these coincide and when points of difference arise. Does *Crimewatch* act as a simple transmission-belt for police demands or is there a clear-cut area of autonomy in which the priorities of broadcasting significantly shape what we see on the small screen? Moreover, whereas the popularity of this form of television is evident, does it really mobilize its viewers? In short, we need to examine the working-out of television's *mediating* role.

The Origins of *Crimewatch*

Crimewatch was first developed in BBC Television's Documentary Features Department, where it has been produced ever since. In Spring 1983, Peter Chafer, who was to become the programme's

---

[15] Rath, C-D. and Jacobsen, D., 'Produzione di figure di terrorismo alla televisione tedesca occidentale', in Ferrarotti, F. (intr.), *Terrorismo e TV*, ii (Turin: ERI, 1982).

[16] The relations between broadcasting and the state during the Northern Ireland crisis are extensively discussed in L. Curtis, *Ireland: The Propaganda War* (London: Pluto, 1984); Rolston, B. (ed.), *The Media and Northern Ireland: Covering the Troubles* (London: Macmillan, 1991); Schlesinger, P., Murdock, G, and Elliott, P., *Televising 'Terrorism': Political Violence in Popular Culture* (London: Comedia, 1983).

producer, and who had a history of involvement in documentary programming on crime and the law, had his attention drawn to the existence of ZDF's programme: 'It was rather like an extended version of Shaw Taylor's *Police Five*, but it had a magical ingredient. Viewers could actually participate in the programme simply by picking up the telephone and giving information directly to police officers whom they could see, live, in the studio.'[17] Chafer and his colleagues had a strong sense, as he put it to us, that 'one could do something with this particular format'. However, there was also a clear perception of how it would need to be different: 'The Germans were inclined in their reconstructions to be rather odd—sometimes it was the rapist's eyes' view of what was going on which I found a bit distasteful—but more importantly for me I was slightly worried about the preponderance of political crime that they were dealing with.' This comment offers first, a professional view on how best to use televisual technique, and second, a moral–political judgement of what programming best suits the British context. The ZDF programme's concern with hunting terrorists was seen as unsuitable, given controversies over Northern Ireland coverage. Peter Chafer pointed to the practical difficulties:

I could never guarantee the confidentiality that people who are, in a sense, informants, which in Northern Ireland has a particular ring about it, I could never guarantee their safety. And it seems to me there's enough trouble there without me actually adding to it. Plus the fact that you never know whether someone has raided a post office because they're anti-social or because they're seeking funds to pursue some political aim.

A further point of difference with the ZDF programme concerned relations with the police. Peter Chafer observed: 'We asked them how far the police determine the content and they said entirely, so we made a little note to make sure that it didn't.' We will explore the ramifications of this claim later on.

Chafer and his Documentary Features colleagues next had to 'sell' the idea both to the police and the BBC. A formal approach was made to the Association of Chief Police Officers (ACPO) during their 1983 annual conference. The then ACPO President, Kenneth Oxford, at the time Chief Constable of Merseyside Police, cautiously offered co-operation in principle if the BBC were prepared to fund a pilot programme. Oxford told us that he had

17 Ross and Cook, *Crimewatch UK*, 9.

persuaded his colleagues, as he had seen 'great benefits' in the idea. However, he had not thought that the German television production 'would be acceptable in UK terms, bearing in mind they're addressing a totally different audience, different culture'.

After winning over the police, Chafer next had to convince the Controller of BBC1, then Alan Hart, to back the programme. An initial investment of £10,000 enabled Chafer and his colleagues to make a pilot programme with collaboration from several police forces. This secured wider support from chief constables. The Controller of BBC1 authorized a budget for three programmes. The first series opened in the Summer of 1984. Once the first programme had gone on the air, Peter Chafer was certain that he had a winning new formula in popular television.

Inside the BBC, doubts remained in some senior quarters about the propriety of *Crimewatch*. Arguments against the format included the view that some sections of the population had suffered at the hands of the police and did not share the programme team's perceptions of them, and that such a programme might increase unreasonable expectations about what could effectively be done about crime. However, as *Crimewatch* rapidly established its popularity without any adverse external reaction, such internal reservations amongst senior BBC executives ceased to be aired. Or at any rate, they have not subsequently surfaced in public.

The Rules of the Game

The emergence of *Crimewatch* in the mid-1980s dovetails neatly with the accentuated concern with 'law and order' politics that characterized Mrs Thatcher's successive governments and which has remained a prominent public preoccupation. Peter Chafer summed this up as follows: 'Ten or fifteen years ago I don't think it would have worked because . . . then we were very concerned as a society about what it was we were doing to people to make them criminal . . . In the last three or four years we've suddenly said to ourselves, "To hell with the criminal, what about the poor bloody victim?"' The rise of law and order politics has brought the police into the forefront of public attention and, as we have demonstrated above, they have become increasingly sophisticated in their media strategies. It would be difficult to envisage the present level of police–broadcaster co-operation without such prior developments.

Unlike programmes such as *Out of Court* and *Rough Justice*, *Crimewatch* is constructed on the basis of assumptions that unambiguously support the fight against crime. It poses no difficult questions about the effectiveness of the police nor about their methods in achieving results, although these have become major issues of public concern.[18]

Within this overarching framework of identification with crime-fighting, police co-operation with *Crimewatch* is based upon a set of mutual understandings with the BBC. On the BBC's side, apart from deciding to steer clear of political crime, a number of other rules of the game have been established. Thus, the *Crimewatch* team are careful to stress their relative distance from the police. The programme's presenters observe that one problem 'has been to ensure that our professional relationship with the police does not become so embracing that it puts in jeopardy the independence of the BBC'.[19] Elaborating on this, Peter Grimsdale, successor producer to Peter Chafer, observed to us: 'We are television programme-makers who use the police and offer police opportunities to appeal for information on crimes they're investigating. At the end of the day we have editorial control, and that's that, really.' For his part, Peter Chafer remarked: 'I've never felt it was the programme's business to be an arm of the police force. I think it is there as a platform to enable the police to make a direct appeal, direct by virtue that it's interactive to the public as a whole, to seek further, new, any information which is liable to be constructive in their task.'

Much hangs on how independent 'editorial control' is interpreted in practice, especially in reconstructing major crimes. In effect, there is an 'exchange' or bargain: an unusual measure of access to information on the part of the broadcasters is traded for publicity required by the police to help solve specific crimes. According to the journal *Police Review*,

concern about the use of dramatic reconstruction to jog the public's memory and at the same time 'entertain' the majority, was allayed by the mutual formulation (by ACPO and *Crimewatch*) of two basic ground

---

[18] 'The programme is deliberately non-controversial, which means it does not tackle police bungling or worse. The recent reconstruction of the murder of 11-year-old Lesley Moleseed in 1975, for which Stefan Kiszko was wrongly imprisoned for 16 years, passed over the circumstances in which he confessed guilt to investigating officers. That would be journalism: not quite what *Crimewatch UK* is about.' Sweeney, 'Where Fear and Loathing Stalk the Set'.

[19] Ross and Cook, *Crimewatch UK*, 156.

rules: first, that anything filmed would be embargoed and could not be used again unless the force involved gave its permission; and second, that the police must reveal all the known facts and their suspicions to the *Crimewatch* team—then the two parties make a mutual decision about what is to be shown to the public.[20]

In principle, therefore, the police have ultimate control over the filmed material screened, although so far as we have been told, once the process of making a reconstruction has been initiated no embargo has ever been applied.

This arrangement implies very close collaboration between the programme team and the police in the making of reconstructions. Usually, a director, researcher, and production assistant are allocated to the story; then

police officers now have to be persuaded to unlock all their secrets . . . Detectives who have learned to mistrust the media with some vigour sometimes find this rather hard. It is equally difficult for our journalists whose instinct is to publish anything that's fit to print, and more besides. So far each side has seen the sense in extending confidentiality and the mutual trust has never broken down.[21]

The broadcasters must attempt to safeguard themselves from being used by the police. Apart from needing to know as much as possible in order to make a credible reconstruction, their insistence on being privy to the details of a given case is to test whether or not a public appeal is really genuine. As Peter Grimsdale observed:

The thing is, we don't want to be seen to be fitting people up: it would call the whole programme into question then. And we also have to be careful because if the case came to court and the defence were to argue in such a way that their client had been tried by *Crimewatch* . . . then we might find ourselves having to go off the air.

The rule of thumb, therefore, is that there should be no major leads or suspects.

Programme Form

Crimewatch has a well-established formula. It runs for 40 minutes; after the opening sequence, the two BBC presenters introduce the programme as giving the public a chance to do something about crime and then (in the style of a news programme) offer a menu of

[20] Diggins, T., 'The Right Combination', *Police Review*, 24 Jan. 1986, p. 187.
[21] Ross and Cook, *Crimewatch UK*, 32.

the main items to follow. Next comes the first main 'reconstruction' of a serious crime, followed by 'Incident Desk', a round-up of several less serious incidents presented by the two police presenters. This is followed by the second main reconstruction, which in turn precedes a brief feature on stolen property. Next comes 'Photocall', 'television's version of the wanted poster', presented by the BBC presenters, which makes use of videos shot by concealed cameras in banks and building societies and of still photographs. Finally, the third reconstruction is transmitted.

Each reconstruction is followed by an interview with the police officer leading the inquiry into the case in question. The public are given the relevant telephone numbers of the police forces concerned, and as information comes into the studio this is relayed to the viewers. Behind the presenters sit police officers and BBC researchers manning a bank of telephones. *Crimewatch* is followed later in the evening by a 10-minute update, giving information about the public response; there is a further follow-up the morning after. The update is suffused by a sense of urgency, as, at times, is the main programme itself.

Despite the varied programme menu, it is the 'reconstructions' that occupy centre stage, as they are the longest items by far, running for up to 10 minutes. The programme's 'founding father', Peter Chafer, has stressed how *Crimewatch* engages in 'documentary reconstruction' as opposed to 'drama-documentary': 'the word "drama" is considered to be rather a filthy word down in the *Crimewatch* office.' The directors were all initially recruited from within the documentary tradition, and it was only after the programme's format had become well established that Chafer 'allowed one or two guest people to come in who had done a bit of drama'. A firm line is therefore drawn between 'fact' and 'fiction'. In Peter Chafer's words: '*Crimewatch* is about a . . . rather unpleasant reality, and therefore I do everything I can to remind people that this is not cops and robbers *à la Dempsey and Makepeace, Cagney and Lacey, the Bill* [or] *The Sweeney*.'

This last remark underlines the realist ideology of documentary production, central to which is the notion of adequately capturing processes and occurrences in the real world. *Crimewatch* self-consciously fits into a realist model.[22] Where documentary

22 For an extensive discussion of the questions surrounding documentary realism

reconstruction is involved, the ability to convince an audience needs to be rooted in the detailed authentication of the events portrayed. Normal journalistic practice involves the production of accounts based upon the use of various forms of source material. *Crimewatch*'s programme-makers have at their disposal a single, authoritative source, namely the police, who have themselves engaged in a prior process of reconstruction based on the taking of testimony from witnesses and the use of forensic evidence. *Crimewatch* makes televisual sense of accounts available to the police. In the realist documentary framework it is precisely the establishing of correct detail that counts in making a reconstruction, as is clear from the following account:

The team ploughs through pages of detailed statements, meets witnesses, where necessary gathers photographs for casting actors, and tracks down props . . . In *Crimewatch* we always use the originals when they are available from the scene of crime, but where something is missing we will go to great trouble to replicate it.[23]

Not only does *Crimewatch* draw upon police research and by reconstructing it turn it into popular television, it has also developed other visual techniques as a means of engaging the audience. The computing skills of producer Ritchie Cogan have been used in developing simplified 'micromaps' to display movements by criminals and their vehicles in the area of a crime. His 'other innovation was more spectacular' and, it is proudly claimed, 'will one day be regarded as a standard tool of criminal investigation'.[24] Following the existing police technique of constructing photofits, Cogan developed the 'videofit', which used a powerful graphics computer to produce a colour image of a suspect's face without the distracting jigsaw lines. Television's visual imperative has thereby been harnessed both to the needs of policing and the journalistic value of offering verisimilitude to the audience.

The videofits are often used in a round-up called 'Photocall'. As Ross and Cook point out, these hi-tech reconstructive techniques are 'television's answer to the wanted poster. We discovered there was a rich fund of photographs of suspects, of escaped prisoners and of criminals caught in the act by security cameras. They made

see Nichols, B., *Representing Reality: Issues and Concepts in Documentary* (Bloomington, Ind.: Indiana University Press, 1991).

[23] Ross and Cook, *Crimewatch UK*, 32.   [24] Ibid. 88.

good television and television made good use of them.'[25] The wanted poster is a staple both of the Western and of the gangster movie and derives from a tradition of representing criminality that precedes photography. Steve Chibnall has noted that the entire history of such representations, one in which fact and fiction substantially overlap, betrays a tension between the commercial imperative to entertain and the expectation that responsible crime news will act as a vehicle of social control.[26]

Crimewatch is therefore part of a long journalistic tradition in which pictorial forms of representation have always been an audience-building technique. The visual representation of the criminal remains central to news-reporting, with the mug-shot arguably becoming 'a universal mythic sign—the face of all the "hard men" in history, the portrait of Everyman as a "dangerous wanted criminal"'.[27] It is within these parameters that *Crimewatch*'s visualization of deviance should be understood.

Selection Criteria and Investment of Resources

Crimewatch actively seeks out stories appropriate to its popular audience-holding goal, with researchers routinely calling each police force about 'major unsolved crimes'. In addition, press reports in both the national and local press are used to select cases to be followed up. 'Moreover', as the programme presenters observe, 'any crime that has hit the headlines is followed up, for though the motive may not be entirely virtuous, *we believe it is in the programme's interests to be seen at the centre of the crime detection business*.'[28] In other words, *Crimewatch* capitalizes on existing media attention as part of its audience-building strategy. The best-known instance of this occurred during the Stephanie Slater kidnapping case when *Crimewatch* broadcast the taped ransom demands made by her kidnapper. Although the police could have used national radio and television news to make their appeal for information, they waited for more than a week after Ms Slater's

[25] Ibid. 111.
[26] Chibnall, S., 'Chronicles of the Gallows: The Social History of Crime Reporting', in Christian, H. (ed.), *The Sociology of Journalism and the Press* (Keele: Sociological Review Monograph 29, 1980), 179–217.
[27] Hall, S., 'The Determinants of News Photographs', *Working Papers in Cultural Studies*, 3 (1972), 85.
[28] Ross and Cook, *Crimewatch UK*, 29, emphasis added.

release to use the next scheduled broadcast of *Crimewatch*. This substantially boosted the programme's image, as the result was the capture within hours of the kidnapper, Michael Sams, whose voice was recognized by his ex-wife.[29]

One major televisual criterion at work in *Crimewatch* is variety: 'We need a spread of different types of cases, not just murder, in different places, not just Liverpool or London, and we need different types of action, not just high-speed chases through city streets. Some cases are too trivial to contemplate, others have only a local interest or point of appeal.'[30] The reference to 'not just murder' is noteworthy, given the programme's tendency to select murder, armed robbery with violence, and sexual crime as the main stories for reconstruction. The *Crimewatch* book, accordingly, selects the following as tales to be recounted in detail: a violent robbery in Essex, a murder in a Scottish village, a violent pub raid in Merseyside, a double murder in Wales, an armed building society robber's activities in Essex, the murder of two young boys in Essex, a series of antiques robberies, and the murder of a shop-keeper in Bristol. These crimes against the person and against property are typical of the popular news story.

A criterion of geographical spread also comes into play. Since *Crimewatch* prides itself on its national appeal, there is an attempt to find stories that represent different parts of the country. Nevertheless, there are practical limits to the national spread, since Northern Ireland presents difficulties because of problems in disentangling the political from the criminal. Nevertheless, a 'straight murder' in the Province can be covered, as in the Inge Hauser case broadcast in June 1988, which concerned a young West German student travelling throughout Britain who ended up murdered in Northern Ireland. Scotland has also been complicated to cover for the *Crimewatch* team because of the stringent application of the Lord Advocate's rules on reporting cases under investigation. Potential stories have usually been offered to the programme only when the crimes have been almost beyond solution.

The problems of reconstructing 'complex fraud' also affect what is selected. 'White collar crime' is generally judged to have less visual appeal (although, for instance, *Crimewatch* has successfully reconstructed the passing of phoney bank drafts). Action stories

[29] Sweeney, 'Where Fear and Loathing Stalk the Set'.
[30] Ross and Cook, *Crimewatch UK*, 29.

are regarded as more attractive for a programme conceived as pop-ular television. Where *Crimewatch* holds itself apart from down-market tabloid journalism is in the producers' concern to try and avoid prurient interest in sexual detail. There is also concern with how violence should be presented.

Finally, a further criterion involves the assessment of risk in committing resources, in particular whether the programme is going to strike a chord with the audience by running a particular reconstruction. A rule of thumb for judging impact is the number of telephone calls received from members of the public as a result of transmission.

Mobilizing the Audience

Crimewatch's high-audience formula derives from the selection cri-teria applied by the production team. Peter Grimsdale put it thus:

Crimewatch has to be a piece of television that caters for people who may not have anything to offer just in order to attract that big audience. *So it has to be a piece of television in its own right which will engage the viewer*—I prefer to use that word rather than 'entertain'—and have pace, and have a sense of drama about it. [Emphasis added]

For the programme to have its mobilizing effect on the casual viewer, *who may just turn out to know something relevant to a case*, it has to be compelling. Peter Grimsdale went on to describe how the programme team tries to produce the requisite effects:

First and foremost, it's a television programme just like *Out of Court*, or *That's Life*, or *Tomorrow's World*, or *The Money Programme* . . . there-fore it needs to have a mixture and balance of items . . . This month we did the sexual assault and murder of a woman in Tonbridge Wells . . . and then we did a reconstruction-stroke-report on the investigation into the so-called Notting Hill Rapist. Now, you could say that perhaps there were similarities there . . . we set out to separate them both in terms of where they were in the programme and how they were treated, so that they were actually quite different items . . . What [the police] wanted to do was to try and encourage . . . people to come forward. We said 'OK, in that case this is how we think you should do it.' For example, it was our choice to have the woman detective doing the [studio] interview because it just seemed apparent to us as programme-makers that if you're going to appeal to women to come forward who have felt uncomfortable about coming forward, that if the police claim that they can offer a

sensitive interview in agreeable surroundings, then we should make something of that.

This tells how *Crimewatch* is constructed in televisual terms and
how the medium might best be used for the purpose of evoking a
public response. The above account also shows how considerable
thought went into projecting the most positive image possible of the
police in the highly sensitive area of sexual crime. As noted earlier,
providing such a service for the police has been part of a package
deal that maintains the programme's singular credibility with them.

The production team's reluctance to say unqualifiedly that
Crimewatch offers a form of entertainment is significant: they
stress their contribution to the public good of helping solve crimes,
and are highly sensitive to the accusation made by some critics that
they are simply using crime as an audience-pulling vehicle. The
charge that gratuitous violence is shown, that the programme
might glamorize crime, or that there might be alleged 'copy-cat
effects' as a result of the reconstructions produced a concerned
rebuttal in the *Crimewatch* book: '*any* reporting of crime (or of
open courts and open justice) shoulders all these dangers. There is
no simple choice between taking and avoiding risks like these. In
any case *Crimewatch* would add only a tiny fraction to the general
outpouring on crime.'[31] There is a related concern to reassure the
public at the end of each programme that fear of crime is greatly
exaggerated: this is condensed in Nick Ross's customary signing-
off: 'Don't have nightmares, do sleep well!' As we shall see, there
is some evidence that such reassurances may misfire for sections of
the audience, notably amongst women.

To hold the audience serves two sets of organizational aims—
those of the police and those of the broadcasters—as is clear from
Peter Chafer's account:

Of course we need results, but for quite different reasons to policemen.
Policemen want results because they know they're going to have to explain
their clear-up rate or lack of it. We don't. But . . . it would be pretty
insufferable if we showed chapter and verse and produced no results,
because critics could quite legitimately say that we were being merely
exploitative for fun or for entertainment.

Crimewatch's own 'clear-up' rate therefore becomes a central justi-

---

[31] Ross and Cook, *Crimewatch UK*, 155.

fication for the choice of a popular television form and functions defensively to rebut potential or actual criticism.[32] The broadcasters' concerns about being accused of producing an entertaining form of factual television do not appear to be shared by the police, who may see the programme as a straightforward entertainment vehicle that happens to be performing a useful function for them, both in helping to solve outstanding cases and in generally portraying a positive image of the service. For example, Detective Superintendent Roy Payne, investigating a murder reconstructed by *Crimewatch*, observed of the programme: 'If it wasn't entertainment and it wasn't watchable they just wouldn't run it. Or if they did run it, they'd run it at some obscure time in the middle of the afternoon when nobody's watching . . . I think the public service element of it would take very, very much a back seat.' Thus from a police perspective both the fact that the programme is highly selective and that it is transmitted during peak viewing hours are seen as key ingredients in its success. So is the relative infrequency of the transmissions, currently running at ten programmes a season.

Concern about how the public might view the role of the police in the programme is typified by remarks made to us by Superintendent David Hatcher, who has been presenting 'Incident Desk' from the start:

Editorial control should be retained—I'd argue wholeheartedly—by the BBC, not as happens in some other countries where the police try and dictate too much what is going to happen on the programme. I think then it ceases to be the kind of television that people want. I hesitated, not to use the word 'entertainment', but that, in essence, is what people are looking for, and you've got to be a realist: without the viewer you get no phone calls, without the phone calls you don't get results, without results why would we want to become involved?

Superintendent Hatcher was selected for his presenter role after competitive auditions involving several forces. His advantage lay in past experience as a press officer in the Kent police, in which role he

[32] Ibid. 159 for the *Crimewatch UK Results*. Exactly the same 'public interest' justification is used by *Crime Monthly*. Simon Shaps (see n. 5) said his programme had 'taken two murderers off the street'. *Crimestoppers* sells itself identically: 'The number of arrests made in 1991, a direct result of *Crimestoppers*, was 1609—more than 60 per cent up on the year before. Over 4,500 crimes were cleared up and property to the value of more than £2,300,000 was recovered. This equates to a monthly average of 134 arrests and almost £200,000 of recovered property.' *CAT: Community Action Trust Newsletter*, 3 (Mar. 1992), n. p.

had made video appeals and half-hourly monthly programmes. His original co-presenter, WPC Helen Phelps, was trained within this public relations framework. Given Superintendent Hatcher's background, his views on editorial control offer an appreciation of the perspectives both of television production and of policing. So far as the police were concerned, he had noticed that some officers 'meet the programme staff no doubt with suspicion and potential hostility' but that 'somehow it's built a credibility with police officers that other programmes haven't done, shown by the fact that officers want to get their cases on'. It was Hatcher's acceptance of broadcasters' sensibilities that made him put 'entertainment' in quotation-marks. Moreover, apart from solving crimes, the less immediate goal of improving the police's image is also a major concern. David Hatcher's conception of his role is this: 'I wanted it to be somebody who could represent a friendly image of the force and represent an . . . open-minded image of a police officer.' This ties in with the police's increasingly sophisticated awareness of the need to use the media for their own ends. Their concern about the public's frequent lack of response to appeals for information has also been thoroughly internalized by the production team.[33]

The desire to mobilize the audience, hold it, and to achieve quantifiable results, therefore, fundamentally informs the construction of the programme. The televisual imperative leads to a frequent change of pace coupled with the tension that comes from 'live' production, a variety of content in order to provide visual interest, and a stress upon presenter credibility.

Audience Research

Both the BBC and the Independent Broadcasting Authority (IBA) have undertaken research on audience-mobilizing crime programmes. Understandably, the BBC's study has focused on *Crimewatch* whereas the IBA's has concentrated on *Crimestoppers*. The BBC's research combines findings from five group discussions, three of women, two of men, with data from its regular national Omnibus survey of 1,000 adults, with a response from 781 persons.[34] The IBA's work is entirely survey-based, focusing upon

[33] Ross and Cook, *Crimewatch UK*, 115.

[34] BBC Broadcasting Research, *Crimewatch UK* (London: BBC, Special Projects Report, SP. 88/45/88/16, Oct. 1988).

three ITV regions, with responses from respectively 544, 448, and 485 persons.[35] A study commissioned by the Broadcasting Standards Council has also investigated the reception of *Crimewatch* in the broader context of analysing televised violence against women. This study made use of fourteen discussion groups with 91 members in all, six of which were based in Central Scotland, eight in the English Midlands, and all of which were entirely composed of women.[36]

The BBC study found that eight out of ten viewers watch *Crimewatch* and that some three-quarters of the audience find it interesting. Respondents drew attention to both its social function in crime-fighting and its individual function of raising personal awareness of crime. The researchers detected ambivalence about the use of reconstructions, in particular, amongst some respondents, concern that these might gratuitously show violence, increase fear of crime, produce 'copy-catting', and encourage voyeurism. However, such worries were evidently far outweighed by audience members' acceptance of the logic of the television producers' programme values: namely, that reconstructions were essential for jogging witnesses' memories, for heightening awareness, and for capturing a large audience. The vast majority of the BBC's sample (82 per cent) found that the level of televised violence in the programme was acceptable. Because it relates to other findings reported later, it is worth noting that where the programme was held to cause fear, this was restricted to *female* viewers only, especially those living or viewing alone.[37]

Of particular interest was the reported narrative appeal of *Crimewatch*, which raises questions about whether the audience really interprets television in terms of mutually exclusive categories of fact versus fiction. The BBC's report also noted that respondents expressed discomfort in using such terms as 'enjoyment' and 'entertainment' to describe *Crimewatch*.[38] Furthermore, the genre itself

[35] Wober, J. M. and Gunter, B., *Crime Reconstruction Programmes: Viewing Experiences in Three Regions, Linked with Perceptions of and Reactions to Crime* (London: IBA Research Department Paper, Aug. 1990).

[36] Schlesinger, P., Dobash, R. E., Dobash, R. P. and Weaver, C. K., *Women Viewing Violence* (London: BFI, 1991).

[37] BBC, *Crimewatch UK*, 18.

[38] Ibid. 16. Also see Sparks, R., *Television and the Drama of Crime: Moral Tales and the Place of Crime in Public Life* (Buckingham, Philadelphia: Open University Press, 1992), 156–9 on the overlap between 'fact' and 'fiction' in programmes such as *Crimewatch*.

creates difficulty, being hard for viewers to place: when asked to categorize it, respondents recognized it as different from other documentaries and from police fiction, and somewhat loosely grouped it with other programmes that have a consumer/public involvement element and style, such as *That's Life*, *Watchdog*, and *The Cook Report*.[39] *Crimewatch* is evidently recognized as a BBC programme rather than a police programme, suggesting that the production team's efforts to present it as editorially independent have paid off.[40] Although respondents accept that it is principally about catching criminals, it seems also to lend itself to a process of learning about crime prevention.[41]

The IBA's findings accord with those of the BBC in uncovering strong public support for crime reconstructions as a means of helping the police. Reconstructions would appear to be highly popular, with an average of 83 per cent of respondents finding them a good idea, and some six out of ten believing that more are needed, although there were strong reservations amongst four out of ten about any concentration on violent crime. Between eight and nine out of ten respondents expressed a willingness to telephone the police if they suspected that a crime was being committed.[42] There is evidently widespread enjoyment of factual programming on crime and the police.

The IBA's research was particularly concerned to establish whether or not worries about *Crimestoppers'* impact on fear of crime expressed in the Grade report were justified. The most pertinent finding was that one in three respondents thought that it had 'made them feel more cautious about going out alone in the dark or that other people had probably also become more afraid of crime as a result of watching the programme'.[43] Although it tends to play down the importance of such fears, the IBA's research does give pause for thought, especially when the issue is explored more thoroughly. The findings of the study commissioned by the Broadcasting Standards Council suggest that over half the women studied felt that some media, especially television and the tabloid press, increased their fear of crime and that over three-quarters thought crime-reporting might increase women's fear of being

---

[39] BBC, *Crimewatch UK*, 7.   [40] Ibid. 27.

[41] Ibid. 21. Though that is not offered as a justification for its existence. Nor, as Simon Shaps pointed out, is it part of the remit of *Crime Monthly* either.

[42] Wober and Gunter, *Crime Reconstruction Programmes*, 6.   [43] Ibid., p. ii.

attacked.[44] *Crimewatch* was said by over half of the respondents to 'increase' their fear of crime, with one-third saying that it made them 'feel afraid'. The attempt by the presenter to reassure at the end of the broadcast by stressing that the crimes shown are unusual and urging viewers not to have nightmares was sometimes viewed with derision and dismissiveness.[45]

The idea that such programmes may generally mobilize audiences against crime and criminals was challenged by the ways in which respondents carefully distinguished between crimes against property and crimes against the person. The women identified strongly with the dangers of personal physical attack but could be quite detached from frauds or confidence tricks, which might even be seen as amusing or worthy of admiration.[46] Some criminals could be admired whereas some victims could be regarded as stupid.

Nor should it be assumed that the police's public relations effort escapes unscathed. The study found widespread scepticism about police effectiveness amongst those whose experience of violence had brought them into negative encounters with law enforcers. Ethnic minorities were especially disenchanted in this regard. Not surprisingly only half the respondents said they would be willing to report crimes, and *Crimewatch* increased confidence in the police in only a quarter.[47]

These latest findings, therefore, cast some doubt on the view that a programme such as *Crimewatch* may mobilize audiences to help the police in an uncomplicated manner. Social groups may interpret television variously in the light of gender, ethnicity, class background, and social experience. The evidence suggests that the broadcasters' research somewhat underestimates the role played by television in generating fear of crime, at least amongst women,

[44] Schlesinger *et al.*, *Women Viewing Violence*, 39–40.

[45] Ibid. 69. A point underlined by Moore, S., 'On Crime and Crimewatching', *Observer Magazine*, 16 May 1993, p. 5. Nick Ross, however, has his own way of self-defensively interpreting these figures. Asked about whether *Crimewatch* caused fear, he replied, 'Well, look, first of all, we've seen research ourselves on Women in TV Violence [*sic*], but of small samples in led interviews conducted by sociologists, I have an enormous amount of scepticism about these findings. Nevertheless, 67 per cent of the women questioned watched *Crimewatch* regularly and thoroughly approved of it.' Hind, J. and Mosco, S., 'Posers: Would Nick Ross Move from a Career in *Crimewatch* to Front a Show Called *Nicewatch*?', *Weekend Guardian*, 30–1 May 1992, p. 37.

[46] Schlesinger *et al.*, *Women Viewing Violence*, 55–6.   [47] Ibid. 71–3.

although, arguably, such fears are to be seen as interacting with prior processes of socialization.

Conclusion

Crimewatch has a privileged relation with its source of information, the police, who have complete control over access to evidence and a determining voice over the possible uses to which this might be put. Thus, although the production team exercise editorial judgement over how the cases that they reconstruct are to be presented in televisual terms, their decisions take place within a predefined framework. The producers also have scope for judgement as to which cases they wish to pursue. But it is in these limited professional spheres that 'editorial control' functions. The BBC team has a symbiotic relation of exchange with the various police forces. Each needs the other. But clearly, although the police would continue to pursue criminals without television, without the active co-operation of the police, no programme such as *Crimewatch* could exist. It is plain that control over access is decisive, and that is where power ultimately lies.

The benefits of this bargain for the BBC lie in the winning formula of socially useful popular television, uncriticized by the police and law and order lobbies. Precisely the same calculation informs *Crime Monthly*, which also sees the world from the police's point of view. Its executive producer has observed that television current affairs programming is otherwise seen by the police as overwhelmingly critical of them.[48] Occasionally, reservations on grounds of good taste and possible adverse effects are expressed by some television critics and academic researchers. As for the police, apart from undoubtedly achieving some results (though obviously a minuscule benefit in terms of the real incidence of crime) the main advantage, at a time of mounting public concern about crime and police effectiveness in controlling it, lies in the widely diffused sense that something is being done. *Crimewatch* offers a generally useful public relations context in which the police are portrayed in an unambiguously positive and sympathetic light.

Crimewatch is close to popular journalism in terms of the selection of types of crime, particularly its emphasis on murder, sexual

---

[48] Simon Shaps, speaking at the 'Making Crime Pay' Training Day (see n. 5).

crime, and robbery with violence, and the general absence of fraud and corporate crime. Its location on the main BBC channel locks it into high audience-seeking goals, particularly so given its prime-time slot after the *Nine O'Clock News*.

Crimewatch has successfully avoided current controversies over the dramatic 'reconstruction' of real events because its form has posed no threat to the law enforcement and criminal justice establishments. Nevertheless, from time to time official concern about the role of media in increasing public fear of crime does resurface. Since the publication of the Grade report, the proliferation of programming dealing with real-life crime cases has triggered a further significant official response, this time from the Chief Executive of the Independent Television Commission (ITC, successor body to the IBA). In March 1993, David Glencross registered his worries about

a new development in 1992 in which real crimes became the subject of drama-documentary—*Suspicious Circumstances, Michael Winner's True Crimes* and *Crime Story*. What we are seeing now is a public revulsion against violence in society which is feeding through to a desire for a greater sensitivity by television programme makers and the makers of films and videos. Members of the Commission expect programme makers and television companies to take full account of that concern.[49]

This intervention, although not directly addressing *Crimewatch* and *Crimestoppers*, none the less bespeaks a growing recognition that changed market conditions in Britain in the wake of the Broadcasting Act 1990 are making 'responsible' tabloid journalism much more difficult to sustain. Some believe that real crime programming might be tempted to follow the explicitly violent and graphic model of the Fox network's *America's Most Wanted*.[50]

[49] 'Television: The Public's View', *ITC News Release*, 24 Mar. 1993, p. 1. Hostility to such programming was expressed in Raymond, B., 'Call of the Wild', *New Statesman & Society*, 25 Sept. 1993, pp. 46–7. For ITC reassurances that the scare about violence is ill-founded, at least so far as both research and viewer reaction indicate, see Monteith, P., 'Rolling Agenda' and Gunter, B., 'Putting the Research into Perspective', in *Spectrum*, 10 (1993), 14–15 and 16–17.

[50] See Hebert, 'The Nightmare of Nark's Corner' and Minogue, 'Putting Real Crime on Prime Time'. For a discussion of crime 'reality' programming, underlining its proximity to drama, see Cavender, G. and Bond–Maupin, L., 'Fear and Loathing on Reality Television: An Analysis of *America's Most Wanted* and *Unsolved Mysteries*', School of Justice Studies, Arizona State University, 1992. The authors argue that such programmes convey a sense of danger, generate audience participation, and rationalize the demand for greater social control.

Although extrapolation from the very different system and circumstances of the USA is not to be undertaken without caution, a general shift down-market is now under way. Moreover, the growth
of 'real' crime television programming has been paralleled by that
of specialized magazines.

It is increasingly evident that crime pays in audience terms,
whether in attracting large numbers for fiction or for factual programming. At this time of writing, *Crimewatch*, *Crimestoppers*,
and *Crime Monthly* have been joined by *Crime Limited*, *Cops*, and
the various programmes mentioned by David Glencross, all drama-
tizing real-life incidents from robbery to rape, and increasingly
important as popular television. *Crime Limited* extends the
Crimewatch stable's formula to examining cases from the victim's
point of view, and has had co-operation from Victim Support. The
official aim is to use reconstructive techniques to diminish fear of
crime rather than increase it. Nevertheless, with traditional public
service goals in broadcasting being increasingly marginalized, the
sensationalist temptation may yet prove impossible to resist.[51]

---

[51] The first case screened by the second series of *Crime Limited* on 8 July 1993
was that of Tessa Howden's murder, discussed in the previous chapter. Of the
series' intentions, Nick Ross said: 'There is a danger of course with these programmes. *Crimewatch* has the danger of increasing fears of crime. I hope overwhelmingly that it does more good than harm.' See Andrew Culf, 'BBC Defends
"Voyeuristic" Crime Series', *Guardian*, 23 June 1993, p. 6.

Conclusion

GIVEN their centrality to public life, crime, and the criminal justice system more generally, simply cannot escape being crucial fields for everyday news-reporting. Consequently, the struggle to define the law and order agenda, and to stake out the moral high ground, is bound to remain an inexhaustible source of political contestation.

In this book, we have taken the field of crime-reporting as a way of concretely studying the workings of the political public sphere. Of course, this is just one of many possible sectors of political debate and action, but it has served the purpose of showing that reporting crime is much more than crime-reporting. Our approach has been to stand back from the customary media-centrism of the sociology of journalism and to refocus it explicitly, by drawing on an existing, somewhat submerged, strand of media research. The media politics of other specialist areas of coverage could be investigated in similar ways.

Our analysis has taken us into a detailed exploration of source–media relations. This has disclosed clear evidence for the existence of an inescapable promotional dynamic that lies at the heart of contemporary political culture. Political actors operating inside a policy arena—and would-be actors who wish to enter it—are all obliged to be serious about media relations. There is no escape from the rationalizing tentacles of communication planning in the quest to control both the construction of messages and their targeting. The animating hope for those involved in the upward spiral of news source sophistication is to shape public priorities by way of capturing the media agenda. Whether this works is, of course, a contingent question, rather than something secured by guarantee merely because of participation in a game that none can refuse to play.

Our study has sliced into one policy arena and shown the centrality of the state machinery as a point of reference for members of a policy network. There is nothing surprising in this. However, it is just as well to be reminded that what is undertaken by key actors such as the Home Office and the Metropolitan Police is a continuous effort at news management and the cultivation of media relations. Telling official stories is not an effortless occupation. Nor is maintaining—or even establishing—the political initiative in struggles over the construction of the news. Journalism is crucial in mediating our understanding of the policy arena—to such an extent that it could indeed be seen as a constitutive and constituent part of it.

We have sought to demonstrate, too, that using source–media analysis offers an important point of entry into the study of pressure group politics generally. In this connection, we have shown how political actors may engage both in competition and co-operation under conditions of inequality. A further complication that emerges from our analysis is precisely where 'official' political culture stops, given the routine use of surrogates for testing government policy. Clearly, this merits further investigation, and raises some potentially far-reaching questions about the relations between the state and civil society.

Our study of the criminal justice policy arena strongly suggests that those with policy expertise have their own way of communicating with themselves. The rest of us may listen in to the passing messages if we are so inclined. For criminal justice professionals and pressure groups, the obvious interlocutors for their causes are the quality press and public service broadcasting. This is evident from how given media are targeted as part of the wider lobbying process in the policy debate. This leads us on to note a more general point. A concrete and highly specific examination of a sector of the political public sphere such as this underlines the special importance of the links between non-official political actors and certain sectors of the media. Within the rather limited circles identified by this study as constituting the policy network in the crime and criminal justice field, many do indeed believe that rational political action and debate are important, but for them the rational public that counts, and the media that service it, are actually limited to the circles of the powerful and influential.

There are good grounds for supposing that this rather restricted set of relations is typical of the more general functioning of the public sphere, and highly characteristic of what we rather generously think of as a democratic political culture. Thus, as we suggested earlier, this is not just an argument about micro-politics, but also has consequences for our understanding of macro-politics. Whilst this may dismay those who envision a political world involving much wider participation, it appears to us a rather unsentimental, empirically founded starting-point for understanding the nature of media politics in what passes for contemporary democracy.

In our case study of the police we show how the key source for routine crime news also cannot avoid the mediatization of politics. For the police, contemporary promotional culture imposes inescapable tasks. The making of a corporate identity constructed upon the idea of service is a touchstone of the police's current crisis of authority and legitimacy. In a sceptical world, all police officers have to be media-wise and become exponents of public facework. Naturally, all of this effort, as in media politics generally, may not invariably pay off, although sometimes, of course, it will. The really important point is to note just how far the image-making impetus has penetrated into the everyday management of police–public relations. It is the putative solution to a problem, namely, an underlying crisis of credibility at a time of intensifying social conflict.

The other side of the source–media relation—that of journalistic practice—has also been demonstrably affected by the promotional dynamic. Usually, given the distorted optic of the sociology of journalism, reporting is seen as targeting sources rather than targeted by them, as subject rather than object. Of course, it is—or can be—both.

In this study, we have shown the growth in complexity in crime-reporting. In its larger sense, it now embraces home affairs and legal affairs. This testifies to the centrality of the policy arena as a routine field of reportorial activity, especially, but certainly not exclusively, for the quality press and public service broadcasting. There has been a need to adapt to new definitions of crime and to the expanded scope of the criminal justice system. Different emphases in different market sectors and in different media express themselves in how the journalistic division of labour is organized inside each news outlet. At the same time, we have found that there are also recognizable continuities in the practice of crime-reporting—not least in the focus on the police—although perhaps rather more scepticism about the probity of this source than previously.

In writing this study, we have found it impossible to avoid addressing the question of 'fear of crime'. It would seem that the management of public anxiety is simply an integral part of the policy debate, and inescapably part of the continuous political struggle over 'law and order'. Thus, for us at least, it is plausible to suppose that the regular fuss about the reporting of crime statistics is not really about public fear at all. It is much more about the right of political parties to use the figures to elaborate political differences. If we are to grasp the issue of 'fear' more surely we should look elsewhere.

In this connection, we have suggested, illustratively, that public anxiety is more two-sided than the dominant, one-dimensional argument about fear of crime would indicate. Policing is there to act as an insurance against public disquiet by way of imposing order. However, the very recourse of the police to the politics of corporate identity bespeaks a general crisis of legitimacy and purpose. In that context, when the police transgress the accepted rules that govern the use of force, this occasions a particular crisis of legitimacy—and that needs serious news management.

The Lovelock acquittal offered a clear-cut example of this process at work, where the evident—and explosive—misuse of legitimate force needed to be explained away as an accident, or aberration of human fallibility. Explicit public concern was manifest in the press and television reporting of the event. But what was so striking was the divergence between two major renderings of the story: the policy discourse at the quality end of the market, and the human interest tale that dominated elsewhere. Human interest news offers a powerful contrast to the relatively closed world of policy-oriented coverage: its priorities differ, as does its likely capacity for engaging the majority of the public in the telling of a story. This was evident too in the coverage by most of the press and some television news of the 'Sleeping Beauty' murder conviction. It is surely here that we should pose questions about forms of popular identification with crime stories, and how this may articulate with the social distribution of anxiety, fear—and, let us not forget, pleasure. Our analysis of popular journalism points to its proximity to fiction, and has raised questions about the role of voyeurism in the detailed reportage offered of sexual crime.

It is precisely the ground of voyeurism and popular entertainment that is traversed by 'real crime' television. Moreover, how such programming works also connects closely with our argument about the importance of source–media analysis. For *Crimewatch* and its siblings a close, and uncritical, proximity to the police is indispensable. The police are the privileged source of information, who trade a positive presentation of crime-fighting (guaranteed nowhere else in routine journalistic output) against the delivery of a large, popular audience. But there are no certainties about what that audience takes from its viewing, as we have seen.

It is increasingly evident that televised 'real crime' is causing anxiety in some sections of the establishment, notably amongst the regulators. It also plays into politicians' worries that such coverage feeds anxieties about mounting crime, as is evident during the ritualized political position-taking over the publication of crime statistics. The police, however, do continue to have a vested interest in such programming, since it is basically on their side. Moreover, its public popularity is likely to ensure its continued presence on the small screen.

As we conclude this book, public concern about crime and crime-fighting is once again at a high. In such conditions, crime reporting is hardly likely to lose its salience as a supplier of tales of seemingly endless fascination. And behind the scenes, news sources will continue to be driven by the promotional dynamic to attain new heights of sophistication in trying to manage the news.

Appendix 1

Newspapers and Television News

Newspapers

The newspapers referred to in this research have been grouped according to three market types: 'quality', 'mid-market', and 'popular'. 'Quality' papers are produced as broadsheets, whereas both 'mid-market' and 'popular' papers are published in tabloid form and therefore commonly grouped together. We have provided newspaper circulations for both 1987 (when the main research was under way) and 1993, when this book was being completed. For those unfamiliar with the London press, we have listed the political orientations of the national daily newspapers referred to in the most recent, 1992, General Election.

DAILY PAPERS	Average daily sale		Political support 1992
	Apr. 1987	Jan–June 1993	
Sun	3,993,000	3,516,902	Conservative
Daily Mirror	3,123,000	2,680,988	Labour
Daily Star	1,289,000	773,052	Conservative
Total popular	*8,405,000*	*6,970,942*	
Daily Express	1,697,000	1,497,070	Conservative
Daily Mail	1,759,000	1,774,578	Conservative
Today	307,000	537,770	Conservative
Total mid-market	*3,763,000*	*3,809,348*	
Times	442,000	365,876	Conservative
Daily Telegraph	1,147,000	1,024,798	Conservative
Guardian	494,000	415,960	Labour
Independent	293,000	346,734	Liberal Democrat, but no full endorsement
Financial Times	280,000	290,134	Labour/Liberal Democrat, against Conservative majority
Total quality	*2,656,000*	*2,443,502*	

Sources: 1. Audit Bureau of Circulation for newspaper circulations; 2. Harrop, M., and Scammell, M., 'A Tabloid War', in D. Butler and D. Kavanagh (eds.), *The British General Election of 1992* (Basingstoke: Macmillan, 1992), 181–2 for newspapers' political alignments.

Television News

The television news discussed in the book is terrestrially broadcast and produced by two organizations, the BBC and ITN. The BBC is a public corporation and ITN a commercial company owned by a consortium of television companies. Both organizations are expected to observe impartiality and balance in their reporting of the news and may not take an overt political stance. The BBC produces news for both of its channels, BBC1 (the more popular) and BBC2. ITN produces news for both of the terrestrial commercial channels, ITV (the more popular) and Channel 4. An indication of major news programmes' audience size is as follows:

TELEVISION NEWS

Week ending 31 Jan. 1993	Audience
Channel 4 News (ITN, C4)	938,000
Nine O'Clock News (BBC1)	6,198,000
News At Ten (ITN, ITV)	6,660,000
Newsnight (BBC2)	1,169,000

Source: BARB/Independent Television Commission.

Appendix 2
List of Interviewees

Police, Home Office, and Customs and Excise

Superintendent Martin Burton, West Midlands Police
Superintendent Pauline Clare, Merseyside Police
Alan Davidson, Bramshill Police Staff College
Chief Constable Geoffrey Dear, West Midlands Police
Tony Diggins, Lincolnshire Police
Inspector Bob Dugdale, Merseyside Police
Chief Inspector Mike Frost, Bramshill Police Staff College
Robin Goodfellow, Metropolitan Police
Graham Hammond, HM Customs and Excise
Superintendent David Hatcher, Kent Police
Asst. Chief Constable Gwynfor James, Greater Manchester Police
Jo Moloney, West Midlands Police
Brian Mower, Home Office
Chief Constable Kenneth Oxford, Merseyside Police
Det. Superintendent Roy Payne, Thames Valley Police
John Stubbs, Metropolitan Police
Robin Thornton, Greater Manchester Police

Professional Associations and Trades Unions

Leslie Curtis, Police Federation
John Dovell, Prison Governors' Association
David Evans, Prison Officers' Association
Harry Fletcher, National Association of Probation Officers
Walter Merricks, Law Society
Mark Potter, Bar Council
T. Rudin, Magistrates' Association

Pressure Groups

Tony Bunyan, Police Monitoring and Research Group
Paul Cavadino, National Association for the Care and Resettlement of Offenders (NACRO)
Geoff Coggan, Preservation of the Rights of Prisoners (PROP)

Frances Crook, Howard League for Penal Reform
Ann Dunlop, Prisoners' Wives Association
Beverley Lang, The Haldane Society of Socialist Lawyers
Leah Levin, Justice
Kate McKay, Society of Voluntary Associates (SOVA)
Bill Mather, Apex Trust
Neil Ockenden, Catholic Social Service for Prisoners
Ann Owers, Joint Council for the Welfare of Immigrants (JCWI)
Una Padel, Prison Reform Trust (PRT)
Joe Parham, National Council for the Welfare of Prisoners Abroad (NCWPA)
Charles Patterson, The New Bridge
Helen Reeves, National Association of Victim Support Schemes (NAVSS)
Isobel Reid, Children's Legal Centre
Mick Ryan, Inquest
Roger Smith, Legal Action Group
Sarah Spencer, National Council for Civil Liberties (NCCL, now Liberty)
Mrs Taylor, Victim
Chris Tchaikovski, Women in Prison
Jo Tunnard, Family Rights Group
Jerry Westall, The New Bridge

Also

Prisoners' Wives and Families Society
Brent Police Monitoring Group
Brian Raymond, solicitor

Journalists, Producers, Editors

Peter Archer, The Press Association
Colin Baker, Independent Television News
Alan Bookbinder, *Out of Court*, BBC Television
Ed Boyle, *Out of Court*, BBC Television
Peter Chafer, *Crimewatch UK*, BBC Television
Neil Darbyshire, the *Daily Telegraph*
Malcolm Dean, the *Guardian*
Bob Dyfield, *Out of Court*, BBC Television
Geoff Edwards, *Daily Star*
Chris Elliott, the *Sunday Telegraph*
Peter Evans, *The Times*
Frances Gibb, *The Times*
Peter Grimsdale, *Crimewatch UK*, BBC Television

A. H. Herman, the *Financial Times*
George Hollingberry, the *Sun*
David Jessell, *Out of Court*, BBC Television
Sylvia Jones, the *Daily Mirror*
Terry Kirby, the *Independent*
Joanna Mead, *Out of Court*, BBC Television
Andrea Mitchell, *Out of Court*, BBC Television
Heather Mills, the *Independent*
Robert Rice, the *Independent*
Nick Rossiter, *Out of Court*, BBC Television
Joshua Rozenberg, BBC News
Kim Sengupta, *Today*
Terence Shaw, the *Daily Telegraph*
Chester Stern, the *Mail on Sunday*
Owen Summers, the *Daily Express*
Stewart Tendler, *The Times*
John Weekes, the *Daily Telegraph*

Several other interviewees preferred to remain anonymous.

Appendix 3
Some Pressure Groups

A number of pressure groups are discussed in Chapter 3. Brief details on those that receive most attention there are presented below.

The Haldane Society of Socialist Lawyers
Aims to provide a socialist analysis of the law and operation of the legal system, to provide information on the law for the labour movement, and to press for law reform, especially the defence and extension of civil liberties. It was formed in 1930.

The Howard League for Penal Reform
Aims to promote constructive policies for crime prevention, and the fair and humane treatment of offenders and victims. Funders have included trusts, charities, and business. It was formed in 1866, and in 1921 merged with the Penal Reform League to form the Howard League for Penal Reform.

Joint Council for the Welfare of Immigrants (JCWI)
Monitors the operation of changes in immigration rules. It supports the cases of families split up due to immigration controls and offers a service of representation in immigration appeals. Funders have included Church bodies, the Commission for Racial Equality, the Greater London Council, charities, trusts, and business. It was formed in 1967.

Justice
This is an all-party law reform society concerned to uphold standards of justice and maintain individual liberties. It takes up cases of miscarriages of justice. It was formed in 1960 and is a registered charity. Funders include trusts, charities, and business.

National Association for the Care and Resettlement of Offenders (NACRO)
Aims to service voluntary organizations involved in the community care of offenders, to manage pilot projects concerned with the care of offenders and the prevention of crime, and to educate the public about the care of offenders and crime prevention. It was formed in 1966. Funders have included charitable trusts, business, and individual benefactors.

National Association of Victim Support Schemes (NAVSS)
Organizes schemes to give victims of crime support, including an information service and advice on legal, medical, and insurance matters. The

schemes are run by volunteers. It was formed in 1979 and is a registered charity. Funders include the Home Office, local authorities, charities, trusts, and business.

Prison Reform Trust

Takes up issues and complaints about the operation of the justice system made by prisoners or their families with the prison authorities. Responds to official and parliamentary inquiries and gives briefings to Members of Parliament. It was formed in 1981 and has charitable status. Funders have included the Greater London Council, trusts, business, and individual donors.

Women in Prison

The prime concern is with the deaths of women in prison. It promotes investigations into issues such as fire safety in prisons and campaigns for better facilities and for improved training and supervision of prison officers. Funding at one time came from the Greater London Council's Womens' Committee. It was founded in 1983.

Source: Interviews/Reports and Accounts. Shipley, P., *Directory of Pressure Groups and Representative Associations*, 2nd edn., Bowker, Effing: Bansen 1979.

Index